DIANA

MYTH AND REALITY

DIANA
MYTH AND REALITY

TED HARRISON

HODDER &
STOUGHTON

First published in Great Britain in 2006

2

British Library Cataloguing in Publication Data
A record for this book is available from the British Library

ISBN-13: 9780340863817
ISBN-10: 0 340 863811

Typeset in GoudyOldStyle by Avon DataSet Ltd,
Bidford on Avon, Warwickshire

Printed and bound in Great Britain by
Clays Ltd, St Ives plc, Bungay, Suffolk

The paper used in this book is a natural recyclable product
made from wood grown in sustainable forests.
The hard coverboard is recycled.

Hodder & Stoughton
A Division of Hodder Headline Ltd
338 Euston Road
London NW1 3BH
www.madaboutbooks.com

CONTENTS

ACKNOWLEDGEMENTS

There is great value in stepping back from events to try to understand what is really going on. Historians always have the benefit of hindsight in a way contemporary commentators never do. To get a new perspective I did two things. First, I looked afresh at the life and the events leading up to the death of Diana, Princess of Wales, having allowed seven years to pass. Second, I took myself far away from the places associated with Diana and wrote much of the book on the Island of Unst in Shetland – my second home.

So my thanks go to my family, wife Helen, and daughter Caroline, for allowing me to do this, as well as to all the many individuals I have quizzed and pumped for information in recent years. Much of what I was told was necessarily off the record, provided as background, and for these briefings I am very grateful.

1

THE
IMPROBABLE MYTH

She came from God and to him she has returned. Like a drop of rain flowing to the ocean.

Diana, our Queen, you will live in our hearts for ever.

The words from just two of the several hundred cards and letters left, together with teddy bears, balloons and bouquets of flowers, at the gates to Kensington Palace – not in the astonishing week of public grief which followed the death of Diana, Princess of Wales – but on 31 August 2005, eight years later.

It was a warm late summer's day, and from dawn to dusk admirers of the late princess – the Dianaphiles – arrived with their anniversary tributes. One American woman, on her first visit to London, said that she had travelled from her home in Phoenix, Arizona specially to be there on that important day in the year. 'I think about Princess Diana every day,' she said. 'When I am at home I sometimes light a candle for her, or wear something Diana-like. She had so much work to do and such a good heart; if she had lived the world would now be a very different place.'

Others, like the members of the Diana Circle, were taking part in what had to them become an annual ritual and pilgrimage. 'I am here to pay homage, because I really loved Diana,' said one Circle member. 'Diana was the most compassionate lady who ever lived. She could empathise with everyone,' said another.

In addition to the messages from the British Dianaphiles, the gates displayed tributes sent from around the world. Australia and the United States were well represented, as were several European countries, notably Germany and Sweden.

Some of the people who spent the day outside the palace had also camped overnight and had lit candles in the darkness. In doing so they were attempting to recreate something of the special atmosphere of eight years before when, in the days leading up to her funeral, tens of thousands had kept vigil in the royal park. As one woman said, when asked to explain her annual pilgrimage to the Princess's former home, 'We do it every year because we have to try to keep Diana's memory alive. As long as I have breath left in my body I will be coming here.'

'We kept vigil through the night,' a couple explained, 'and we do the same every year because we have to try to keep Diana's memory alive. There are certain people within a certain family that just want to eradicate her from history, but we'll be here next year and the year after that.'

There were men and women, although the women appeared to outnumber the men by at least two to one. While the Dianaphiles are of all ages and colours, women in their mid-forties (the age Diana would have been in 2005) are noticeably well-represented.

Many people, as well as leaving tributes and messages, stood awhile in private prayer. There was also a short service led by the former curate of nearby St Mary Abbots Church. In his address, in the course of what has now become an annual act of remembrance and worship, Father Frank Gelli described Princess Diana as 'a wonderful, caring philan-thropist'.

He recalled how she would sometimes come into the church and sit at the back and pray. He read a passage from St John's Gospel and offered special prayers for Diana, Dodi Fayed and the Princes William and Harry.

At one point an official opened the ornate gates and allowed some of the visitors into the palace garden.

It was in the main a solemn day, although a few of the Dianaphiles brought picnics and lent something of a carnival atmosphere to the occasion. Many wore bright summer clothes and one man, a well-known sight at British royal and patriotic events, was resplendent in red, white and blue topped off with a Union Jack sunshade on his head. There was also just a hint, a suspicion of anger in the air. Some of the notes left at the gate contained derogatory remarks aimed at Prince Charles' new wife, dubbed 'Cowmilla'. Others expressed views on the new memorial fountain which loyal Diana supporters believe to be a shoddy and inadequate memorial to the Princess – their Queen of Hearts.

Several people voiced the opinion that it was particularly important to pay their respects to Diana again this year in view of the recent civil wedding of her former husband, the Prince of Wales, to his former mistress Mrs Camilla Parker Bowles.

One message taped to the gates had the simple, stark message, 'Adulterers will be punished on judgment day.'

Father Gelli felt that 2005 had been an unhappy year for some of Diana's loyal supporters, who had felt a sense of personal hurt and betrayal when the Prince of Wales remarried, and two members of the Diana Circle confirmed the priest's view.

'Every year is hard but it's been more so this year because Charles married . . . I can't even say her name. Diana is our Queen of Hearts.'

'You never forget your Queen of Hearts. Camilla, they will forget her, she's rubbish, but not our Diana.'

Four years earlier the cards and messages left at the gate had been fewer in number, but even more vituperative – Mrs Parker Bowles, not surprisingly, being the recipient of most of the venom. In 2005, while there were signs that attitudes towards the new Duchess of Cornwall[1] might have been softening, there was no diminution in the devotion to Diana, Princess of Wales. Judged by the numbers of tributes left, devotion to Diana, having appeared to wane in the first years after her death, seemed to be on the increase again.

Royal and social observers who had viewed the events following Diana's death as an aberration, an uncharacteristic softening of the British stiff upper lip, an emotional blip in the steady progress of constitutional monarchy, a mercifully brief sign of public immaturity, now need to reassess that view. Devotion to Diana appears to have taken root. Her memory has not been erased. After eight years she still looms large as a potent force capable of shaping the future of the monarchy and as a symbol of comfort to many thousands of people.

Yet it is a Diana of fantasy and imagination that is the focus of adoration. Many of those who now place flowers at the gate, or write prayerful messages to Diana, have followed the ups and downs of her life from the moment she first caught the attention of the world's media as a shy teenager through to her death. Few of today's most devoted Dianaphiles however knew her as a real person. Like many of the saints of the Christian church, the Diana of public veneration has been constructed by the popular imagination from some unlikely raw material.

'Most saints were once real people,' wrote Pierre Delooz, 'about whom objective facts may be established: their sex, their place of birth, and particularity of their death . . . but . . . all saints are more or less constructed in that, being necessarily saints for other people, they are remodelled in that collective representation, which is made for them.'[2]

In other words, saints might be based on real people, but the objects of veneration that they become are manufactured by the people who venerate them according to their various spiritual needs and imaginations. The most obvious example is that of the Virgin Mary. There are barely half a dozen references to her in the Gospels: the annunciation; the birth of Jesus; the flight into Egypt; the time she lost the young Jesus to the scholars in the temple; the miracle of turning the water into wine; and the crucifixion. Yet, from those few references, the Marian Tradition has evolved. Over the centuries the Roman Catholic Church has developed a pivotal role for the mother of Jesus which in some instances takes the form of an entire Marian cult. Mary is associated with hundreds of different places and causes. She is Our Lady of . . . whatever group invokes her name.

There are signs that devotion to Diana, as an unofficial saint, is evolving in a similar all-purpose manner. In some instances she is already being portrayed as a modern-day Madonna. She was the virgin bride selected to be the mother of a king. She became the woman of sorrows. She is representative of the iconic feminine. Unlike Mary, however, Diana has not been remade as a woman without sin. That would not be possible given her public confessions of weakness and failure. So the Diana of myth follows another common saintly tradition: a woman whose healing strength and spirituality may be apprehended through her public displays of vulnerability.

If Diana is being mythologised, how many Diana devotees might there be? Solid numbers are hard to come by although the many sources of circumstantial and anecdotal evidence suggest she is currently venerated by many tens of thousands of people worldwide. The evidence is admittedly unscientific and not yet substantiated by any reliable statistics. There has been no census of Diana followers, but there are dozens of stories on offer.

A man selling souvenirs at Windsor, who makes his living from the thousands of tourists who come to see the castle every year, notes that the Diana brand is by far the most popular with his customers. Items showing Diana's image easily outsell those linked to other members of the royal family.

An internet site[3] accessed by Diana devotees has over 1600 current tributes.[4] They are posted at the rate of around three a day. 'There's not a moment we don't think about you', writes one typical contributor addressing the Princess herself. 'One day when the angels sing and God asks what have you done with your life, you'll look back with pride at the journey you took for the people', writes another.

A poll on the same site conducted seven years after Diana's death found that 81 per cent of respondents were still in mourning for the Princess, although it has to be pointed out that the sample is self-selecting and inevitably slanted.

There are chatrooms and web-rings and a wide range of Diana memorial websites, most of which are being continually updated with Diana news. Snippets of gossip about Princes William and Harry, the latest rumours from France about the circumstances of her death, or uncomplimentary remarks about the new Duchess of Cornwall are shared.

Judging by the scale of the internet interest, together with the continuing sales of newspapers and magazines featuring the Princess, plus the trade in relics and souvenirs (a personal, uncontroversial letter written in Diana's handwriting to a friend, can fetch £20,000 at auction), it is undeniable that there is a large body of people who remain fiercely loyal to Diana. It is a loyalty that spills over into devotion. The late Princess is treated as a kind of modern saint with each of her followers bringing to their devotions their own unique collections of needs, longings, expectations and fears. Many Dianaphiles have small shrines to the Princess in their homes where, from time to time, they will sit in silence, gathering their thoughts under what they feel is the Princess's protection. The shrine will be arranged perhaps with a group of photographs of Diana, a vase of flowers and a candle.

Most devotees of Diana are sincere, level-headed and keep things in proportion. Others have incorporated Diana into their own fearsome worlds of imagination. To them, the dead Diana has become a figure of complete fantasy.

Her image and memory have been borrowed, adapted or hijacked by what seems like an army of fanatics and obsessives around the world. There are hundreds of strange contemporary rumours that circulate and thrive in cyber-space. They involve aliens, the Antichrist, the occult, Nostradamus and conspiracy theories of all kinds. Many of them today have shape-shifted to incorporate Diana.

Few ideas come more obsessive than the ones held by those convinced that a secret cabal of establishment figures is attempting to control the minds and spirits of the entire human race by setting up a new world government. This will be heralded and achieved, say the proponents, by and through the establishment of a new world religion. When Islam is discredited and Christianity has run its course, then a worldwide devotion to Diana will replace all organised and established faiths – or so they believe.

Diana will be identified with the Mother Goddess; with Mary, Mother of Jesus; with Mother Earth; and with all the other faces of the ancient Goddess Diana.

Princess Diana will be seen as the saviour of the poor, the protector of the weak, the healer of the sick. Diana, Princess of Wales, will be transformed into a Saint and then merged with the ancient Goddess Diana.

The familiar images of the People's Princess will adorn the walls and altars of the Temple of Diana. They will grace the halls of the churches, mosques and synagogues that have been rededicated to the Goddess Diana. The Goddess Diana will have the face of Princess Diana, and in the minds of the Devotees, the Goddess and the Princess will be one and the same. Patterning their doctrines after Christianity, Princess Diana will be both the daughter of the Goddess and the Goddess Herself![5]

There is plenty of bizarre speculation to be explored and it would make for amusing reading if it were not for the fact that every rampant website represents the sadness and paranoia of its writer.

The more mainstream followers of the Diana legend, by contrast, write poems, make cards and collages, meet for coffee-mornings and buy every book and magazine with any mention of the Princess. They visit Althorp, the Spencer family home, and observe anniversaries. They pin their hopes for the future on Prince William continuing his mother's work. Yet even this group is not immune to speculation and most harbour suspicions that the Princess's death was not a simple accident.

One dedicated follower of Diana and regular visitor to the gates of Kensington Palace wrote a poem to mark the eighth anniversary that contained these lines:

Untimely death then shook the world 'midst universal
    mourning.
Was it accident? Or murder? The truth is sought
    unyielding.
The long awaited inquest looms, to solve this awesome
    tragedy.
Nothing but the truth will serve, to validate our history.[6]

Diana now has an established place in history. By convention, specific periods of British history are named after a ruling monarch or royal house; thus much of the nineteenth century is known as the Victorian era and the architecture of the eighteenth century is referred to as Georgian; the sixteenth and seventeenth centuries are synonymous with the ruling houses of the time, the Tudors and Stuarts.

In similar vein, the last twenty years of the twentieth century were the Diana years.

* * *

There is a tendency for larger-than-life characters of history to become legends around whose lives stories are told, retold and embroidered: Queen Boadicea; Kings Arthur, Alfred, Henry VIII; and great national leaders and warriors such as Drake, Nelson, Wellington and Churchill. As the centuries pass it becomes increasingly difficult to untangle the fact from the fiction. Not that it matters, for it is the stories themselves that are important. The sagas and stories from history give to the modern generations a sense of heritage and a feeling of belonging. The character chosen to represent an age gives that period its identity. Arthur represents a time of chivalry; Henry VIII epitomises the brutality of his age; Nelson represents sea power and Britain's maritime heritage; Churchill epitomises defiance against the odds.

So what does the age of Diana represent? It was a time of rapid change during which the established social values, the governing codes of morality, and the norms of religious practice and belief were challenged or overturned. It was a time also of huge technological advance, especially in the field of communication. Mobile telephones, the internet and cheap-price air travel were in their infancy when she married but were well-established, widely-available tools of modern life by the end of the century. It was a time too when many groups in society felt left behind or alienated by the speed of change. The life-stage on which Diana acted her part was one of constantly shifting scenery. She needed to combine many roles, some of which appeared to contradict each other. She was both a modern media celebrity and a fairytale princess. She is recalled as the virgin bride and the promiscuous playgirl. She was widely admired for her physical beauty, yet she abused her body by slashing and starving it. She was rich and beautiful and yet received the devotion of the poorest and least fortunate. The Princess appeared oblivious to her own inconsistencies and was well suited to represent an age of both change and contradiction.

So, how did the unremarkable teenage daughter of a British

aristocratic family, with no special claims to intelligence or talent, come to haunt the imagination and memories of millions of people around the world and carve for herself a unique place in history?

Normally a biography starts with a birth and ends with a death, but in the case of Diana, Princess of Wales, her story starts several centuries before her birth and, eight years after her death, has failed to reach a conclusion.

The facts of her life have been chronicled and recorded in great detail. During her life she was photographed more than any other living person. She granted interviews to journalists and therapists, both on and off the record, in which, without embarrassment, she discussed her emotional and mental state. The intimacies of her love affairs have been exposed to public view and speculation. Some of her closest confidants and advisers have published their own personal recollections and have added fuel to the fires of gossip, intrigue and curiosity. The circumstances surrounding her death have been (and continue to be) examined in minute detail and despite numerous assurances, many people remain convinced that her death was not simply a tragic accident.

It is only now, with the benefit of hindsight, that sense can gradually be made of all the accumulated information and that the information can be placed in its context. The Diana story has been an evolving legend. As time passes and the Diana of folk-tale becomes increasingly divorced from the Diana of flesh and blood, so the myths and legends have taken greater hold. Time is both a great healer and an inventor.

The Diana of mythology remains an influential force. Much charitable work continues in her name. In world terms, her memory is a powerful and perpetual reminder to governments and their armed forces that landmines are an unethical form of weaponry. She has also been described as an icon of femininity in a world dominated by masculine values and testosterone-fuelled politics.

For the British royal family Diana is a continuing, spectral presence.

It is said that Anne Boleyn haunts the Tower of London. She was a young royal wife who met a brutal end on the orders of her husband.

The ghost who haunts Macbeth is that of Banquo, the man whose murder he planned in order to gain the crown.

The House of Windsor is also haunted, by the spectre of a young woman, who died in mysterious circumstances. There is nothing the Royal House can do to exorcise this troublesome spirit. Her shadow is perpetually cast across the business of the family firm.

Her face is seen everywhere. In newspapers, on television, on the covers of magazines, on pink cards left on the gates of royal palaces and inescapably in the features of the young man who will one day be King – William, Diana's first-born son.

The ghostly metaphor is an apt one, for a spectre can take many forms and serve several purposes. It can serve as a reminder of deeds long past which have never been forgotten or forgiven; it can represent vengeance, and the inescapable fact that all past deeds have consequences; it can be reproach from beyond the grave; or a demonstration of how things might have been. The spectre can goad and torment, and can never be wished away.

The ghost is also a reminder of the world of the spirit. While Princess Diana was very much of this world, she was a physical woman who touched and hugged, shopped and partied, danced and swam, she was also intuitive and fascinated by the plethora of spiritual options offered by the New Age. She believed in fate, omens, astrology and 'energies'. Today, while her earthly remains lie in their island grave at Althorp, she lives on in spirit in the minds, imaginations and obsessions of thousands of people.

And curiously, as organised religion has declined, the style of spirituality offered and exemplified by Diana has grown. Understanding the impact made by Diana in life, and the

11

influence she continues to exert after death, involves an examination of a range of political, sociological, psychological and constitutional factors. But significantly, it also involves an investigation into how spiritual ideas and religious language, while remaining rooted in the spirituality of the ancient and primeval, have evolved over the last twenty-five years. It is from this process of change that the Diana of modern myth and imagination has emerged.

Through this retelling of a familiar story it will be seen how the myth was created, with Diana herself helping to create her own legend. With that in mind, it is then possible to look to the future, to explore where the Diana of myth and legend goes from here, for it is unlikely that she will simply fade from memory. Will she continue to grow as a figure of obsession and fantasy? Will she become the focus of a new form of religious practice? Will she, through her son, facilitate profound and lasting changes within the institution of the British monarchy?

2

THE DISAPPOINTING DAUGHTER

Nineteen sixty-one was a year of grave international tension. At the time of Diana's birth, many millions of people in both the west and east felt fearful and vulnerable. The news was dominated by Cold War politics as the two super-powers, the American and Soviet blocs, eyed each other with mutual distrust. It was the year The Berlin Wall was raised to prevent the citizens of Communist East Berlin fleeing to the Capitalist West. It was the year the American president advised all prudent Americans to build themselves a bomb shelter. The threat of nuclear war felt very real.

In Britain, despite threats looming on the international stage, many aspects of life seemed reassuringly secure. Much would change in the coming years, but in 1961 steam engines still pulled trains on the rural branch lines; London commuters wore bowler hats to work; policemen walked the beat; shoppers used shillings and old pennies; theatre and cinema entertainment was carefully censored lest anything immoral be shown; television was in black and white; hereditary peers sat by right in the House of Lords; and supermarkets, motorways and credit cards were dreams of the future. Even the population profile was different with a higher proportion of young people and substantially fewer old. The forty years after 1961 saw a 50 per cent increase in people of pensionable age.

There were however stirrings of social change. New music had recently arrived from America heralding an upheaval in popular culture. The Beatles had not as yet been formed, but Elvis had arrived on the scene. The British music chart was still pretty tame with acts such as the Everly Brothers exporting records across the Atlantic, and Frankie Vaughan and Helen Shapiro being the home-grown chart-topping stars. The language, as always was evolving. The slang of the Second World War was on its way out and new words were coined for and by the younger generation, the teenagers, as they were now called.

On the fashion front, women's trouser suits and Chelsea boots were coming into vogue. At the Palace of Westminster, despite having been returned with a substantial parliamentary majority two years earlier, the British Conservative government was in decline after ten years in power. Deference was being gradually challenged by satire. The aristocracy was being challenged by the meritocracy.

Diana was born on July 1st of that year. Her father was Viscount Althorp, known as Johnnie. He was the heir to the Spencer earldom. Her mother, Frances, was the daughter of the fourth Lord and Lady Fermoy. Diana was born into the English aristocracy, and in particular into a family with a pedigree and claim to a centuries-old position in society, rivalling, if not exceeding, that of the ruling royal family, the House of Windsor. Her place of birth was Park House on the Sandringham estate in Norfolk. Sandringham is one of the Queen's main homes and so the Spencer heir's family and the Windsors were neighbours.

The Spencer family was genuinely wealthy and owned land and works of art valued at tens of millions of pounds. The family's historic stately home is Althorp in Northamptonshire. The Spencer fortune could be traced back five hundred years and was founded on the wool trade. In fitting with their social position, Diana's parents married in Westminster Abbey in 1954, almost exactly a year after the coronation of Elizabeth II. There were 1700 guests, including most of the royal family, and it was generally regarded as the society wedding of the year. Johnnie was at the time a Queen's equerry and had at one stage, it is said, been on the list of potential suitable husbands for the Queen herself. An equerry is not a royal servant like a butler or valet, but someone of higher social position who acts as companion, friend, attendant, guide, organiser and counsellor to a person of high royal position.

Frances was aged eighteen at the time of the wedding. She had been presented at court as a debutante and had received the traditional upbringing of her social class. Her presentation had been arranged and managed by her mother, Ruth Fermoy who was described by Frances's biographers as 'an unbending perfectionist with exacting standards and impeccable manners'.[1]

To present herself for marriage at the age of eighteen was, in the 1950s, precisely what was expected of the daughter of a peer. In upper-class circles there were two unwritten rules concerning a young woman's function. 'First and foremost, she must marry in the blossom of youth. Then she has to produce, and preferably at the first attempt, a son and heir.'[2]

Johnnie, as the heir to the earldom and in keeping with his class and the age in which he lived, was hoping the marriage would provide him and his family with a son. It was important to him and his own father that there would be a new generation to carry forward the Spencer name and titles. In normal circumstances under the British system of primogeniture, daughters did not inherit titles. However, in one rare exception to the rule, provisions were made for the earldom created for Prince Philip's uncle, Lord Mountbatten of Burma, to pass on his death to his daughter. And of course in the major exception to the rule, if a king has no son, a daughter can inherit the throne.

The fact that Diana was a girl was both a matter of disappointment and concern. What is more, she was the third daughter, and at the time of her birth, the third surviving of the couple's four children. A brother, John, had been born eighteen months earlier, but he had only lived for a few hours. He had been whisked away at birth and his mother had never been allowed to see him.

Today she would have been encouraged to see and hold her child, even in death. Then it was considered best for the mother that she have no contact. The death certificate stated that the infant had died of extensive malformation. For the rest of her life the circumstances of John's birth and death caused Frances sorrow and pain. What was particularly hurtful was the fact that all decisions were taken by the midwife, doctors and her husband without consultation. They treated John 'as if he had never happened. But I'd had him on board for nine months. He was mine . . . I was responsible from the beginning to birth. That is a mother's part, and only hers.'[3]

Adding to her distress, following John's birth, Frances was required to undergo intrusive medical tests to determine whether there was any reason why she was not able to give birth to a healthy male child.

In many cultures, greater value is given to male children than to female. In some Middle Eastern societies, for instance, two sheep are sacrificed for a boy, only one for a girl. In some cultures unwanted female babies are left in the cold to die. There are Chinese orphanages devoted to abandoned girls. In the more 'civilised' world of the mid-twentieth-century English aristocracy, the demand for male children was also strong, although the recriminations when a healthy boy baby failed to arrive, were more subtle and focused on the mother.

The medical tests proved to be such an unpleasant experience for the young bereaved mother that she retreated into a kind of half-life.

As she herself said, 'It was obvious that I was considered the reason why John was not able to survive. So when I became pregnant the next time I was fiercely aware what was expected of me. I suppose it was a form of protection, but I decided I would keep the pregnancy to myself until I was a bit further on.'

Disheartened, exhausted, worried and deeply saddened, Frances needed to get away. So later that summer she took the two children to the seaside in Devon for a few days . . . to try to find the courage to announce the news of another potential Spencer heir . . . Then one night she awoke in terrible pain.

Something had gone horribly wrong . . . She sat on the cold bathroom floor and sobbed. There, alone and afraid, she miscarried the child that only she knew about. The one blessing in the dreadful event was Johnnie's absence, and thus the lack of reproaches and admonishment.[4]

Frances informed no one of the miscarriage until years later when, after her husband's death, she told her then-adult children.

Later that year Frances became pregnant again, her fourth conception in five years. Diana's birth was straightforward. She arrived at the family home Park House on the Sandringham Estate in Norfolk to the sound of applause. Nothing to do with the birth – there was a cricket match going on nearby and at the moment Diana arrived a batsman completed a century.

Yet, to the wider family, her birth was an anticlimax and triggered what with hindsight seem like mean-spirited displays of disappointment. Instead of rejoicing at the arrival of a new family member, the Spencer family was not best pleased that Diana was the third healthy daughter and not the first healthy son. In one version of the story of Diana's birth, a bonfire prepared for lighting by her grandfather as a beacon to announce the arrival of an heir to the Spencer titles and estate, was left cold. In another story, it is said that so determined were her parents that their new child should be a boy that they had no girls' names in readiness for a daughter. It is certainly a fact that Diana was the only Spencer child not to have a member of the royal family as a godparent. She was christened at the local church – unlike her brother, who was, three years later, baptised in Westminster Abbey with the Queen as a godmother.

Diana later told of how she would visit the grave of John, the Spencer son who died in infancy eighteen months before her own birth, and ponder how, if he had lived, she herself would never have been born.

The story of Diana's childhood has been told many times. The standard version of the story, as shaped and encouraged by Diana herself, has it that while born into the privileged surroundings of the English aristocracy, she lived in a home where she was deprived of normal emotional comfort.

And the key reason for this was the breakdown of her parents' marriage. For although Frances eventually did her dynastic 'duty' and produced the male heir – Charles Edward Maurice, the ninth Earl Spencer who would thirty-three years later deliver the oration at his sister's funeral – by that time the marriage had been irreparably damaged. She and Johnnie separated when Diana was six and the young girl was left as the mother substitute, so Diana later described, to comfort her younger brother as he cried himself to sleep at night.

At the moment of her mother's departure from the family home Diana sat alone on the floor at Park House, her home since birth. She recalled how she listened to the sounds of her mother packing. Eventually she heard her mother's footsteps on the gravel and the car driving away. Then there was silence.

The long-term psychological and emotional damage caused by the departure of their mother can only be a matter of speculation, but it is a fact that in later years two of the daughters developed eating disorders and two of the children themselves had broken marriages.

The Spencer divorce was a bitter affair and something of a scandal in its day. Earl Spencer fought for custody of the children. Today it would be normal for a court to award custody of children to a mother, unless there were overwhelming reasons not to. In the 1960s it was sufficient for a peer of the realm, in collaboration with his mother-in-law, Lady Fermoy, to attack Frances's reputation in court as a deserter and adulteress, for the children's upbringing to be entrusted to their father.

Years later, in telling her own story, Diana described how she was, as a consequence of the court's decision, brought up by a succession of nannies. Some of them she liked, but some physically abused her and her brother. One literally banged their heads together. Not surprisingly she and Charles also treated many of the nannies badly. They misbehaved and tormented them. The two children saw them as having usurped their mother's place. As a single parent Johnnie did his best, but found no easy rapport with Diana and her brother Charles. They certainly lacked for nothing material. They had extensive grounds in which to play and in many ways lived a highly enviable life within the royal orbit. At Christmas, when the royal family was in residence, the young Spencers were sometimes invited to tea or to watch a film at the main house. Diana therefore was not unfamiliar with the world of royalty, yet recalled later how, even at a young age, she found the atmosphere of the royal home 'strange'. She resented the Christmas duty. Not even the treat of watching a film was much compensation as it was invariably the same one, *Chitty Chitty Bang Bang*.

But was the departure of Frances quite as stark as it might appear? Frances's own account of events differs from the Spencer family version. Diana's version, as told in adult life, leaves out several important details mentioned by her mother. Her parents, it seems, initially agreed to a trial separation. It was at a time when the two older girls were safely at boarding school and Diana and her younger brother Charles were taken by their mother to London. For a while the two young children attended a school in London and returned to Park House at weekends and holidays. It was only when Frances suggested a divorce that Johnnie took the first step in the custody battle. It was only then that the children were enrolled at a local Norfolk school and he refused to allow them to return to London.

Frances was shocked by her husband's actions, but felt powerless and physically afraid of him. As the lawyers became involved Johnnie became more angry and entrenched in his position. He felt hurt by his wife's wish to live with another man and concerned that his social standing, and connections with royalty, might be harmed if he ceded any of the blame for the break-up of the marriage. He called his wife, 'the bolter', and found a vital ally in his redoubtable mother-in-law. In court Frances accused Johnnie of cruelty. The judge granted the divorce on the grounds of her adultery with Peter Shand Kydd. Relations between Frances and her mother were strained for many years. Lady Fermoy's decision to side with her son-in-law in court is hard to understand, but is best explained by considering how implacably traditional and aristocratic she was. Her view would have been that although people of their social position might want to leave their husbands, abandon their children and have affairs, and often did, they never did so in such a way as to cause a scandal. It was her philosophy that outward appearances and public decorum were always to be rigidly maintained.

The divorce was finalised on 29 April 1969 and three days later Frances married Peter Shand Kydd at Westminster Register Office.

When Diana's grandfather died, the Spencer family moved to Althorp. Johnnie succeeded to the family title, stately home and estates and Diana became 'Lady Diana' as the daughter of an Earl. In due course the new Earl Spencer was to remarry. His second wife has been portrayed by Diana as an ambitious and pushy stepmother who was loathed by all four children. Raine, the daughter of the romantic novelist Barbara Cartland, was nicknamed 'Acid Raine' by the children. She took complete control of the management and redecoration of Althorp. Only in later years, after Raine had nursed Johnnie through a serious illness, was there a slight thawing in the relationship between the new wife and the Spencer children. In fact Lady Sarah was in due course to marry one of Raine's cousins. But the thaw was only slight and Diana never forgot the anger she felt towards the woman her father chose when he remarried.

As a teenager Diana did little of note at school, achieving nothing academically, although she enjoyed dance and music, played the piano, and was a good swimmer. She did however discover and develop her one special talent, her capacity for displaying empathy towards those less fortunate than herself. She found she enjoyed being in a caring role. She made house visits to old people in the vicinity of the school and befriended patients at a local psychiatric hospital.

It was the idea of Ruth Rudge, the headmistress of West Heath School, that her pupils work in the community. Diana willingly mucked in, doing chores, shopping, cleaning, listening and befriending. As in later life she never took on the day-to-day grind of responsibility for anyone's needs, but offered herself in short, intense bursts of concern and activity.

At school Diana was normally well behaved, unlike her sister Sarah who was expelled for drinking alcohol. Her fellow pupils however recall Diana as having a nasty streak in her makeup. As one pupil recalls, 'that look, which everyone now thinks is so sweet. It's anything but sweet. She used to make the younger girls tremble with that look. It meant, "Watch out, you're in big trouble." It always meant that she was really furious about something . . . she had quite a temper . . . and she made sure she always got what she wanted.'[5]

During her time at school, as she read romantic novels and pondered her future, Diana nurtured a sense of destiny that she would eventually marry a man of importance to whom she would give her love and virginity. It was, arguably, at boarding school that she honed her skills in planning and scheming. It was certainly where her quick-wittedness evolved and where her professed disinterest in matters intellectual became evident.

> She spent every prep reading Barbara Cartland romances
> . . . The girls bought stacks of the books and rotated them . . . We all hoped that we'd grow up to live a life like a Cartland heroine . . . She had this emotional hunger for passion and romance, for being wanted and needed, and didn't give a stuff about passing exams . . . She had absolutely no intellectual curiosity . . . All she wanted was to be liked and loved. She's a creature of the heart, not the mind.[6]

She was however physically active and fit. As well as being a swimmer and dancer she played tennis and other sports. Photographs taken of her in her early teens show her to be slim and elegant and notably tall. It was her height that was eventually to rule out her chances of pursuing a career in dance.

On leaving school Diana had a short spell at a finishing school in Switzerland and then moved to London. She took on various jobs to make money, but was in no serious financial need. Her family had ensured that she had her own flat and she sublet rooms to her girlfriends. She found she was especially good with children and took part-time work child-minding and at a kindergarten. She also worked like Cinderella for her older sister, cleaning her flat and washing her clothes. She was typical of a generation of young upper-class women of the early 1980s who became known as the 'Sloane Rangers'. They were well connected, independent and lived a privileged social life.

The term was invented by authors Peter York and Ann Barr for *The Official Sloane Ranger Handbook* and quickly entered the English language in its full or abbreviated form.

Sloanes had wealthy parents, had been to private schools, were not especially intellectual, but were fond of shopping for high-status and expensive brands. They mainly did their shopping in the Knightsbridge area of London. They favoured jobs with public-relations companies, charities and estate agents, but did not see paid employment as their long-term calling. They had both a way of walking and a pitch of voice that marked them apart. As their mothers before them, their aim in life was to find a rich husband, who of course would come from the same social class.

When talking about her early years and schooldays, the events Diana focused on were mainly those that reinforced the image she wished to portray. She wanted the world to know that she had had an unhappy childhood. Diana herself, when recording tapes for the author Andrew Morton, focused on the memories which were most consistent with the image she had, and wished to project, of herself as the unwanted child, victim of emotional neglect who could, despite her royal status, empathise with the lonely, the unwanted and the neglected of society.

Did she give a balanced picture of her youth? The truth of the matter is now immaterial. All recollections of childhoods contain times of joy and times of trouble and the adult is left to construct his or her own image of childhood from these fragments of memory. Siblings raised in urban poverty where hunger and beatings were commonplace are often known to look back with a seemingly misplaced nostalgia, concluding, 'We were poor, we had nothing, but we were happy.'

Diana chose the opposite approach. She had wealth, status and all the material benefits of her class. She mingled with royalty and lived in one of the country's grandest stately homes, yet recalled hers being 'a very unhappy childhood . . . Always seeing my mother crying . . . Too many changes over nannies, very unstable, the whole thing. Generally unhappy and being very detached from everybody else.'[7]

In the early days, around the time of the wedding and shortly afterwards, Diana had not started to brief the press off her own bat. The writers of sugary prose who were fed nuggets of information about her childhood from other sources, painted a very different picture from the one that would emerge later at Diana's instigation. They knew of the divorce of her parents – it was a talking-point in its day – but suggested it was one of the few setbacks she faced in an otherwise happy upbringing.

> The much publicized custody battle between her father and . . . mother . . . offered one stain of scandal on an otherwise shining escutcheon . . . Amateur psychologists wondered whether this early family tragedy had not contributed to the Princess's evident realism, and the resilience with which she had so cheerfully withstood all the pressures attendant on her most extraordinary courtship and marriage.[8]

Lady Colin Campbell, writing only two years after Diana's wedding, and drawing on her own society sources, described how, after making the adjustment, Diana settled in to life at Althorp. 'The servants remembered her as a happy and well-behaved teenager without airs and graces. She often came into the kitchen to talk to them and practised her dancing for hour after hour on the black and white marble floor.'[9]

The circumstances under which the young Lady Diana Spencer became the Princess of Wales have been described many times. The story has become something of a folk legend. Diana herself encouraged the version that she was deeply in love with the prince, but that he, as she learned only later, was less committed to her. He had another woman and was only interested in marrying her out of duty. He had, it was implied, deceived her into marrying him.

'In my immaturity, which was enormous, I thought he was very much in love with me.'[10]

'I loved my husband and I wanted to share everything with him, and I thought that we were a good team,' she told Martin Bashir in the celebrated *Panorama* interview.[11]

24

Several years later it certainly became clear that the image of the 'fairytale' royal marriage being pedalled at that time was a highly misleading one. Not that the writers of the time knowingly distorted the truth; they and their readers did not then want to hear anything that would spoil the moment. When a prince marries a princess, do they not live happily ever after? The prince is not expected to be yearning for another woman and the princess is not expected to be suffering from an eating disorder. It was several years before the facts emerged.

One highly plausible suggestion that emerged later, and one that Diana herself did little to encourage, was that she actively planned to engineer the proposal and ensnare the Prince into marriage. She was not the 'shy Di' of the tabloid press, but a scheming and ambitious young woman, who had several times dropped into conversation with her friends that she intended to become Princess of Wales. 'She has the will-power of ten devils,' said one school friend. She had seen her elder sister being courted, and then dropped, by the Prince, and strongly fancied her own chances. She assessed the Prince's strengths and weakness and how to use his insecurities and vanities to her best advantage. She had for years dreamed of a great destiny and she was inwardly confident that she had the necessary determination and had practised the necessary wiles to shape it her way.

There is an account of Lady Diana Spencer staying at Birkhall, the Queen Mother's highland home near Balmoral. She was there with her grandmother, Lady Fermoy, a long-standing friend of the Queen Mother. Diana had not been there for more than a few days before

. . . everyone at Balmoral was saying how lovely she was. It was a short hop from that to how suitable she was, and how wonderful it would be if The Prince of Wales married someone like her.

Diana, however, had to play her part if she was going to

win the game of being 'royalised'. At Birkhall she did this to perfection. She stuck to Prince Charles 'the way deodorant sticks to your armpit,' says someone who was there with them. 'She had abandoned all reserve . . . You could tell by the way she looked at him, how she spoke to him, how she followed him around, how she laughed that little bit too much and in general behaved towards him. She did not behave badly. Far from it. She was very careful how she trod. But it was plain for all to see that she was throwing herself at his feet, metaphorically speaking of course, and saying, "I'm in love with you. Acknowledge me or abandon me." It was just the right tactic to use with Prince Charles, because he really is very soft-hearted and would never knowingly hurt a fly.'[12]

She was undoubtedly in love with the Prince of Wales, but was her romance with the title as much as the man? If she had known then what she was to learn later, about what life as a princess was really like, what joining the Windsor family firm truly involved and what being married to Charles would have in store for her, would she have been so determined?

The answer could well have been yes. Thousands of young people dream of being famous. Not famous for being outstanding in any field of endeavour, but simply being famous for the sake of being famous. The lure of being a celebrity is especially attractive to those who have no specific talents. Public recognition and adulation is one way to feel loved and wanted. The fact that fame has its downside is undeniable. The pressures from the media, the temptations of fame – the risk of addiction and long-term unhappiness – are widely reported, but those dreaming of fame seldom weigh the risks.

For most young 'wannabees' today, the road to fame is television. Getting on *Big Brother* or a musical talent show is the goal. While many contestants enjoy little more than their allotted fifteen minutes in the limelight, some find they have those indeterminate qualities required to catch the imaginations of viewers. They go on to carve out a career for themselves as 'C' list celebrities. In 1980 ephemeral fame was available as a pop star, model or socialite. Diana could have gone down that route, but she was uniquely placed through her connections and position in society, to aim for the jackpot. To be Princess of Wales.

If indeed Diana was working to a cunning plan, Charles took some time to respond to the teenager. They met several times over a two-year period as Diana was invited to join various royal social gatherings. The invitations had been initiated by Diana's family contacts. Diana's brother-in-law was a member of the Queen's secretariat and her grandmother was one of the Queen Mother's inner circle. It was as the royal family themselves began to see this attractive and apparently suitable young girl as a possible bride that pressure built up on Charles to respond. Luck was with Diana. She was the right person in the right place at the right time. There was a general sense within the nation that not only was it high time Charles married, but it was a good time to have a display of royal colour as a diversion and entertainment. What better than a public re-enactment of the Cinderella story? And who better than Lady Diana Spencer to take the part of the young, beautiful and enchanting young woman who is transformed into a princess? And there was certainly no room in the script for the uncomfortable truth that Prince Charming was already in love with someone else, Mrs Camilla Parker Bowles, the wife of his sister's former lover.

The wedding took place in the summer of 1981, when in Britain a Conservative government was dishing out spoonfuls of bitter-tasting economic medicine. 'There is no alternative,' insisted Prime Minister Margaret Thatcher as unemployment rose and traditional manufacturing industries closed. Around the world the Cold War continued to provide a backdrop of tension and uncertainty, with President Reagan claiming the moral high-ground in the nuclear stand-off. Through the early 1980s, the Soviet Union was commonly referred to by Western leaders as the 'evil empire'.

For the British inner cities the summer of 1981 was a time of tension and trouble. There were riots in Brixton and Toxteth. Thus the wedding was an escape. It was just the right circus, spectacle and public entertainment needed at the time. The arrival of Diana, commentators observed, gave the monarchy new and, some would argue, much needed glamour, for the royal firm was getting a bit stale and badly in need of new blood. None of the new generation of royals had charisma. The Queen had been on the throne nearly thirty years and while no one was openly complaining about her and there were few, bar a handful of oddball political activists, calling for a republic, the daily grind of royal visits, investitures and social fixtures lacked sparkle. For the Queen, who ran the family firm, hers was not supposed to be a glamorous business. As one constitutional expert put it,

> ... the real business of our monarchy is not mere glamour. It lies in the professionalism of the Queen as our Head of State, the hard but rewarding charitable slog of the Prince's Trust, the gruelling journeys undertaken by the Princess Royal on behalf of deprived children. This is the core work of the Royal Family. This is where its value lies and where, in seemingly small, unromantic ways, it continues to strengthen the bonds of nationhood.[13]

The day of the wedding arrived: 29 July. Crowds cheered along the route as the bride made her way to St Paul's Cathedral in London. The nation was en fête. Street parties were organised with even more gusto than they had been four years earlier for the Queen's Silver Jubilee. Not even when Diana stepped out into view in a crumpled wedding dress did anyone dare to voice a note of discord. Three quarters of a billion people watched the ceremony on television. 'All couples on their wedding day are royal couples,' declared the Archbishop of Canterbury. 'This is the stuff of which fairy tales are made.'

What else could he say? He could not share the reservations he later voiced. 'I remember Richard Chartres[14] saying – a very observant man – when they came to see me for the first time, and there was a general conversation, with Richard present, about the arrangements and things, Richard said to me, "He's seriously depressed. You can tell from his voice." We thought it was an arranged marriage, but my view was, "They're a nice couple, and she'll grow into it." '[15]

And what could he have done if he had known the bride's true feelings? She had realised her greatest ambition. She had triumphed. She had won the coveted prize, she was about to become Princess of Wales; but where was the happiness that was supposed to go with it all? Princesses live happily ever after, don't they?

'I don't think I was happy,' Diana was to recall later,

On Monday we had gone to St Paul's for our last rehearsal . . . and I sobbed my eyes out. Absolutely collapsed and it was collapsing because of all sorts of things. The Camilla thing reared its head the whole way through the engagement . . . I had a very bad fit of bulimia the night before. I ate everything I could possibly find . . . and nobody understood what was going on . . . I was sick as a parrot that night. It was such an indication of what was going on.[16]

It took several years for the truth to emerge, but when it did, at the time when Diana was involved in a battle for the hearts and minds of the public, it played into her hands. When she gave her version of her childhood, her word was accepted. When she described her marriage as she saw it and how the royal establishment had cold-shouldered her and how her husband had been persistently unfaithful, she was believed. She never had to spell out explicitly to her public, but the implication was always there. They lied to you over the wedding, they cannot be believed now.

In the *Panorama* interview she gave fourteen years after the marriage she even suggested, somewhat disingenuously, that she too had been mislead. 'My husband and I were told that the media would leave us in peace after the engagement. But that was not the case, and we found that a deep interference. In the course of time one suddenly realises that one is just a good saleable commodity. That people want to make money from oneself.'[17]

The Diana of myth familiar today was created in several stages. The story does not begin, as one might suppose, with the poor little rich girl dreaming of her prince. That image is a later creation. The story begins with the requirements of a ruling house to find a suitable virgin bride for the heir to the throne.

Much had changed in British society from the time of Diana's birth to that of her marriage. One institution however had altered little: the monarchy.

When Diana was born, less than half a century ago, the Prime Minister was the son-in-law of a Duke, and was shortly to be succeeded to the highest political office by a fourteenth Earl. When the Princess married, the Prime Minister and Leader of the Conservative party was the daughter of a Lincolnshire grocer.

Diana's first twenty years spanned a period of immense social and spiritual change within British society. Only eight years before her birth the nation had celebrated the coronation of Queen Elizabeth II, during which the peers of the realm paid their monarch homage and revealed, in front of millions of television viewers, the feudal reality of the British constitution. British people are not citizens, but subjects of their monarch.

The service took place within the context of a celebration of Holy Communion to emphasise and symbolise how the established order had the authority of God.

In the sixties and seventies many of the old religious and political certainties were replaced by new forms of popular spirituality and a new socio-political agenda.

The royal family, however, had not changed with the times.

When she married, the expectations placed on Diana were similar to those that had been placed on her mother. An older man was required to extend his dynasty and needed a young woman of child-bearing age to produce a healthy heir. After that, if she was decorative and supportive, all very well. She might even grow over the years to become a matriarchal figure dedicated to good works and the maintenance of the status quo.

Unlike the royal family, many within the old aristocracy had been forced to move with the times. Not so long ago, the royal family was just one of several great families in the nation. The Earls, Marquises and Dukes considered the Windsor line to be German interlopers into English society. One hundred years earlier many of the grandest families of England lived a similar lifestyle to that of the monarch. Many were considerably wealthier. They shared the same lifestyle and pastimes. They were governed by the same moral code. It would have been unthinkable for daughters of the great houses to live the lives of Sloane Rangers, living in London flats and having jobs! But for the aristocracy the twentieth century was a debilitating period. Death duties, democracy and two world wars took their toll, undermining the great families' power and wealth.

Not that the great families were completely destitute or without influence, things had not gone that far. Many, like the Spencers, remained powerful and very wealthy in assets, if not cash. By 1981 however, the Windsor family remained uniquely untouched by the financial and social pressures of the time. For instance, the Queen at that time remained the only person in Britain not required to pay income tax.

The world of mass culture had also played a part in undermining the traditional aristocratic values and culture. Diana read romantic novels as a teenager. She watched television soap operas and bought girls' magazines. Through the message of the media she had access to the values and expectations of ordinary people. She listened to popular music with lyrics about romantic love. Barbara Cartland novels led her to believe she would one day find her perfect man to whom she would give all her love and from whom she would receive similar love and devotion. Under the old moral code aristocrats in unhappy marriages stayed together for the sake of appearances. Adultery was condoned, indeed sanctioned as a release of tension, but divorce was rare and carried with it a social stigma. During Diana's childhood – a seminal decade of social upheaval as the sixties are now considered – things changed. Her own parents' divorce, while a scandal in its day, was an early sign of that change. Diana and her siblings had watched their mother leave the confined space of an aristocratic marriage for the open ground of a relationship based on love and mutual attraction. Within royal circles the changes came some fifteen to twenty years later.

As W. F. Deedes noted in his pen-picture of Diana published after her death, at the time of the wedding in 1981 the court of Queen Elizabeth II was 'understandably' slow to change. 'Monarchy, in my view, must adapt cautiously to modern ways. In nations moving as fast as we did in the last century, there needs to be a balance struck between change and continuity. So this wedding took place against a social background different from that of earlier royal occasions.'[18]

At the start of the 1980s, Prince Charles was still living by the old royal moral code, despite the fact that he was the subject of much popular gossip and his sex life was under the scrutiny of the tabloid press. It had been instilled into him to put duty before love. If love happened, all well and good; but his duty was to find a young woman to bear him children and perpetuate the dynasty. She could not however be any young woman. She could not be a woman with a past, in case the tabloid press found former lovers willing to tell intimate tales. For mystical and religious reasons, which were never spelt out, she had to be a virgin. She had to be drawn from one of the suitable royal houses or aristocratic families of Europe. She had to be white, Protestant and ready to 'be good'. Until he found the right bride it was perfectly acceptable for him to have wide sexual experience. There was no requirement on him to stay chaste. Indeed his 'honorary grandfather', as Prince Charles called Lord Mountbatten, had positively encouraged him to bring young ladies to stay at his home at Broadlands in order to sow his wild oats.

> Broadlands offered an environment in which the Prince could at least spend a little time in the company of an unattached young woman shielded from the prurience of reporters speculating about the honour of his intentions. In his role as a surrogate grandfather Mountbatten was quick to appreciate that in no other way could the heir to the throne make more than a nodding acquaintance with the opposite sex, let alone dally in private like any other adult of his age. Over the years, therefore, he took it upon himself to welcome at Broadlands a number of potential inamoratas – whose names were never trawled through the gossip columns – taking care, by one means or another, that they were given the opportunity to be alone with the Prince.[19]

Almost thirty years later, six revealing letters from his bachelor days were offered for sale on the internet auction site eBay for $72,000. This was much to the Prince's embarrassment, as they were love-letters to a girlfriend written at a time when he was also seeing Camilla – now his second wife, the Duchess of Cornwall.

The letters came from a collection of royal memorabilia owned by a dealer Alicia Carroll. Five date from 1976, when Charles was a junior naval officer with 'a girl in every port', and one was sent in 1980, a year before he married Lady Diana.

In the 1980 love-letter, Charles complains about not being able to sneak women into his hotel rooms while on tours for fear of being caught by the press. An earlier letter tells how he longs to spend more time with the woman to whom he was writing and another says he hopes they can be together when his ship visits Canada. It reads, 'I wish I could come roaring across the Atlantic to make you less lonely.' And referring to the pressure on him to wed, he complains, 'I will just have to get married and then all these people will relax a little.'[20]

Ironically when Prince Charles first began to think of Diana as a potential wife in July 1980 it was her words of concern about the death of Lord Mountbatten that first touched him. 'You looked so sad at his funeral,' she had said as they sat together at a barbecue. Were the words spontaneous or rehearsed, part of her scheme to lure the Prince or an instinctive response to his look? Who knows? Later, it was at Broadlands, where Prince Charles had been encouraged to have his early sexual experiences, that he and his young bride were to spend the first two nights of their honeymoon. By then Broadlands was the home of Lord Mountbatten's grandson Lord Romsey.

In the period before his courtship of Lady Diana Spencer, as Prince Charles entered his early thirties, the pressure on him to marry grew stronger. Potential princesses came and went with great regularity. There was much talk, many names were suggested, but few met the stringent requirements. The Prince had the support of two strong women, Camilla Parker Bowles, previously mentioned, and 'Kanga' Tryon. They gave him the love, affection and support he needed. In time-honoured aristocratic manner their respective husbands were willing to share the affections and favours of their wives with the Prince. Both Kanga and Camilla were aware of the Prince's requirements for a fecund virgin with no discernable, or at least threatening, ideas, expectations or opinions. He needed a womb with no views, a presentable brood mare who would do what was required of her and impinge on his life as little as possible.

As the field of possible royal brides narrowed, one young woman presented herself with the right pedigree and qualifications. The seemingly shy and bashful third daughter of the eighth Earl of Spencer.

She was inspected by the Prince's female friends and pronounced acceptable. Camilla interviewed her and was relieved to discover she did not hunt, leaving it open for her to continue seeing Prince Charles when riding to hounds. In a serious misjudgement of character by Charles's friends, Diana was pronounced 'a mouse' and therefore quite suitable. In royal circles she was also deemed suitable. She had the right breeding and background. A medical examination confirmed what other discreet enquiries had suggested: she was a virgin.

Importantly too Diana met with the approval of the Windsor matriarch, Queen Elizabeth the Queen Mother. She was reassured by the knowledge that Diana was the granddaughter of her long-standing friend Ruth Fermoy.

Meetings between Charles and Diana were carefully engineered. In the autumn of 1980 Diana was invited to join a house party at Balmoral. It was an opportunity for Charles to inspect his potential bride over a longer period and for Diana to continue to fall in love with her prince. She still addressed him as 'Sir', but a relationship was beginning to take shape. It was at Balmoral that Diana first became the quarry of the press. She was spotted watching Charles fishing. Despite hiding behind a tree she could not escape for long. Within days Lady Di, as the popular press dubbed her, was the most sought-after woman in the kingdom.

As the photographers laid siege to her flat and to the kindergarten where she worked, Diana developed the strategies of guile, cunning and charm that were to serve her well in later years. She captivated the press pack and through their publications the nation and the world. Lady Di was popularly acclaimed as the next Princess of Wales.

There was considerable pressure therefore on Charles to get on with the job and propose to Diana. Prince Philip made it clear to his son that if he were to marry her it would please his family and the country.

The Queen Mother's biographer Hugo Vickers believes that the Prince of Wales felt that he was being bludgeoned into matrimony by his father. He misinterpreted a 'thoughtful letter from the Duke of Edinburgh, which warned him not to dally with Diana's affections and risk compromising her, as a virtual command to marry her'.[21]

'Faced with what he regarded as a parental ultimatum he felt emasculated, cornered, compelled almost to do what he did next. He telephoned Diana and suggested they meet. On Friday 6 February at Windsor Castle, the Prince of Wales, aged 32, asked Lady Diana Spencer, aged 19, to marry him.'[22] She accepted. After the proposal Diana returned to her West London flat at Coleherne Court. She let her flatmates in on the secret and next day telephoned her parents. A few days later she left on a prearranged trip to Australia during which, as she was later to reflect, she was surprised not to hear from the Prince.

One royal observer suggested that if Charles had failed to marry Diana, having once introduced her as a 'possible' bride, he would have suffered a severe loss of popularity.

From the moment of the announcement of the engagement Lady Diana Spencer was taken into royal keeping. She had been brought up next door to Sandringham and had lived in Althorp, one of England's most stately homes, yet nothing could have prepared her for the shock of royal life. It was like going back in time. She was taken from the familiar sur-roundings of her London home and the convivial company of her girl friends, initially to live at Clarence House, the Queen Mother's London home. Her daily routine was abruptly overturned. Ostensibly to protect her from the prying cameras of the paparazzi she was taken into a form of gilded protective custody. In reality it was to shut her off from her old world and prepare her for the duties of her new existence.

Before I knew what happened I was in Clarence House. Nobody there to welcome me. It was like going into a hotel . . . I was told I was expected to be at Clarence House. And I'd left my flat for the last time and suddenly I had a policeman. And my policeman the night before the engagement said to me: 'I just want you to know that this is your last night of freedom ever in the rest of your life, so make the most of it.' It was like a sword went in my heart.[23]

It was a price that the young Diana accepted was worth paying, not to become a princess, but for love. Always one to rewrite her own history, she convinced herself that all along it had been Charles she had wanted, not the title. Nurtured by her years of reading romantic fiction, Diana believed she had found her Prince Charming and that he loved her.

It was not long before doubts set in. She recalled the cold atmosphere of the royal household and the lies and deceits. On her arrival at Clarence House she found a letter from Camilla addressed to her. It was an invitation to lunch. Diana wondered how Camilla had been privy to the information as to where she would be staying. Only later did it occur to Diana that Charles might have been sharing every move, intimate moment and development in their courtship with another woman.

In the days leading up to the wedding, other events aroused Diana's suspicions that her fairytale prince was not as devoted to her as she was to him. He sent Camilla gifts and had intimate phone calls with her. It was alleged many years later that Prince Charles had spent the night before his wedding with Camilla. The Prince's authorised biographer Jonathan Dimbleby referred to the allegation in a footnote. The allegation was reported by the *Daily Mirror* correspondent James Whitaker and was based on comments made to him by the Prince's former valet Stephen Barry. Dimbleby noted that Barry was now dead and that he was 'never able to rebut the charge against either his employer or his own integrity'.[24] Dimbleby did not however report any denial of the allegation from the Prince himself.

Dimbleby did acknowledge however that in the hours before his wedding Prince Charles was in 'contemplative mood, not at all elated but aware that a momentous day was upon him, clear about his duty and filled with concern for his bride at the test she was to face'.[25]

The heir to the throne had reason to be troubled in his conscience. In the preamble to the wedding service, couples are warned not to embark on marriage for inappropriate, wanton or ill-advised reasons. Yet here he would be, standing before the altar of St Paul's Cathedral, in full view of his mother's subjects and as the next Head of the Church of England, taking an oath which he knew he could only part-ially endorse in his heart. He was to embark on a honeymoon with a naive young wife, whose mind was full of romantic hope, and take her virginity in a manner reminiscent of an act of droit du seigneur. He would be doing this with the full knowledge and support of the woman he truly loved who would be in the marital bed with her own husband. A strange way for a member of a royal family dedicated to the upholding of Christian family values to behave.

The only hint the public had at the time that the marriage was not a fairytale love match was that curious codicil added by Prince Charles at the time of the engagement photocall when asked if he was in love. 'Yes,' he replied, 'whatever that may mean.'

A few shrewd observers sensed trouble ahead. Hugo Vickers noted in his diary of 22 April 1981: 'The Royal Wedding is no more romantic than a picnic amid the wasps. Prince Charles has been mucking about with Camilla Parker Bowles and is said to have told the Queen angrily: "My marriage and my sex life have nothing to do with each other" . . . So what love there is emanates from Diana.'[26]

As Diana walked down the aisle she was so in love with her husband she could not take her eyes off him, or so she later recalled. She spotted Camilla Parker Bowles in the congregation and even thought to herself, 'Let's hope that's all over with.'[27] When asked by Martin Bashir if she was completely happy at the start of her marriage, she replied, 'Absolutely.'

The euphoria was short-lived. Her feeling of 'tremendous hope' was dashed by day two of their honeymoon. 'It was just grim.'[28]

On the tapes recorded for Andrew Morton she blamed her husband for this change. In her *Panorama* interview she blamed 'pressure from the media'.

Consistency was not Princess Diana's strong suit. But whatever the reason for the early deflation of her hopes, it is now generally agreed, with the benefit of hindsight, that it was a mistake for Prince Charles and Lady Diana Spencer to have married. The marriage took place for a variety of plausible, but misguided reasons. A few friends counselled against it at the time, but Prince Charles felt he had no option. The public was clamouring for a wedding. The dynasty needed one. The immediate royal family was pressurising Charles to make up his mind. Diana's family relished the idea of a union between the houses of Windsor and Spencer. Diana, at least to begin with, thought it would bring her happiness and fulfilment.

The Spencer family, it is claimed, have nursed ambitions to be at the heart of the British royal family for three hundred years. Lady Diana Spencer was descended from the Stuart House on five counts, including one legitimate one, and could claim a more ancient royal bloodline than the Windsors. In the early eighteenth century, Sarah Duchess of Marlborough, the former close friend and confidante of Queen Anne, attempted to marry her granddaughter, also Lady Diana Spencer, to the then Prince of Wales. A bribe of £100,000 is said to have been offered.

This time no bribe was required. Even Prince Charles's closest female friends supported the match. They considered Diana to be in love and had no doubt that she would agree to his proposal. As everything lined up, two key questions were overlooked. Were the couple compatible? Did they enter the union with the same expectations? Two modern questions, which under the old moral code of the aristocracy did not need to be asked. If compatibility was there and expectations matched, that was a bonus, but not a requirement of a successful marriage.

Those brought up in cultures where arranged marriages are

the norm were not shocked or surprised by the circumstances surrounding the marriage of the Prince and Princess of Wales. People raised with the expectations and values of the modern Western world, however, felt cheated and deceived when the facts of the wedding later emerged. How could the Prince have been so callous? How could he have been so cruel to his young bride? Surely a man should marry a woman by choice and in love?

Yet those same people, who on the wedding day cheered for, as they then believed, a couple in love, were not as modern and enlightened as they might suppose. While believing in and supporting contemporary ideas of romantic love, they were also endorsing the primeval instincts of their distant ancestors. Why was the wedding of interest? Why was it watched on television by millions? Why was it a day of celebration? Not because the couple were celebrities or heroes, but simply because he was royal and she, by marriage, was about to become royal. And royalty is an ancient and primitive institution, with an ancient and primitive attraction.

There is no way that Lady Diana Spencer could have evolved into the 'Queen of Hearts' without first marrying into the Royal House of Windsor. For all her physical allure and perceived qualities of compassion, had she not married Prince Charles, she would probably be alive today and a nobody. So what is it about royalty, even in the twentieth century, which through marriage and association transformed a rather unexceptional citizen into a fairytale princess possessed of astonishing gifts of empathy and beauty?

3

MAGIC AND
MYSTERY

Diana's early years of marriage were confused and miserable. Only the births of her two sons provided joy. If her own account of events is to be believed, she suffered the neglect of a selfish husband who cared more for his mistress than his wife. As a consequence of his behaviour she experienced bulimia, depression, threw tantrums, shouted and screamed for help, attempted suicide, demonstrated several other symptoms of self-harm and lived a lonely and misunderstood life.

At the same time, whenever she ventured out, she experienced a tide of devotion that both astonished and terrified her. It was far, far greater than anything she might have anticipated. To want to be famous is one thing, to be Princess of Wales and the focus of unrelenting attention and devotion is taking fame to another level entirely. The extent of the adulation took the royal circle by surprise. It also took her husband by surprise and Diana later suggested that he became increasingly jealous as her popularity grew. 'We were on our honeymoon in Australia and . . . I noticed that the media concerned themselves more with me than with him. I found that unfair, I wanted to share it with him. It upset him. It lead to jealousy from many sides and resulted in complicated situations.'[1]

Some of the places she visited in the early months were not bastions of monarchy. When she and Prince Charles went to Wales, some Welsh Nationalists had prepared banners carrying the message, 'Go home English Princess'. For a young English aristocrat to charm the socialist Welsh valleys was a tall order. Yet Diana triumphed. Tom Davies reporting for the *Observer* noted,

> Seasoned analysts of the Welsh psyche are having trouble sorting out why the Welsh have fallen so abjectly and hopelessly in love with Princess Diana. For three days and 400 miles last week there was the astonishing sight of a whole nation having a nervous breakdown on rain-swept streets. Choirs sang, harps tinkled forth and grown men cried. One old man in St David's cried, pulled himself together and burst out crying again.

Behind the scenes it was Diana who was weeping. She was unwell, both as a consequence of her pregnancy and of her bulimia, and she was overwhelmed by the emotions of the crowds. Several times she said she could not go on, but Prince Charles insisted she had to. She yearned for her old uncomplicated life in her flat with her friends. Her misery was compounded by the fact that when she overcame her fears and did her duty, including that of giving a speech in Welsh, she received not a word of praise from her husband.

Despite the unhappiness of her real life, her public persona had become an enormously powerful image. In the days of the mass media and the cult of celebrity, someone had emerged who was both a 'double-A' celebrity and who was also touched by the magic and mystery of royalty.

As a royal wife she was the successor to Queens Mary, Alexandra, Caroline and other names from history. As a star she was in the Hollywood galaxy along with Marilyn Monroe, Judy Garland, James Dean and Elvis Presley. And she had emerged when, thanks to modern means of mass communication and entertainment, the royal family was itself becoming an ingredient in the diet of mass culture. Indeed, within a year of the marriage the first fictionalised versions had been filmed by rival American television networks. 'Rose-tinted versions of the romance . . . culminating in the fairytale wedding and the balcony kiss. Little known look-alikes played Charles and Diana.'[2]

Prior to and at the time of her engagement Diana's superstar qualities had remained hidden. At that time comparisons had been made between Diana and another earl's daughter who had married into the family, the Queen Mother. But compared to Diana, the Queen Mother's popularity as it evolved was benign and unthreatening to the Royal House. True, the Queen Mother had an impressive capacity to mythologise herself, as A. N. Wilson put it 'to project a personal myth onto a credulous world . . . In spite of being a very rich woman who all her life had been pampered by servants and enjoyed everything handsome about her . . . she also managed to be the "Queen Mum" supposedly never happier than when condescending to East Enders and sharing the humble plight of her loyal subjects.'[3]

The Queen Mother myth however was one which helped bolster rather than undermine the monarchy. During the Second World War, when the myth evolved, it was a useful public relations ploy. The King and Queen nurtured a homely image and when Buckingham Palace was bombed Queen Elizabeth remarked that she could now look the East Enders in the eye. Monarch and subjects had suffered together.

Post war the Queen Mother myth became merely a charming and endearing vanity. Diana's equal gift for self-mythology, her power to make the public see her in her own terms, was of a different kind and magnitude and one which, when its true extent emerged, was not considered to be to the royal family's advantage. When the spotlight was on Diana, the rest of the royal family, the Queen included, were in the shadows. It took some time for the Diana effect to be recognised in these terms, both by the royal family and Diana. Certainly, in the early period following her wedding, the reactions and adorations of the crowds to Diana's public appearances were thought to be good for the monarchy. She added colour to the institution. It took some time for the point to sink in that the crowds were not interested in the monarchy as enhanced by its new member, but only interested in Diana herself. It was as if the magic of monarchy had not merely rubbed off on, but had been transferred from the Windsor family to her. Royal advisers had little understanding of what was happening and Diana herself was confused. In the early months she had not developed the strategies for coping with and manipulating the public responses that she used to powerful effect later on.

Diana lived a double life. In public she could do no wrong. She attracted huge attention wherever she went. People wanted to see her and touch her. The clothes she chose to wear set fashion trends. Her face set a new standard for beauty. But away from the crowds she was wracked with self-doubt. It seemed to her that her fairytale prince was cold and unsympathetic and far more interested in his gurus, his state duties, his pleasures and his mistress than in her.

Added to this she was living in royal palaces where everything was governed by tradition and protocol. Her body was undergoing the transformations of childbearing and the effect of this on her general health was not good. She was prone to sickness and, after the birth of her children, to post-natal depression. She tried to comfort herself with food, but then in fits of self-loathing induced herself to vomit the food back.

Diana was later to think of her bulimia as an addiction, and when she eventually conquered it she likened her achievement to that of an alcoholic who gives up drink. 'Like any addiction you know that one day it can come back and haunt you . . . The thing about eating disorders is that people think it's about fitting into a small dress or whatever, but it's not. It's in the head, it's about self-esteem and all that. It's difficult to explain it.'[4]

Diana described bulimia as a secret self-infliction:

One feels bad and because one is of the opinion that one has no value, one fills the stomach four or five times per day, sometimes even more often, and one feels good. That is as though one is being hugged, but that only lasts for a short time. And then one is so disgusted by the bulging stomach, and vomits. And this repeats itself time and time again – a destruction of the true self. It was completely normal for me to come home and go straight to the fridge. It was a symptom for all the things that were happening in my marriage. I cried, I screamed for help, but with the wrong signals . . . If one has bulimia then one shames oneself. One hates oneself. One doesn't mention it to other people. The unhappy fact is that one doesn't lose or put on weight. One can act as though everything were normal.[5]

The bulimia started only a week after the engagement. She maintained that a casual remark by Charles that she was on the chubby side was the trigger. Between February and July she lost a substantial amount of weight and her waist reduced from twenty-nine to twenty-three-and-a-half inches.

Her behaviour was noticed.

People were saying I gave my husband a hard time, that I was acting like a spoilt child, but I knew I just needed rest and patience and time to adapt to all the roles that were required of me overnight. By then there was immense jealousy because every single day I was on the front of the newspapers.[6]

Some people in the public eye never read the papers. Some actors are famed for never reading the critics. Politicians often get given digests of the day's reports prepared by civil servants and never get to read the papers themselves. These digests are often diplomatically censored to flatter or protect the minister. Diana however was an avid newspaper reader. 'She scoured every tabloid newspaper for photographs of herself almost, so it seemed to those about her, as if hoping to discover her identity there.'[7]

She focused in particular on two or three of the popular titles. She admitted later that she found press criticism hard to take. She took any adverse note about her dress sense or her demeanour to heart. She was desperate not to let down the royal family, yet her concerns were out of proportion. By and large the media coverage was more than simply favourable. It was outstanding in its praise, adoration and continuing fascination. To newspapers, magazines and television Diana was the undoubted star far outshining the other members of the royal family. Yet still she felt unsettled by criticism, however mild or slight. Fame had not delivered its promise. In public she was loved and adored, but out of the public gaze, shut off from contact with anyone other than the royal family and the palace staff, fame was no answer. A lack of self-confidence plagued her. The love showered on her by the world seemed synthetic and unreal when reported back to her in the newspapers. It was no substitute for the true affection of deep human contact. She sensed that her public adored the myth and not the real Diana.

'For photographers Diana became the pot of gold at the end of the rainbow,' observed one time Fleet Street editor, W. F. Deedes. 'They could not get enough of her. At first it was exciting for Diana, but it soon became exacting. Two high walls enclosed her, an overexcited and insatiable news media and the formidable group of men and women who served the Queen. Diana lost touch with many of her old friends who might have jollied her along.'[8]

She made several half-hearted suicide attempts. She cut her wrists and, when four months pregnant with William, threw herself down the stairs. She was badly bruised but not seriously injured.

> When no-one listens to oneself everything is possible inside one's thoughts. One feels pain inside and tries to injure oneself on the outside because one wants to receive help. The people are of the opinion that one just wants attention, although one has already got enough attention from the media. But I called for help so that I would be able to carry on playing my role. I mutilated myself. I couldn't cope under the pressure any more. I mutilated my arms and my legs.[9]

Although Prince Charles was not present during any of the suicide attempts or sessions of self-mutilation, Diana was, she later admitted, trying to get her husband's attention. She wanted him to listen to her. But he accused her, she claims, of 'crying wolf'.

Initially all the indications are that Prince Charles had been sympathetic, but as time went by he became increasingly confused and impatient with his wife's histrionics. To him, life in the royal family with its customs and duties was second nature. Surely Diana must have known what was to be expected of her: Had her father not been an equerry? Had she not lived at Sandringham and been on the periphery of royal affairs all her life? He was to underestimate the gap between the world of the royal family and the ordinary lives of other people. Despite her close royal connections, despite being a member of the ancient aristocracy, Diana had experienced as a young adult what it was like to live a normal life, albeit a relatively affluent and undemanding one. She had ridden on the tube, run her own bath, walked the street without being stared at, gone shopping, carried money and taken spontaneous decisions about her life. For Prince Charles everything he had ever done had been planned, had been special and privileged, and he knew no other way of living.

Not even choosing a wife was something he could be permitted to do without duty impinging. She had to be selected with care and then willing to adapt her life to his. And if his way of life included spending summers in a bleak Highland castle, riding to hounds, meeting tedious municipal officials and staying in close touch with his mistress, then that was the way of life to which Diana had to adapt.

For all her apparent qualifications the woman Charles married was not the 'mouse' he had first taken her to be. In her confusion and uncertainty, says Charles's biographer Jonathan Dimbleby, she was unpredictable and contradictory. Not only did she have tantrums and an eating disorder, she had a disconcerting personality trait which emerged in the early days of marriage and which she never overcame. It was her tendency to form intense, intimate relations with people, friends and staff alike, and then, without any apparent reason, or on some perceived minor slight, to drop that person from her life entirely or turn on them as enemies. If that person suffered a particularly brutal fall from grace, the Princess had an imaginative and vindictive capacity for vengeance. When her equerry Patrick Jephson fell out of favour he received a malicious text message accusing him of having an affair. He deduced the message could only have come from his employer.

As will be seen, it took seven years before there was a turning point and Diana discovered the resources and skills to take command of the situation. Part of the process involved inventing an image for herself with which she felt comfortable and which she could turn to her advantage. It was not a simple image, but it contained some very powerful elements. In 1993 A. N. Wilson said that her 'confused self-image', included the icon of Diana the Martyr.

In the mythology the carefree, innocent . . . was snatched by an older and more cynical man, who did not love her and who forced her to be the smiling bride, however cruel and cold he was towards her. Bravely, because this experience (added to the trauma of her parents' divorce) had taught her to understand suffering as few people did, Lady Di was able to stretch out healing hands to sufferers the world over. A tireless charity worker, our Saint was there in the midst . . . Not since Queen Anne had touched and allegedly healed the sick, had such claims been made by a Royal Personage.[10]

The supposed ability of the monarch to be able to cure diseases was an example of the survival of one of the ancient and mystic aspects of kingship. 'The belief in royal healing powers could, of course, be related to the idea of the king's . . . Christ-like character, although it may well have been a reflection of a more primal sense of the religious aura and magical power of the monarchy.'[11] The disease for which the royal touch was said to be most efficacious was the King's Evil, or scrofula, the inflammation of the lymph nodes. Henry II was recorded as having practised healing and the tradition continued through to the Hanoverians. The Stuarts in the seventeenth century were especially diligent in exhibiting their healing powers.

Unlike the Queen, Diana was a tactile person. As she met people in her line of duty, she did not restrict her contact to the proffer of a gloved hand. Diana hugged and squeezed and took children on her lap. And in doing so created iconic images for the photographers in attendance. She was seen in poses reminiscent of classic paintings of the Madonna with the Christ child.

Her 'touchy-feely' style was a huge departure from normal royal practice and protocol. Even in her lifetime claims were made that she had healing powers. Betty Palko, a psychic who was often consulted by Diana, said in 1996 that the Princess had the healing power of angels at her fingertips.[12]

While for many years members of the royal family, especially female members, had lent their names to charities and visited the sick, Diana took this traditional royal role, extended it, and then monopolised it.

Her different style was quickly noticed. It was visual and photogenic. Essentially she was doing what the Queen and many other members of the royal family have done for years, simply visiting hospitals and touring wards. Yet the way she performed the duty was so very different.

On one visit to a hospice she sat on the bed of a man dying of AIDS. She held his hand and then when the man began to cry she hugged him. It was an impulsive move. 'It was just so touching because he clung to me and he cried. Wonderful! It made him laugh, that's all right . . . I felt so comfortable in there. I just hated being taken away.'[13]

In 1987, when Diana first took an interest in AIDS, it was generally believed that the condition was highly contagious. Thunderous and apocalyptic television advertisements warned people of a potential epidemic. Patients, who were largely members of the gay community, were socially and medically shunned. Furthermore, some religious fundamentalists viewed AIDS as a punishment for those who had indulged in unnatural sexual practices. Medically there was still much to learn and AIDS patients were isolated and cared for by nursing staff who wore protective gowns, masks and gloves.

In this climate of apprehension and fear, Diana agreed to open a new purpose-built AIDS ward at a London hospital. Not only that. She made a conspicuous point of shaking hands with a patient and doing so without wearing gloves. The simple gesture changed the public's attitude towards the disease at a stroke. From that moment AIDS was viewed in a more understanding and sympathetic manner. Any residual stigma was entirely removed when she later cuddled a baby with AIDS.

In addition Diana also undertook unofficial, out-of-hours visits to hospitals. Although the press was seldom in attendance, word of her nocturnal and spontaneous visits to AIDS and children's wards quickly spread. She made repeat visits to several patients and wrote letters to cheer them when she was unable to see them in person.

Often what differentiated a Diana visit from that by any other royal was her ease of conversation. She never stood on ceremony, did not expect to be addressed as 'Ma'am', and she either chatted in an easy familiar style, or entered into a deep empathetic discussion.

There are numerous anecdotes to relate about the effect Diana had on those she visited. Often her involvement triggered a period of recovery. Patients who were depressed, or needed a new purpose, target or fillip, found that Diana's interest in their illness provided just the right stimulus.

Joy Bradbury was eleven years old when she underwent open-heart surgery. She was on a ventilator, drifting in and out of consciousness when Diana first visited her. She woke to find the Princess by her side. 'Until that moment Joy had not even had the strength to smile and her eyes had appeared listless to the nurses who were caring for her. Suddenly a smile crept across her face and her eyes lit up.'[14]

Joy's mother described it as a magical moment and said that Diana gave her daughter the will to live. By her presence, Diana had made Joy and the family feel special. And furthermore Diana stayed in contact to monitor Joy's recovery. And later, when she was well, Joy remained on Diana's Christmas-card list.

Four years before she died a Diana myth was well established. More cynical writers mocked it, but millions believed in it. The potential was there for a Diana legend, or a Diana cult to emerge. As this author wrote in 1996,

> No more powerful deed can trigger a legend than young death or martyrdom. Prince Charles, it is said, has often accused her of feigning 'martyrdom'. Her dramatic suicide attempts have been reported and one can only speculate on the powerful potential of a Diana cult if the Princess should by any ill chance meet an early end. She would no doubt become a figure as powerful as Evita, President Kennedy and Elvis Presley combined.[15]

It was revealing of the Queen's isolation from the world that she wrote to Hillary Clinton after Diana's death, 'I don't believe that anyone could have anticipated the scale of the public out-pouring of grief.'[16]

The Queen cannot however be entirely blamed for her failure to realise Diana's impact; royalty is of necessity set apart from the world. Its ancient purpose is to be set above, a link between earth and heaven. It is this mystical role that gives royalty the enduring qualities that no celebrity can claim by right.

In the early days, the Welsh crowds and others who turned out to see the new Princess of Wales, were enraptured by Diana's youth and novelty. True, she had been promoted to the position of a major world celebrity, but she was also a symbol of the enduring qualities of royalty. Built into the mystique of royalty is constant rejuvenation. One king dies, another succeeds. 'The King is dead, long live the King' is the cry when a new monarch is proclaimed. The origins of kingship are found in the ancient social rites associated with the seasons of the year, death of the old and the birth of the new. In Diana's youth and fertility it was possible to see new growth and potential.

'These aspects of sacred monarchy were clearly apparent in Celtic societies where the king was seen as possessing special powers of healing and divination and as upholding the moral and spiritual order of the people.'[17] A rule characterised by a 'mystical entity from which radiated harmony' brought fertility to the land and prosperity to the people, while the opposite brought about natural disasters.

There is one simple way to demonstrate the ancient power of royalty even in the modern world. It is to ask, what might have become of Lady Diana Spencer if she had not married the Prince of Wales? Despite what was said of her in later years, there was much about her that was ordinary. She was a bit on the tall side, her looks were not classic, her voice was unremarkable. Her connections, family wealth and title would have given her a good start in life. She would never have experienced a lifestyle below that of 'comfortable'. She would in all probability have married a young man in the higher echelons of society. Her photograph would not have appeared on the front cover of every major newspaper and magazine, but she would have had her portrait in *Country Life* at the time of her engagement and later, on a regular basis, in her local county magazine. Her children may well have gone to Eton. She might, like her mother, have divorced. If not, her royal connections might have qualified her for a position at court, as a lady-in-waiting perhaps, following in her grandmother's footsteps. It is not improbable that her career path would have been with a charity, in a paid or voluntary capacity. If she had died tragically young in a car accident it would have been a sad time for her family, but not a major national event. And no one would have questioned the official explanation for the accident.

It was the act of marrying into a royal house that elevated Diana. It endued her with intangible and ancient qualities. Instinctively she did things that were to revive the magic of royalty, a magic that the House of Windsor was on the verge of losing. Only later did she come to realise what acts and deeds worked particularly well. Only with hindsight can one start to identify why her actions resonated at a deep level. In the early days she simply did what came naturally to her, and it was instantly noticed that there was something different about her. She did not act as other royals did. She was not stiff, formal and hidebound by protocol. The Queen and other members of the royal family had become rather dull. Diana was spontaneous and vivacious.

From the start many people found in Diana a touch of magic and a glimpse of Camelot. She was someone around whose image it was easy to weave tales. She could be a metaphor for a return to a golden age. As one member of the British Order of Druids observed to the social anthropologist Marion Bowman on the day of Diana's funeral, Diana had brought the ancient British bloodline back into the royal family. 'The British people warmed so much to Diana because they instinctively recognised the true royal, their real monarch.'[18]

'It was clear the royal family had acquired a valuable new asset', wrote Robert Lacey at the time. 'Accomplished and charming though the young royals like Prince Charles and Prince Andrew might be, they were almost too smooth: quirkiness and spontaneity had been polished out of them by their meticulous royal upbringing. This new recruit has chirpiness and originality.'[19]

Since the days of Queen Victoria, as political power ebbed away from the monarch, the British royal family has nurtured its role as the model family. It has seen itself as setting an example of loyalty and duty in family as well as national affairs. The image was seriously dented in 1936 when the King, Edward VIII, decided to marry a divorced woman, Wallis Simpson. The combined force of government, church and public opinion forced him to abdicate. He was succeeded by his younger brother. To repair the damage of the abdication, the new royal family concentrated on playing the role of model family and played it to perfection. During the years of the Second World War and the period of austerity that followed, their public displays of ordinariness and domesticity hit precisely the right note.

When the present Queen succeeded her father in 1952 she and her family formed a neat domestic unit – husband, wife and two young children. She was a serious woman for whom duty was all-important. She was protected from the realities of life by protocol and courtiers. She was a woman of faith who sincerely believed that God had given her a solemn vocation in life. The ancient words of the coronation of 1953 reinforced this belief, as they invoke ancient rites and biblical precedent.

Be thy head anointed with Holy Oil: as kings, priests, and prophets were anointed. And as Solomon was anointed king by Zadok the priest and Nathan the prophet, so be thou anointed, blessed, and consecrated

Queen over the People, whom the Lord thy God hath given thee to rule and govern, In the Name of the Father, and of the Son, and of the Holy Ghost. Amen.[20]

Hers was not to be a reign of flamboyant gesture. Personal popularity was not of importance. She had a calling from God to perform conscientiously her ancient duties for the welfare and good of her subjects. In private she lives a curious life that blends extraordinary privilege with the entirely mundane. Who else pours her breakfast cereal from a Tupperware container as she is serenaded by a personal piper? She has intimate access to affairs of state, including a weekly audience with the Prime Minister of the day. She has met all the important people on the world stage of the last half century. Yet her real interests lie in country pursuits, keeping corgis and breeding racehorses.

She greets ambassadors, confers honours, performs the arcane and curious rituals of state, embodies all that is required within her royal vocation, without encouraging or displaying any of the magic or mystery.

Yet displaying magic and mystery is the ancient purpose of royalty. The monarch as the go-between twixt God and the people can be traced back to pre-industrial cultures. Its roots lie in the Shaman of hunter-gatherer tribes. They were both healers and priests who through ritual and by virtue of descent and inherited powers communed with the gods and provided physical and psychological healing to the community. These Shamans, medicine men or wise women, came from a caste or oligarchy and had the secrets transmitted to them through the family. As societies became more urban, the Shaman became the sorcerer kings. During various stages of evolution monarchs have been demi-gods, warriors, philosophers as well as healers. As the gods themselves do not show themselves, kings and queens must act vicariously to enable the people to have a glimpse of the numinous.

The theme of monarchy looms large in the Bible and the British character has been much influenced over history by the Old and New Testaments. Much of the ceremonial and ritual associated with the British monarchy today is based on Old Testament practice and precedent, claims the theologian Ian Bradley.

> This is particularly true of the coronation service in which the central sacred act is the anointing of the monarch with holy oil. The anthem which has been sung at the most solemn moment of the crowning of every English sovereign since Edgar in 973 is taken directly from the account in the first chapter of the first Book of Kings of the coronation of Solomon by Zadok the priest and Nathan the prophet.[21]

The music composed by Handel to which the anthem is now sung is today a highly popular, classical work.

> More broadly the Old Testament provides one of the main sources for our understanding monarchy as having an essential sacred and spiritual character. There are those who take it as a literal model and who see British monarchs standing in direct descent from King David and having a special covenant with God as rulers of his chosen people.[22]

If the British royal family would not admit to this overtly, there do nevertheless exist ample reminders to her subjects of the Queen's special religious calling. Every coin spent has imprinted on it in an abbreviated form that the Queen reigns by the grace of God and is the Defender of the Faith.

When Diana joined the royal family by marriage, there still lurked somewhere in the collective mind of the British people – even in a land with a fading adherence to formalised Christianity – a latent, spiritual understanding of monarchy.

Something of the Old Testament concept of monarchy survives, as an institution that derives from God, with whom the monarch stands in a close and special relationship.

Monarchy is still perceived as a sacred institution, with kings and queens 'having a close and intimate involvement with the nation's public worship and a high and solemn calling as both the principal channel for, and the human model of, God's rule of righteousness and justice'.[23]

In being prepared for her coronation the young Queen was schooled in the biblical precedents. She was given a programme of daily Christian readings and meditations to prepare herself spiritually for the day. She prayed in her first Christmas broadcast for 'wisdom and strength' to carry out the solemn promises she would be making.

Over the years there have been some disreputable monarchs. Henry VIII was a bully and tyrant. Many of the Hanoverians were debauchees and lechers. The Queen's own uncle, Edward VIII was vain and self-centred and had Nazi sympathies. So the constitutional theory has been developed that the person of the monarch should not be confused with the role. However unworthy of reverence a monarch might be as an individual, the office and calling remain untainted. The flip side of that theory is that however dull and uninteresting the monarch might be as a person; the potency of the office should not be diminished.

By 1981 when Diana married Charles the monarchy had not lost its potent magic and mystery, but it lay dormant. The Queen had settled into middle age, conscientiously performing her duty, but with little imagination or flare. The young royals were objects of curiosity and gossip, but exhibited few charismatic qualities.

The royal wedding was the occasion for a reawakening of Britain's mystical relationship with royalty. Not that Diana would have intellectualised it that way. That would not have been her style or interest.

Like 1961, the year of Diana's birth, 1981 was again a fearful year. The tensions of the Cold War had not gone away. Indeed the nuclear stand off was entering a new phase. For many years the threat of nuclear war had been real, but somehow in Britain the threat seemed removed from daily life. It was theoretical rather than imminent as the weapons and silos were kept out of view. By the early 1980s plans were well developed to base a new generation of weapons on British soil. The cruise missiles would be launched from mobile units that would leave their silos and travel to launch sites around the countryside. Convoys of military vehicles practising for war became a common sight on the roads in southern England. A main base for these missiles was Greenham Common in Berkshire where in 1981 a women's demonstration against the deployment of these highly conspicuous weapons turned into a full-scale peace camp.

As suggested earlier, Diana's wedding to Charles was as welcome a diversion from the concerns of Cold War politics as it was from the other social problems besetting the nation. How much more comfortable to celebrate a fairytale wedding than to contemplate nuclear annihilation or inner-city injustice. A new Princess of Wales, the promise of a new family, all so much more comforting than the alarming fact of political life that American nuclear weapons were being driven along the highways of Britain and young men were setting light to cars in south London and Liverpool.

But the wedding was more than simply a pleasant diversion. Deep within the human psyche other forces were being stirred. They were the primitive forces of archetype. Diana represented certain timeless emotions that lurk within all people. Normally they surface as stories and legends. In Diana they could fix on her as a living story.

The first archetype was the least accurate but, superficially, the most appealing. Diana was Cinderella. She had lost her mother when young, had acquired a 'wicked' stepmother, cleaned the house of her sister and was eventually transformed into a princess. The fact that Diana was never a kitchen drudge, being paid a fair wage for her short spell as a domestic cleaner to her sister, and saw a great deal of her mother and very little of her stepmother, should not be allowed to get in the way of the fairytale.

* * *

The second archetype is however more complex and profound. Diana was the virgin bride destined to give birth to a future king.

In its best-known form this legend is found in Christianity, although many Christians would argue forcefully that the story of the nativity of Christ is history and not myth, if myth is understood to imply that the story is fictitious. As the New Testament relates, the Christ-child was conceived miraculously. Mary was impregnated by the Holy Spirit and Jesus had no earthly, biological father. Some Christians say that Mary remained a virgin and earned herself a special and exalted place in heaven; others say she later gave birth to other children. The biblical evidence has been interpreted in different ways.

The story of the Christ being born to a virgin can be traced back to the Old Testament book of Isaiah and a passage later quoted by St Matthew the Evangelist, 'Behold a virgin shall conceive and bear a son.'

Throughout history and across cultures, virginity has embraced mystical qualities. Even in the twentieth century it was clearly seen as necessary that the new bride of the Prince of Wales had to be a virgin. When the satirical magazine *Private Eye* threatened to research Diana's past boyfriends, her uncle offered a quote to a well-known royal correspondent to confirm his niece's virginity. 'Lord Fermoy's exclusive to James Whitaker created a sensation. Never before had an uncle of any prospective bride of any well-known member of the royal family, privately or publicly commented on the intactness of his niece's hymen . . . The royal family didn't bat an eyelid.'[24]

How the uncle knew such an intimate detail was never revealed.

Virginity symbolises both purity and the promise of fertility. When Christianity synchronised with the Roman Mithraic Cult and other pagan belief systems in the early centuries after Christ, the mystique of virginity became absorbed into it. This happened most notably when the

Roman midwinter festival was adopted as the birthday of Christ. The winter solstice was believed to be the date of the nativity of the sun. In other parts of the ancient world there were similar festivals. In Syria and Egypt the celebrants retired into certain inner shrines and emerged at midnight with the cry, 'The Virgin has brought forth, the light is waxing!' The Egyptians represented the newborn sun as a baby.

In another parallel pre-Christian myth, Attis was said to have been a humble shepherd boy loved by Cybele, the mother of the gods, the Asiatic goddess of fertility. The birth of Attis, as Sir James Frazer points out, was said to have been miraculous. His mother, Nana, was a virgin who conceived by placing a ripe pomegranate in her bosom.[25]

The Queen of Heaven, whose worship was denounced by the Old Testament prophet Jeremiah, is said to have been the wife of the Babylonian ruler who claimed that her son was born to a virgin. Even in modern times the story has its equivalents. In a fable about the birth of Elvis Presley, fans say he was born in a house little bigger than a stable and a strange blue light shone across the sky at the time of his arrival. When he was conceived his earthly father Vernon is said to have blacked out and been taken out of his body to allow a supernatural impregnation of his wife to occur. Elvis, say his fans, went on to become their King! One implication behind the legend is that if a virgin conceives then no ordinary man is the father. The father must therefore be a superman, god or demi-god.

The earthly son of a monarch can make no such claim, yet socially the man is set apart. Charles was given a strange and unique upbringing to prepare himself for the day when he would be anointed with holy oil and take upon himself the sacred duty of kingship. What had to be certain in the days before DNA testing was that a child was truly the son of his or her father and that the bloodline had not been intercepted or contaminated.

In some Christian traditions the mother of Christ is raised to the role of a demi-god. Mary is vested with a position of unique privilege as the mother of the redeemer of the world. If a collective unconscious is at work, as Jung has suggested, and the human mind constructs and acts upon archetypes, it comes as no surprise that in Prince William, the public has found a redeemer. Following Diana's death, a substantial body of public opinion supported the suggestion that Charles should be bypassed and William become the heir to the throne.

Increasingly the prayers and cards offered at Kensington Palace gate on the anniversaries of the death refer to William: 'May God keep him', 'May he grow to be like his mother'. There is no great calling for a republic, despite widespread disappointment with the House of Windsor. The monarchy, it is felt can be redeemed and revived. William is the favoured means. It is his destiny to restore the magic and mystery of the monarchy.

He may indeed be a wise young man, but the expectations placed on him are huge and probably unrealistic.

A third archetype comes into play when examining the life of Princess Diana. It is one also identified with Mary. The woman of sorrow who knows what it is to suffer. In Diana's case she did not grieve for the death of a son, but for the death of a marriage. Or, in a variation on the same archetypical theme, she is the suffering wife; hurt, cheated and abandoned.

Before the separation and divorce there were years of rumours that the marriage was an unhappy one. Diana chose to confirm the rumours in several ways, the most striking and powerful being the moment she chose to be photographed sitting alone in front of the Taj Mahal. It was in the course of a visit to India by the Prince and Princess. Twelve years earlier the Prince had been so impressed by the beauty of the famous building, a seventeenth-century tomb erected by a Mogul emperor in memory of his wife and sometimes described as a temple to romantic love, that he had said one day he would return with his bride.

As it happened the Prince found himself committed to deliver a speech to a forum of Indian businessmen on the day in the schedule when the Princess was shown the Taj Mahal. She took full advantage of the photo opportunity. She posed alone 'before one of the world's great monuments to love, the image both suggested an unbearable isolation and administered a fearsome rebuke to a loveless and errant husband. For most British reporters . . . this was almost the only significant event of the entire royal visit to India.'[26]

She wished to be seen as the archetypal wronged wife betrayed by an uncaring husband. Or, to turn the fairystory around, she wanted the world to know that she was the woman who kissed a prince and he turned into a toad.

4

THE WOUNDED HEALER

The story of Diana's life from wedding to separation follows two parallel tracks. On the one track was the world megastar, never failing to turn heads and set fashion standards.

Increasingly she took on traditional royal duties, as president or patron of various charities. From tentative beginnings she developed a unique style of involvement that made a substantial contribution to the work she sponsored. She employed the magic of royalty in ways that had almost been forgotten.

As well as being involved with big-name charities such as the Red Cross, she lent support to numerous unpopular or unglamorous causes: eating disorders, drug addiction, homelessness. When she wanted to be, she was an intelligent contributor of ideas, and conscientious and hard working. She took the trouble to learn a speech in sign language for a deaf audience. She was a prolific writer of letters. No day was ever complete without writing the required thank you letters or notes to cheer up some of the children or hospital patients she had seen that day. While other members of the royal family might ask a member of staff to write, and a typed letter 'the Queen commands me to thank you for . . .' would be sent, Diana usually wrote letters in her own clear bold hand and often signed 'with love Diana'.

The second track of her life was troubled and initially hidden well from view. The bulimia, the post-natal depression, the raging anger she felt about Charles and Camilla, the lack of self-confidence and the exhibition from time to time of her capacity to sever friendships and harbour grudges.

Over the years the two tracks in her life came more and more to impinge on each other. She discovered how to use her public image to further her private battles. New skills she acquired to cope with public life were employed in her private life and she grew in self-esteem. Her intuitive spiritual life took on a new purpose. Her self-perceived public calling as someone who brought comfort to the sick, dying and despised, enabled her to shape in her own mind a picture of herself. It was this self-image that would sustain her. This picture, a mythic picture, which she also did much to promote to the media, gave her another archetypal role to play: that of the wounded healer.

The wounded healer was one who in ancient societies underwent a quest for knowledge during which he or she had to endure painful trials and overcome suffering to become spiritually transformed. It was a shamanic vocation undertaken for the benefit of the tribe and, as suggested earlier, in many studies of the origins of royalty, the shaman are described as priest-kings and the forerunners of monarchs.

She also drew strength from her encounters with others in her caring role and found them therapeutic herself.

Eventually, when the separation was announced, the two tracks of Diana's life – the public and the private – had substantially merged and she started life afresh. She set up her own home with her own staff and her own court with her chosen band of advisers who were expected to give her 100 per cent loyalty. She was, according to Paul Burrell, who had been hand-picked from Prince Charles's staff to join hers, a new woman.

That was yet to come. First of all, Princess Diana had to perform the duty for which she had been selected. She gave birth to her two sons within little more than three years of her wedding. With the birth of two healthy children she had delivered on her dynastic promise. She presented the House of Windsor with 'an heir and a spare'. When she discovered she was pregnant it was, Diana later admitted, 'an incredible relief. I think that the whole country felt the same as me. It was really a huge relief for me.'[1] She would no doubt have had in mind her mother's unhappy experience at failing to produce a healthy son on demand.

The eldest child William was born on midsummer's day, 21 June 1982, after a difficult and unhappy pregnancy. The descriptions given later by Charles and Diana of the circumstances of the birth and their joint and separate reactions to the arrival of their son were in sharp contrast to each other. Charles authorised Jonathan Dimbleby to publish extracts from a private letter he had sent to his godmother shortly after the event.

> I am so thankful I was beside Diana's bedside the whole time because by the end of the day I really felt as though I had shared deeply in the process of birth and as a result was rewarded by seeing a small creature which belonged to us even though he seemed to belong to everyone else as well!

Diana recorded this recollection of events.

> When we had William we had to find a date in the diary that suited Charles and his polo. William had to be induced because I couldn't handle the press pressure any longer, it was becoming unbearable . . . I was sick as a parrot the whole way through the labour, very bad labour. They wanted a Caesarean, no one told me this

until afterwards. Anyway, the boy arrived, great excitement. Thrilled, everyone absolutely high as a kite – we had found a date where Charles could get off his polo pony for me to give birth. That was very nice, felt very grateful about that! Came home and then postnatal depression hit me hard . . . Boy was I troubled . . . tears, panic all the rest of it.[2]

If the pregnancy and birth had been difficult, so was the post-natal period.

To wake up in the morning and simply have the feeling that one really doesn't want to get up, one feels misunderstood. I had a bad conscience. I had never experienced that before. But when I analysed it I could see that the changes from the past few years had caught up with me.

I was the first in this family who had had such a depression, who had cried in public. And that was naturally disturbing. One had a new label that one could place on me. Diana is not balanced, is unstable, weak.[3]

Prince Harry was born on 15 September 1984. The two years between the brothers were, their mother later described, such a pain that much of it she had blotted from her mind. Although she did admit that for six weeks before the birth she and Charles were closer than they had ever been before and would ever be again. At the moment of their second son's birth however, in Diana's words, 'bang, our marriage went down the drain!'[4]

Initially Charles expressed disappointment that she had produced a boy and not a girl and then he noted disparagingly that the newly arrived infant had red hair. In that moment perhaps Diana saw her own father expressing his bitter disappointment at her birth. When Charles shared his thoughts with Diana's mother Frances she told him sharply to be thankful that his son was healthy and normal.

Later there was speculation that it was at that moment Charles realised the child was not his. Many rumours have circulated that Diana's affair with James Hewitt had started earlier than either ever admitted. There is undeniably a superficial physical resemblance between Harry and Hewitt. On the other hand, photographs of Diana's own father as a young man also have a look of Hewitt. Undoubtedly Hewitt had met Diana before Harry's birth. There is video evidence of him at a polo match attended by the Princess. Also, around nine months before the birth of Harry, relations between Charles and Diana were, it is alleged, at a particular low as Charles was spending an increasing amount of time fox-hunting. It was through hunting that Charles engineered the opportunity to spend time with Camilla.[5] In the absence of published DNA evidence it would appear from all known circumstances that the Prince's red hair and general appearance can be traced to Spencer and not Hewitt genes. Claims that a DNA test was done and endorsed Prince Charles's paternity[6] were made by Simone Simmons, a former adviser to the Princess, but never officially confirmed. Yet to fuel speculation on the other side, in a television interview given in 2005 by an emotional James Hewitt and conducted under hypnosis, Diana's former lover admits that their relationship started far earlier than had been previously suggested and before the birth of Prince Harry.[7]

At this stage it is in no one's interest to pursue further the idea that Prince Harry might be James Hewitt's child. Prince Harry is in all family and legal senses Prince Charles's son and second heir. If any evidence exists to suggest otherwise it is bound to be known somewhere in the secret archives of state. The royal family is the most carefully monitored family in the country. Every member is accompanied by a police protection officer and even private telephone calls are monitored, as both Prince Charles and Princess Diana were to discover. As things stand at present those who might have access to sensitive information, should it exist, see nothing to gain from making it public. .

Apart from her trip to Wales, Diana was broken into her royal duties relatively gently: visits to the ballet; the twenty-fifth anniversary of the London Film Festival; Remembrance Day at the Cenotaph; and her first solo engagement – switching on the Regent Street Christmas lights. Her diary in her first year might have been a great deal busier had she not become pregnant. In the event the light royal duties she did perform were an agony as she battled with morning sickness, bulimia and the increasing tensions in her relationship with her new husband. She sensed the real, or imagined, judgement of the royal family on her. Diana, she felt, was being seen as a problem, and the sympathy of the family went out to Charles who was having such a hard time.

The attitude of the world's media did nothing to help; every press photographer viewed Diana as 'the prize'. Nothing sold quite so quickly or handsomely to newspapers than photographs of Diana. She became used to hordes of photographers and barriers of flash bulbs at every public engagement. It was the feeling of being relentlessly pursued off duty as well which became debilitating, and she was irked by the fact that she was being used as a trading commodity, her image bought and sold for commercial gain. Editors were summoned to meetings at the palace, Diana's mother Frances wrote to the press asking for restraint, but to no avail. When Diana was five months pregnant, prying telephoto lenses even caught her on a private beach in a bikini.

Reading her own accounts of the early years of marriage, they appear very self-absorbed. Her pregnancy coincided with Britain going to war, but no mention is made of the Falklands conflict. From April, when the Argentineans invaded the remote South Atlantic British settlement, through to July and the service of thanksgiving for victory held in St Paul's Cathedral, the nation was transfixed by the conflict. Compared with other military conflicts the casualty rate was not high, but for the family of every serviceman and woman involved it was a time of extreme worry. Diana's own brother-in-law, Prince Andrew, was directly involved as a helicopter pilot, but Diana's accounts of the period focus on her sickness, eating disorder, her concerns about Charles and Camilla and preparing the apartment at Kensington Palace into which the family moved as a London base a few weeks before William's arrival.

By contrast, Prince Charles followed events in the Falklands closely. He was frustrated at being so far removed from the action and unable to contribute. To compensate he devoted as much time as he could to boosting morale from a distance and in greeting troops on their return. 'Having felt extremely guilty and frustrated that I could do nothing during the South Atlantic operation, the least I could do was to try and show all the returning servicemen how much we appreciated their efforts.'[8]

Interestingly, several years later, during the Gulf War, Diana followed events very closely. Her attention was caught by a new interest in military and diplomatic affairs, but also by the fact that her lover James Hewitt was serving in the war zone.

In those first, self-absorbed years of her marriage Princess Diana seems to have thought of little but herself, her immediate engagements, her clothes and problems with her husband, his mistress and her in-laws. It is fair to say she was a loving and much-loved mother and so her sons also absorbed much of her time. But as for the outside world, in none of the unofficial interviews she gave about the state of her mind and marriage did she ever refer to such events as miners' strikes or the IRA bombing campaigns. The economic disparities of the Thatcher era passed her by. It was the time when three million people were unemployed while a new breed of high earners nicknamed 'yuppies' were earning huge salaries. The 'haves' flaunted their money and were epitomised by the grotesque comic creation of the comedian Harry Enfield who strutted the stage brandishing wads of notes and boasting he had 'loadsa money'. Diana might have seen this world on the television, but it was not one that appears to have mattered to her.

Diana's indifference to outside events cannot be solely blamed on her own introspection. As a member of the royal family she was deliberately protected from the realities of life. The royal family is positively discouraged from showing an interest in political issues, as Diana was to learn much later when she left the protection of the royal circle and began to take an interest in the landmine campaign.

And royal protection does far more than provide a shield from disagreeable political and social facts. It creates an unreal world within its protection, a kind of luxurious prison, within which Diana was confined.

From the moment the engagement to Charles had become official, Diana's life had been taken over by the royal system. The Camilla problem and her difficult pregnancy did not help, but even without those additional concerns, the transition from Sloane Ranger to Princess of Wales would have been difficult. The royal family lived according to a rigid routine and Diana was expected to fit in. But to her, Balmoral in the rain was not an enticing prospect, although to the Queen and Prince Charles it was comforting and familiar. Court protocol was also a bind with officials being sticklers for convention. Diana tried to shape her own life, but it was always an uphill struggle. She attempted to make changes, but Charles appeared stuck in his bachelor ways. During one row he even said that he had his parents' permission to live a separate life if, after five years, the marriage was not working out. His valet Stephen Barry left and his private secretary as well. Diana was blamed, but vigorously denied that she had precipitated the departures.

For a while Diana also succeeded in persuading her husband to see his friends from his bachelor days less often. She thought of them as hangers-on and sycophants who did nothing to the marriage. The Prince even got rid of a Labrador dog the Princess took exception to in an effort to placate his wife.

For both Diana and Charles the period between the birth of William and the birth of Harry was difficult. She was troubled, moody, angry and disturbed. He was confused with no idea what to do for the best. He suggested treatments and therapies, but none seemed appropriate to Diana.

Yet in the middle of this period the couple undertook a demanding, and triumphant, forty-five day tour to Australia. They left in March 1983, taking Prince William with them. When the Queen had undertaken her world tour shortly after her coronation, Charles was left behind with nannies. Diana insisted that her son would not be separated from her.

Diana was astonishingly popular in Australia and the popularity often appeared to be at the expense of respect for her husband. 'In Australia the princess had pulled vast crowds and charmed the media with the beauty of her smile and her radiant aura', wrote the Prince's biographer Jonathan Dimbleby.

> So infatuated was the throng at every walkabout that as they got out of the car to 'work' the crowd, an involuntary moan of disappointment would rise from that part of the crowd which turned out to be nearest to the prince and furthest from the princess. Even as they drove through the streets the prince could hear the cries of disappointment, 'Oh no, she's on the wrong side.' It sapped his confidence . . . His distress . . . was compounded by the placards and cartoons which exaggerated the mild protuberance of his ears which had caused him such agony as a child . . . He could not resist a spasm of anguish as he confronted the fatuous remarks and insults.[9]

There is a convergence between the account given by the Prince's champion Jonathan Dimbleby and the Princess's Andrew Morton. Morton writes of the Australian tour that the public reaction to the couple served to drive a wedge between them.

> The crowds complained when Prince Charles walked

over to their side of the street during a walkabout. Press coverage focussed on the Princess; Charles was confined to a walk-on role. It was the same later that year when they visited Canada . . . As a former member of his household explained: 'he never expected this kind of reaction. After all he was the Prince of Wales. When he got out of the car people would groan. It hurt his pride and inevitably he became jealous. It was all very sad.'[10]

The observations serve as a reminder that princes are human, prone to human feelings of hurt and resentment. Behind the title and the position there is an ordinary man capable of envy and hurt. Most outsiders would look at the circumstances and have little sympathy for the Prince. His perceived slight is but a small price to pay for a life of wealth and privilege. Yet Prince Charles knew no other world than that of being the centre of attention. On previous visits to Australia he most certainly had been the centre of attention. Girls had flocked to him. He took his demotion by his wife with bad grace. It did nothing to help a marriage already troubled by distrust and illness.

The pattern of the first years of marriage was set. In public Princess Diana was an international star. In private she felt cooped up by the restrictions and impositions of being royal. She felt inadequate to the tasks being expected of her and unappreciated by her husband who she suspected, rightly as it turned out, of being in love with another woman. Her body was undergoing the hormonal changes of two pregnancies and she found her escape route from her troubles in a form of self-harming illness: bulimia.

Slowly however she found ways of coping and taking control of her life. She turned the imposition of being constantly shadowed by protection officers to her advantage by forming close friendships with several of them. She discovered ways she could use her public reputation to her own advantage: firstly by extending her own role as a 'healer' into a two way process; and secondly by learning the dark art of public relations and spin-doctoring to be able to manipulate the message of the media in the way she wished.

While this did nothing to save the marriage, for Prince Charles turned to Camilla for comfort and support from an early date, it did provide Diana with a double purpose. It enabled her to carve out her own unique niche in public life, which survived after her divorce and it gave her the weapons she needed to pursue her private war against Charles and his mistress.

There have been few previous members of the royal family who have enjoyed a strong popular rapport with the public. Queen Caroline and Princess Charlotte are two examples from two hundred years ago. Diana was unique however because her rapport was developed in the era of mass communication. She combined the magic of monarchy with that of celebrity stardom. Her particular strength was being very photogenic. Some people complain that photographs never do them justice; others find that the camera persistently flatters them. Diana was one of those who could never be photographed badly. She once complained about a photograph taken of her without her permission or knowledge when she was exercising at the gym. When it appeared in the tabloids she was angered by the fact that there had been a breach of trust and the photograph had been taken sneakily. Despite the photograph having been snatched when she was entirely off guard, it is still a picture of a fine, fit, attractive woman and in no way uncomplimentary.

'The camera loved her and she responded to it so well that her image became one of the best-known in the world', wrote Jeffrey Richards.

> She also achieved the elusive blend of being ordinary and extraordinary at the same time, which is often the secret of stardom. As a princess, a multi-millionairess and a jet-setting international celebrity, Diana was obviously extraordinary. But she was ordinary too, in her humanity and vulnerability.'[11]

What irked Diana about the photographers who pursued her through life was that she could never be rid of them. She enjoyed posing for the accredited press corps and often used their attentions to make a point. The paparazzi however were a different matter. As was seen on the night of her death, wherever she went out in public a pack of unofficial photographers swarmed after her. The celebrity paparazzi make their living from the photographs that their quarries, normally celebrities of various ranks, do not want taken. The objective is to capture a moment the star would prefer the tabloid readers did not know about – in the course of a secret tryst or on a bad-hair day. Diana was in a league of her own as a celebrity and any picture taken of her off duty, whatever story it told, was one that could sell for thousands of dollars around the world.

Arthur Edwards of *The Sun* is one of Britain's leading tabloid royal newspaper photographers. He first met Diana when she was a shy nineteen-year-old, and he was also a member of the press pack following her around the Mediterranean when she was holidaying with Dodi shortly before she died. The occasion of the first meeting of photographer and Princess was completely different. She was then still 'new' news and her likeness was not yet instantly recognisable. Edwards only recognised her because she was wearing a necklace with a 'D' on it. He asked her to pose for a photograph and she did it perfectly, as Arthur recalls:

> During her courtship with Prince Charles she was often besieged by photographers outside her West London flat and I was only able to help her once when she was surrounded by French photographers and was about to breakdown and cry.

A few weeks later she got engaged to Prince Charles and by then she was dealing confidently with the royal photographers. She needed no one's advice on how best to cope. She had made few mistakes and those few she had made she learned from quickly. It was not a good idea, for instance, she discovered during an early photocall, to stand directly in front of the sun. The resulting picture, though modest and charming, made it appear that she was wearing a see-through skirt.

> However, she did have a lot of problems with the paparazzi who continually pestered her whenever she left the safety of Kensington Palace. They buzzed round her like mosquitoes and she felt she would never be free of their attentions.[12]

In Arthur Edwards's view, Diana knew how to manipulate the press and was very clever at it.

> But a certain section of the press hunted her, which could send her into a deep depression. By and large, she was in control and handled herself brilliantly.

> She took us to Angola, Bosnia, Aids clinics in Harlem, and the slums of Rio de Janeiro. By highlighting these huge problems hopefully we did some good. If this is how she manipulated the press, then she did a very good job.

> But you can't have your cake and eat it. If you try to control what newspapers say about you, you are in for a big shock. They are not PR sheets for Buckingham Palace, Number 10 Downing Street or anybody else. They say it how it is and they do not mind whose feelings get hurt. Occasionally this happened to the princess and she did not like it.

> I personally felt sorry for Diana. Everybody stared at her wherever she went – even the policemen who were supposed to be protecting her could not take their eyes off her. She was simply a very gorgeous lady and sadly

she had to suffer this endless scrutiny whenever she appeared in public.

There were however some times when I felt ashamed to be part of the same profession as some of the other photographers.[13]

Several members of the royal family have had moments in their lives when they were paparazzi prey. Prince Charles – in particular when he was a bachelor and there was an insatiable interest in who he might be courting; the Duchess of York at times when she was being especially outrageous was also the focus. It was a paparazzi telephoto lens that captured intimate and embarrassing photographs of Fergie holidaying with her financial adviser. For sixteen years, Diana was only truly free of paparazzi pressure when safely in her own home. To compound her problem, the 1980s and 90s were the decades in which the media became more intrusive and less willing to impose self-restraint than at any time in the history of mass worldwide communication. For the first time politicians began to talk in terms of legislation to curb press intrusion. Many appeals were made by the Palace press officers for restraint, but if they had any effect it was short-lived. Anyway, the British tabloid editors argued, how could they be expected to exercise restraint when it was often, especially by the early 1990s, members of the royal family feeding them with stories.

The problem was not confined to Britain. It was worldwide and a function of increasingly cut-throat competition between popular newspaper titles for readers in a steadily declining market. The veteran journalist W. F. Deedes blamed Rupert Murdoch, whom he described as republican and iconoclast. His British tabloid, *The Sun*, was in a fierce circulation war with its main rival, the *Daily Mirror*. The tabloids thrived on sensation and their editors knew what was required of them. W. F. Deedes concurred with the view that in the 1980s 'the British tabloid press was changing character. Its new face had sharper fangs and a more derisive smirk.'[14]

As a young bride, and before she learned how to turn media interest to her advantage, Diana had no one to whom she could turn for advice or understanding about dealing with the persistent unwanted attention of the press. Who else had ever been in her position? Shortly after she had married she had met Princess Grace of Monaco, the film actress who had through marriage become a member of one of Europe's smaller royal dynasties. She offered sympathy, but little practical advice. Things will only get worse, she warned. And any hope Diana might have had to nurture that friendship ended in 1982 when Princess Grace was killed in a car accident. Attending Princess Grace's funeral was Diana's first solo engagement abroad.

While Diana is reported to have got on well with Princess Margaret, who might also have been able to offer some advice about how to deal with gossip and unwanted attention, both at court and in the media, it was not a relationship that offered much practical guidance. Princess Margaret had never known what it was like to have lived outside the royal circle. She did not have Diana's ability to make contact across the British class divide. While she let her hair down within her select arty circle, she was always prone to stand on ceremony. She would never have allowed any of the familiarities Diana encouraged from her staff.

The Queen Mother was also unhelpful, but for different reasons. Her close relationship with her grandson meant that in any dispute she sided with Prince Charles and her sense of duty was such that she was exasperated by Diana's inability, or unwillingness, to put on a dutiful face in public, whatever her private feelings and emotions.

Diana's relationship with Prince Philip was subject to many misunderstandings. Not a man to show his emotions, he found Diana's open display of her feelings difficult to comprehend. When the marriage between Diana and his son had reached rock-bottom he wrote her a series of letters in which he attempted to offer even-handed, but direct and unsentimental advice. He signed them 'Pa'. He certainly attempted to help his troubled daughter-in-law, but did not have either the relevant experience (he had not married into the royal family in quite the same circumstances), nor the required gifts of diplomacy.

Diana read the letters as reprimands and was angered and hurt by their contents. He acknowledged that Charles had been difficult and did not condone his relationship with Camilla, but he also confronted her with some home truths. 'He invited her to face the facts. Essentially he wanted to make Diana think about her marriage, long and hard. And he did. He also made her cry. When Diana received the letters she was at her most vulnerable and volatile.'[15]

As soon as one arrived Diana would read it briefly and then start crying before sharing its contents with her friends. Often she had not read the letter carefully and was upset by an inference that had never been intended or made.

The letters might have been more effective if they had been sent early in the marriage, rather than right at the end when matters were probably past repair. Although the disintegration of the fairytale marriage began almost as soon as the couple had left the cathedral as man and wife, it might have been saved in the early days if the underlying problems had been recognised. However in the early stages of a marriage, whether royal or not, no couple is in a frame of mind or position to examine their relationship dispassionately.

Two years after Diana's death Gyles Brandreth raised the subject of Diana in a conversation with Prince Philip:

'The public view of you, for what it's worth, is of a grouchy old man, unsympathetic to his daughter-in-law . . . but you wrote . . . kind letters, concerned, fatherly, caring letters explaining how you knew first hand the difficulties involved in marrying into the royal family.' He smiled at me. 'The impression the public have got is unfair' I said. He shrugged. 'I've just got to live with it', he said.[16]

There were four problems that can be seen with hindsight: first, the relationship between Prince Charles and Camilla; second, the popularity of the Princess of Wales outshining that of the Prince; third, the fact that Diana, despite her privileged aristocratic upbringing, had nevertheless known what it was like to live outside the gilded prison of royalty, where a different set of values operated; and fourth, Diana's bulimia and her state of mind.

In the event, as one royal writer put it, the Wales's marriage became 'a grim tragedy':

> She was not happy, and simmering beneath the surface were the fires of revenge. She had never been convinced that Prince Charles loved her, and never ceased to be suspicious of Mrs Parker Bowles.

> It is commonly said that the Princess of Wales was too young and did not know what she was going into. This is only partly true. She knew about Camilla Parker Bowles, but, not unreasonably, she thought that once she was married she had at least a chance with the Prince. As one who worked at the Palace at the time put it: 'No one told her romance wasn't part of the deal.'

> The Princess of Wales became more and more popular, the media interest in her only grew . . . She depended on her existence on being the 'Cinderella' choice of the Prince of Wales. She had a unique natural touch, possessing in full measure all the gifts of the best-loved princesses in history. She was good with the sick, good with children and good with old people. She became a living icon, outdistancing the Royal Family to whom she owed her public being.[17]

The way Diana reinterpreted the royal role did not go down well with the royal family or her husband.

When she wowed the dance and show business world by

appearing onstage at the Royal Opera House with ballet star Wayne Sleep, the Prince was far from amused. The Princess of Wales and Wayne Sleep had secretly rehearsed a routine to the song 'Uptown Girl'. On the night however it was presented in such a way as to appear to be quite spontaneous as Diana and Wayne took to the stage together.

> The audience let out a collective gasp of astonishment . . . They took eight curtain calls. Diana even dropping a curtsy to the royal box. In public Prince Charles confessed himself absolutely amazed by Diana's display; in private he expressed his strong disapproval of her behaviour. She was undignified, too thin and too showy.[18]

Diana reported that she found his negative response to any of her initiatives very debilitating.

She also found him unsupportive and unsympathetic when her eating disorder appeared to interfere with her royal duty. On a visit to California, during which she was eating almost nothing, she fainted. She was taken by her lady-in-waiting to a private room to recover. Afterwards Prince Charles told her with some irritation that if she was going to faint she should have done so in private.

From 1984 the Princess and Prince led increasingly separate lives. By 1986 when, as Charles later said, his marriage had irretrievably broken down, he was again seeing, and sleeping with, Camilla Parker Bowles.

For a while the royal couple attempted to put on a public display of unity, but it was becoming increasingly less convincing. Charles went more and more frequently to Highgrove, a short drive from the Parker Bowles's house and Diana preferred when she could to stay in London.

As time went by the only things they had in common were the two children and the need to do their royal duty. But more and more the Prince and Princess 'worked' less and less as a unit. Days and weeks went by when they had no diary dates in common at all.

The engagements they were obliged to fulfil together proved strained and embarrassing. The situation continued for eight years. Media, court and society observers began to realise that something was wrong. The ever-watchful press pack noted the telltale signs of strain: the failure of the couple to make eye contact and the absence of any evidence of mutual affection. Sometimes even looks of hostility from Diana and exasperation from Charles that neither could hide.

Not only was the media watching, they were participants, drawn into the sad conflict. The sympathies of the popular press were largely with the Princess. Despite her frequent protestations that the media was intrusive, sapped her privacy and often made her life unbearable, she made it her business to charm selected journalists. She gave them discrete brief-ings, met and chatted with them, phoned them and ulti-mately, in the case of Andrew Morton, provided the scoop of a lifetime. Charles's advisers counselled him to show his warmer more endearing side, to be seen with his sons more often, behaving in a natural fatherly way. But the Prince could not win. The press and Diana were capable of taking advant-age of any situation to show him up as a thoughtless husband and indifferent father.

The most blatant example of this behaviour occurred in 1991 when Prince William was involved in an accident at school. He was struck on the head by a golf club and needed hospital attention. Holding his mother's hand he was wheeled into theatre for a seventy-five-minute operation under general anaesthetic. She was there with him when he woke and she stayed close by as his post-operative condition was closely monitored. His father meanwhile, having satisfied himself that his son was in good hands, had left the hospital to attend the opera. It was all in the line of duty as he was hosting a gathering of European Commissioners and officials.

The popular press, with no discouragement from the Princess, spared no words in condemning the Prince. 'What kind of Dad are you?' asked *The Sun*. When the Prince was made aware of the public's wrath, he accused Diana of 'making an awful nonsense about the severity of the injury and affected innocence about the possibility that the future heir to the throne could have suffered brain damage'.[19]

For a while Diana found a companionable ally in Fergie, Sarah Ferguson who married Prince Andrew and became the Duchess of York. The wedding took place on 23 July 1986 and Fergie was described by one royal friend as a breath of fresh air.

The relationship between Diana and Fergie was not always an easy one. They gossiped and compared notes about life as a royal spouse. They larked around, notably on Prince Andrew's stag night when they attempted to gatecrash his party dressed as policewomen. Yet Diana also found it difficult to cope with feelings of envy. Fergie appeared far more popular within the family. As the breath of fresh air, she could be counted on to liven up proceedings even at Balmoral. While Diana was seen as a problem, Fergie was seen as 'fun'. When they were on good terms the friendship was close. Yet, in the end, in a manner that was typical of Diana, she cut Fergie out of her life. The pretext was trivial, but the consequences were vengeful. Diana refused to speak to Fergie or even allow their two children, first cousins, to continue their friendship.

Three months before Diana died, Fergie described what had happened:

Because I put in my book that I once caught verrucas after borrowing her shoes . . . and because I thought Charles was an extraordinary man . . . Diana just cut me off. I haven't spoken to her in eighteen months. She won't take my calls or reply to my letters. And worst of all she won't even let me see the boys, which is so upsetting. I loved seeing William and Harry, and so did my girls. It's not fair that they can't see their cousins. I have tried everything, but she can be so obstinate. I've said how sorry I am, but she won't listen.[20]

In due course Diana was to seek solace, excitement and, she hoped, happiness through male companionship and sexual partners.

Best known was James Hewitt, an army officer who is now referred to in contemptible tones as a rat and the man who betrayed Diana. His mistake was threefold: first to have an affair with Diana; second to leave her, or so she felt, in order to continue with his army career; and third to talk about his affair and his love for the Princess when their relationship was finally over.

It all started innocently with Diana asking Hewitt for riding lessons. But he quickly noticed that Diana was unhappy and in need of affection. When he took Diana to his mother's home in Devon it gave her a rest from the restrictions of court life. He got on well with the princes and, unlike Charles, convinced Diana that she was attractive and desirable.

Diana also formed close relationships with her police protection officers. One in particular was Sergeant Barry Mannakee. Diana came to rely so heavily on his support and encouragement that Palace officials suspected that he and the Princess were becoming inappropriately close. He was removed from his post in 1986 and a few months later died in a motorcycle accident in what Diana believed were suspicious circumstances. After his death Diana believed she made clairvoyant contact with him. To supporters of Prince Charles, the idea that a police officer would be deliberately killed for having a close relationship with a member of the royal family was absurd and that the Princess should harbour such thoughts was evidence of her own mental instability and paranoia. Dianaphiles take the opposite view. If the Princess suspected dark deeds in relation to Barry Mannakee's death, it lends credence to their concerns that she too was murdered. Diana, it was reported in 2004, spoke about her relationship with Barry Mannakee on tape and those tapes are now in the hands of the British police team investigating the Princess's death on behalf of the coroner.

Her relationship with her penultimate lover is generally believed to have been her most important. It is also the liaison about which the least is known. The heart surgeon, Hasnat Khan, had no wish to find himself in the eye of a media storm and great care was taken to keep every meeting secret. Diana visited Pakistan to meet his family, the most recent trip being in the May before she died. Everything came to an abrupt end that summer however. Diana characteristically cut him out of her life and turned her attention to Dodi Fayed.

Ten years earlier however Diana was still far from being the confident and independent woman she was to become at the end of her life. Three events happened in 1988 that proved a turning point in her life. The first demonstrated to Diana that she had the confidence and ability to take charge of events. The second showed her how she could tackle her bulimia, and the third that she could tackle the Camilla problem face on and feel stronger and better for it.

It took the tragic death of a friend to convince Diana that she had the inner resources required to control her life.

Diana, Charles and family were taking a skiing holiday at Klosters in the course of which their friend, the former Queen's equerry, Major Hugh Lindsay, was killed by an avalanche. And another friend, Patty Palmer-Tompkinson, was badly injured. Diana did not witness the accident, but was like everyone else in the party, very shaken by the news.

In her account of what happened next, it was she and not Charles or Fergie, who were both present, who took charge. She insisted that she and Charles return home with Hugh Lindsay's wife, despite the Prince preferring to continue with the holiday. 'There were tremendous arguments about that',[21] Diana recalled. The Princess looked after many of the practicalities and, says Andrew Morton, 'felt absolutely in command of a very trying situation'.[22] Diana directed that Major Lindsay's body be removed from the hospital and flown to RAF Northolt. She then invited his widow, who was expecting their first child, to stay at Highgrove and spent many hours talking and weeping with her.

Needless to say Prince Charles's biographer Jonathan Dimbleby has provided a different account. It was Charles who remained calm and controlled as he waited with Patty Palmer-Tompkinson for the rescue helicopter. The Prince was keen to ensure that the guide did not take the blame for the accident and he issued a press statement emphasising that all the party, 'including myself, was skiing off the piste at our own risk'.

> To the lasting dismay of all those affected, the facts of the disaster were persistently to be distorted. In what appears to have been a conscious effort to damage the Prince . . . he was widely accused of . . . causing the tragedy.[23]

Whatever the exact turn of events, the tragedy had a profound effect on Diana. Morton noted, 'It taught her that not only could she cope with a crisis but that she could also take control and make significant decisions in the face of opposition from her husband.'[24]

Around the same time, as she felt more confident in herself, she found the mental strength to seek help for her bulimic condition. She was recommended to a specialist in eating disorders who promised her that within six months she would be transformed. With his help and guidance she succeeded in controlling her illness and described the effect as being born again. She lapsed a few times, but normally only when she was staying at Balmoral, a royal home for which she felt a special horror.

The third transforming event was the one where Diana decided to face Camilla. It was the occasion of Camilla's sister's birthday and after dinner Diana buoyed herself up for a confrontation.

'I was terrified' she later admitted. 'I said, "Camilla, I would just like you to know that I know exactly what is going on between you and Charles, I wasn't born yesterday" . . . it wasn't a fight, calm, deathly calm and I said to Camilla: "I know what is going on, don't treat me like an idiot." '25

Afterwards Diana said that on returning home she wept all night, and in the morning, while she still felt the old jealousy and anger, 'it wasn't as deathly as before'.

The year 1992 was one of double significance. It was the year her father died and the year in which all the anger and frustrations concerning her marriage spilled out into the open through Diana's cooperation with the journalist Andrew Morton. His book, published that year, and quoted from above, remains to this day the most complete record of the Princess's own feelings, memories and motives.

When the book first appeared it was only admitted that *Diana: Her True Story in Her Own Words* was authorised by her friends. The exact nature of the close collaboration emerged later. The book was in fact based on tape recordings made by the Princess during the summer and autumn of 1991. She spoke openly about her bulimia, her suicide attempts and her feelings for the royal family and her husband. She considered herself, Morton wrote later, to be a prisoner trapped inside a bitterly unfulfilled marriage, shackled to an unsympathetic royal system and chained to a wholly unrealistic public image of her life.

> Everywhere she went she was followed by a bodyguard, her every movement was logged while every visitor to her home was noted and checked. She believed she was under constant surveillance.[26]

Was this self-pitying image an accurate reflection of her lot? It is true that being a member of the royal family is to be trapped in an unreal world. In exchange for wealth, adulation and status, freedom is sacrificed. Royalty is public property. In times past kings and queens could not go to bed or take a bath without being watched by the court. Today, the democratic representatives of the public feel justified in taking a close interest in everything the members of the royal family do. The police and security services, which act as eyes and ears of the state, monitor every move. It is also the case that when Princess Diana was in the USA, the American secret services collected information and bugged her calls.

It can be no coincidence that private and intimate telephone conversations by both the Prince and Princess were recorded. The attempts to claim that the Camillagate and Squidgy tape-recordings were made by amateurs who overheard the conversations by chance are utterly unconvincing. It seems highly plausible that the nosey retired bank manager who reportedly listened to other people's phone calls was only able to hear and record the Squidgy tapes because the security services wanted him to. If it were normally so easy to tap into private phone calls there would be dozens of transcripts of such calls from all manner of celebrities flooding onto the market.

For one highly intimate royal conversation to have been accidentally recorded is improbable, but two in the same month stretches improbability beyond all possibility.

Indeed, to underscore the point, there was a third recording made, a private conversation between Fergie and Prince Andrew.

The Conservative MP Geoffrey Dickens attempted to ask a parliamentary question, but was told matters relating to the security forces were out of order. The quality of the recordings and the circumstances in which they were made and released could only point to one conclusion, he claimed, that rogue elements in MI5 and MI6 were at work.

The sequence of events strongly suggests that the Squidgy tapes, which by the date of their release in 1992 were three years old, had been leaked by members of the security forces loyal to Prince Charles as an act of retaliation for the damaging revelations made about the Prince in Andrew Morton's book. Others in the security services loyal to Diana responded by leaking the tapes of Charles's late-night conversation with Camilla, which had also been kept under wraps for three years, as a further tit-for-tat move.

In the Squidgy tapes Diana was heard talking to a close male friend James Gilbey, who called her by his private term of endearment, 'Squidge'. They were flirty, but not sexually explicit, and Diana is heard talking off microphone both to Prince Harry and to Paul Burrell. Their quality to shock has subsided over the years, but when they were first heard they were an exciting and dangerous window on the Princess's world.

From the royal family's point of view the truly horrific revelations came not from the tapes, but from Diana's book. It was felt that to collaborate with a journalist in producing an intimate account of a royal marriage was both unprecedented and utterly deplorable. Staff members of the royal household who have written relatively harmless memoirs have in the past been ostracised by the royal household. That a senior member of the family should make her innermost feelings available to readers of the tabloid press was nothing short of horrendous. Diana appeared to be breaking every taboo in the book of royal etiquette. Her behaviour was viewed as inexcusable, and the more so in that it was a calculated act of vengeance designed to inflict the maximum damage on her husband.

It was not so much that she spoke of her bulimia, of her husband's unfaithfulness, the cold protocol-bound royal court, her interest in astrology and medium, her tears and tantrums. What was abhorrent to the Queen, Prince Charles and the royal courtiers, was that she had spoken at all.

5

THE BEGINNING
OF THE END

It is announced from Buckingham Palace that, with regret, the Prince and Princess of Wales have decided to separate. Their Royal Highnesses have no plans to divorce and their constitutional positions are unaffected. This decision has been reached amicably and they will continue to participate fully in the upbringing of their children.

On 9 December 1992 a formal announcement was made by Prime Minister John Major to a hushed House of Commons. The pretence was over.

The Queen and Duke of Edinburgh, though saddened were understanding and sympathetic, the Prime Minister told parliament, and then added a sentence which was to provoke much subsequent discussion.

The decision to separate has no constitutional implications . . . and there is no reason why the Princess of Wales should not be crowned Queen in due course.

Historians interviewed immediately cited the case of Queen
Caroline and warned of embarrassing scenes to come. By
tradition, the Queen Consort is also crowned at the
coronation, however Queen Caroline was living apart from
King George IV and he had no wish to have her by his side in
Westminster Abbey. He failed to get parliament to agree to a
divorce, but succeeded in physically barring her from
attending the coronation at Westminster Abbey.

John Major had chosen his words carefully and had had
private interviews with both the Prince and Princess beforehand. Palace lawyers had examined every constitutional
aspect of the separation and, on the assumption that it would
not inevitably lead to a divorce, advised accordingly.

Both Charles and Diana had also met separately with the
Archbishop of Canterbury, Dr George Carey, who regarded
himself as the royal family's 'parish priest'. He later wrote
that his conversations with both wounded people revealed

> the depths of pain and undisguised loathing, mingled
> with nostalgia and love, that are often present in dying
> relationships. Neither Charles nor Diana made any
> secret of the sadness they both felt, and the deep
> emotional estrangement that went with it. In my opinion
> the relationship was doomed and it was my pastoral duty
> to bring a Christian perspective to bear.

Lord Carey was later criticised for discussing in public what
had been private conversations, but he was well aware that
the marriage was not simply a private matter between the
two, but 'the talking point of the entire world'.

The Archbishop's comments revealed that he was aware
that the two people he was counselling had both admitted
adultery and he could not appear to condone the behaviour
of either party in this regard, as he had a duty to uphold the
moral teaching of the church. 'Some in the church wanted me
to raise my voice in condemnation of . . . adultery. To have
done so would have been a betrayal of my pastoral duty.'[1]

Diana later insisted that she had not wanted a legal separation. 'I come from a family with divorced parents and I didn't want to have to experience that again.'[2]

Before the announcement was made she went to see the two children, who reacted 'like all children do, with lots of questions. I hope that I was able to console them.'[3]

There were numerous detailed issues to sort out. If the Princess continued to carry out public duties would she be provided with the facilities to do so? Would she be able, for instance, to use the royal train or aircraft of the Queen's Flight?

Crown lawyers were, Diana's private secretary Patrick Jephson noted, even-handed. They were wary of how Diana might use her new-found freedom to undermine Prince Charles's work and reputation, but did not wish to restrict her work.

> She got practically everything she wanted in the separation agreement, including – against her husband's wishes – the continued presence of her office alongside his in St James's Palace.

> Once the agreement had been settled, in legal terms the Princess was left in a very favourable position. Her role as a mother had been reinforced as the parent with day-to-day care of the children. She would now have the apartment at Kensington Palace entirely to herself . . . Her finances . . . were ample.[4]

From Prince Charles's point of view, perhaps the most important part of the agreement was that Diana would no longer view Highgrove as her home. He could retreat there as often as he could arrange it and invite his own friends to join him there, with Camilla acting as hostess.

The arrangement might have lasted some time, for both parties gained space and neither had lost face.

As 1992 – the royal family's 'annus horribilis' to quote

the words of the Queen – drew to a close, there was hope all round that from the new year things could get better. In the words of Paul Burrell, 'the Princess embraced the start of 1993 as if it was going to be the best year of her life'.[5]

However while the lawyers continued to negotiate the fine print of the agreement, the underground battle of briefing and leaking continued unabated. Only a few months after the Prime Minister's announcement, more extracts of the covertly recorded telephone conversations Diana had had with James Gilbey found their way into the public domain. Diana was heard to say: 'I don't want to get pregnant.'

'Darling, that won't happen, OK?' Gilbey had reassured her. 'You can't think like that. Nothing will happen, darling. You won't get pregnant.'

'I watched EastEnders today,' Diana said. 'One of the actresses had had a baby. She thought it was her husband's. It was another man's.'

To which Gilbey responded, 'My octopus, kiss me, O God. Is this feeling not wonderful? Do you like it too?'

And Diana answered, 'Yes, a lot.'

The recording had been made in December 1989, yet that particular extract was only 'released' after the separation. It was quickly followed by the leaking of another secretly recorded, and now notorious, telephone conversation dating from the same month and year. The tabloids published the most sensational extracts just after the announcement of the separation. This recording featured a private conversation between Prince Charles and Camilla Parker Bowles. It was intimate and embarrassing and included the notorious exchange that was to etch the recording in the public memory.

Camilla says that she needs Charles all the week, all the time, to which Charles replies, 'I'll just live inside your trousers or something.' Camilla jokes, 'What are you going to turn into, a pair of knickers? You're going to come back as a pair of knickers?'

'Or,' says the heir to the throne, 'God forbid, a Tampax. Just my luck!'

The dirty war continued. The tactics employed during the years of open matrimonial warfare between the Prince and Princess have since been likened to those employed by the Soviet propaganda machine to discredit dissidents during the Cold War – particularly in the way the Prince's camp attempted to have Diana labelled as 'mentally unstable', and in the use by both camps of private telephone calls intercepted by the security forces.

The damage inflicted however was not shared. Somehow it was Prince Charles's unguarded conversation which shocked the most. Diana emerged with a reputation not only intact, but strangely enhanced. While the revelations hastened the decline of her pristine image, in its place something more durable grew.

> Here was a young woman with flaws who nevertheless aspired to something better. Rather like her bulimia, a secret some might regard as shameful actually became a scar which she bore with acceptance of her own fallibility.[6]

The Princess was privately much embarrassed by the Gilbey tape, but the Prince did not benefit from his wife's embarrassment. The fact that he was shown in his own tape to be in a happy relationship himself 'only made the public reaction more disapproving'.[7] The tape had been known about for several months before it was published and some journalists had even hinted that its publication would be so damaging to the Prince that he might have to renounce his claim to the throne. Indeed the tabloids showed restraint in holding back from publishing for so long.

With the publication of the tape, the Archbishop of Canterbury considered that any hope of a dignified end to the marriage had been destroyed. In the event Charles attracted more ridicule than outrage. Over three decades the public mood had relaxed on questions of sexual explicitness. Although interestingly Diana's own reaction to the Tampax reference was one of genuine shock at its crudeness.

93

Throughout 1993 there was further unseemly jostling for public attention between the Prince and Princess and as always the Princess won any public relations' contest hands down. When she took Princes William and Harry to Thorpe Park, pictures of the three of them getting soaking wet on a flume ride appeared in every newspaper. In a single set of images she declared to the world, when my sons are with me they have fun. Implying of course that with their father life was staid, old-fashioned and boring. It also helped her reach across the class divide. Prince Charles, when his staff arranged photo opportunities with his sons, chose exclusive settings such as ski slopes or a Scottish riverbank. Diana chose a place accessible to everyone. Tabloid readers could go to the same theme park enjoyed by the Princess and experience the same rides as the two Princes. It helped reinforce that aspect of the Diana myth that appealed to many women, that she was 'one of us'.

More significantly during that period she began to nurture her more serious side. No longer would she simply be a celebrity fashion icon, a walking clothes-horse. She began to address and identify with serious issues. She also took steps to develop her public-speaking style, to give it greater clarity and confidence, and engaged a coach.

The first subjects she tackled were domestic ones and those that women in particular could identify with. She attended a well-publicised conference on domestic violence, spoke movingly and from direct personal experience on eating disorders and attended a conference on the plight of women with mental health problems. 'It can take enormous courage for women to admit that they cannot cope . . . As their world closes in on them their self-esteem evaporates into a haze of loneliness and desperation.'[8]

Listening to her that day and chairing the conference was the writer and broadcaster Libby Purves. She articulated what many women were increasingly thinking, that the Princess 'is one of us. A wife, a mother, a daughter who has known problems in her own life and who has courageously used these experiences to comfort other people.'

The Princess was no longer confining her public work to lending support to uncontroversial charitable work. She was beginning to venture into the realms of gender politics. Susie Orbach, the author of the book *Fat is a Feminist Issue* was a therapist that the Princess often visited. Following her death, this theme was pursued by Beatrix Campbell in a book she titled, *Diana, Princess of Wales: How Sexual Politics Shook the Monarchy*. On the feminist.com website a writer, identified only as Amy, described Diana as

> . . . very much a feminist in that she set out to be her own person. She acknowledged her weaknesses and those of society and worked to overcome them both. She was vulnerable and heroic. She seemed very true to herself and less likely to live entirely by a party line. She dared to be an individual in spite of societal structure that wanted her to be a conformist, a stereotype.[9]

Diana the feminist is yet another dimension to add to Diana the myth.

Diana's overseas itinerary in 1993 was also busy with visits to Zimbabwe and Nepal. Because the trips were not official royal tours, they were far less sanitised. Diana was enabled to see life in the raw and on emerging from one hut in an impoverished Himalayan village she said, 'I will never complain again.'

From her staff there was a shared, though smothered, snort of incredulity at her reaction. Yet as the phrase travelled the world, her public took her at her word. 'Serving up such an appetising sound-bite was talent enough', observed Patrick Jephson. 'Getting so many people to take it at face value was verging on genius. The trouble was, the one person who should never have taken it at face value – herself – swallowed it hook, line and sinker.'[10]

The Princess's words can be seen now to have had a particularly hollow ring in that at the same time she was vowing never to complain again, she was involved in an acrimonious dispute with her brother, Charles, Earl Spencer. She was wanting a second home, a rural retreat, to enable her to get away from Kensington Palace at weekends and her brother had offered her the four-bedroom Garden House on the Althorp estate. She began to plan the décor – pale blues and yellows were suggested – but before the matter advanced further Earl Spencer had second thoughts. He became anxious about press intrusion and other security issues, and withdrew the offer.

He wrote to his sister to explain and then telephoned her. Diana slammed the phone down and wrote him an angry letter. He returned it unopened. Their friendship was damaged forever. 'Proud and impulsive, neither would back down, and the quarrel between them became a complete impasse', their mother's biographer later wrote.

> Diana felt let down, while Charles felt misunderstood. Caught in the middle, Frances, like many mothers, tried to see things from both sides. She felt however that Diana and Charles were adults and had to fight their own battles.[11]

The battle became spiteful. Paul Burrell describes how the Earl asked for the return of the Spencer tiara that Diana had worn on her wedding day, saying it should revert to 'its proper owner'. Diana sent it back. The ill-feeling between the siblings continued until Diana's death, which is why Paul Burrell was astonished to hear the Earl at Diana's funeral describe his sister in such affectionate terms:

> Fundamentally she had not changed at all from the big sister who mothered me as a baby, fought with me at school and endured long train journeys between our parents' homes.[12]

In Zimbabwe Diana was to continue to develop her public

image as empathetic carer. Her staff took care, however, to share details of her itinerary in advance with both her sister-in-law the Princess Royal, who was much involved with African-based charity work, and the Queen. Diana visited the Red Cross, Help the Aged and Leprosy Mission projects. She wept at an orphanage she visited. All the children were under five years old and had AIDS.

Reflecting on the tour Patrick Jephson underlined a comment in the *Daily Telegraph* which he sent to his boss: 'Too much of what cynics call the Mother Teresa routine could lead to compassion indigestion by the media, however well choreographed it all is.'[13] In Zimbabwe too, Diana had become aware how she could be stereotyped by the media into the role of a patronising 'lady bountiful', an image she knew instinctively to resist. She felt uneasy when photographed handing out food. It was the wrong image.

On the surface, the first year of her independent life was going well and when in August the separated couple met to discuss the possibilities of some degree of reconciliation or greater cooperation, Diana was emboldened to make the one demand she suspected her husband would not be able to agree to: that he avoid any further contact with Camilla.

Beneath the surface Diana's initial burst of enthusiasm was running out of steam. She was getting bored with the run-of-the-mill royal duties that had been written into her diary months ahead. She was also becoming increasingly lonely. With her sons away at boarding school or staying with their father, she would often return from public engagements to her empty apartment at Kensington Palace. Paul Burrell, her butler, described how she would sometimes invite him to stay with her to chat over the day or watch television just for the human company. She had no shortage of friends and lovers, and spent hours on the telephone, aware of course that even the most innocent of her calls was most likely being monitored. She was too famous and recognisable simply to pop out to a restaurant with friends in any normal way. She liked to find things to do at night and much of her unofficial visiting of the sick was done in the small hours of the morning. This met her chronic need to feel wanted. Yet she still had many hours to brood and feed her introspection.

Additionally she continued to battle with her particular private demon – jealousy. In addition to her simmering envy of Camilla she was developing an obsession with Tiggy Legge-Bourke. Tiggy was employed by Prince Charles to help look after the boys when they were with him. She was very popular with them and enjoyed playing boisterous games. Diana felt that she had usurped her role as a mother. She believed Tiggy to be part of the royal plan to wrest her sons from her by stealth. The day came when vengeance was taken. Diana addressed a vicious and calculated remark to Tiggy at a party. Tiggy was left devastated and weeping. Afterwards, she sent a solicitor's letter to the Princess demanding an apology for making false allegations.

At the time Diana took considerable pleasure in her remark. What she had done was to help stir a groundless rumour that Tiggy had had an affair with Prince Charles that had resulted in a pregnancy and an abortion. Diana had greeted her sons' friend and professional companion with the words, 'Hello Tiggy. How are you? So sorry to hear about the baby.'

'Horror paralysed Tiggy's face,' was Paul Burrell's description of the effect Diana's remarks had. And he reported his boss's gleeful words to him afterwards, 'Did you see the look on her face, Paul? She almost fainted!'[14]

Diana never overcame her feelings of jealousy. In May 1997 Tiggy was invited by Prince William to an open day at Eton. Photographs showing Tiggy drinking champagne and smoking in front of Prince William 'sent his already annoyed mother off the dial'.[15]

She instructed Michael Gibbins in her office to telephone the main newspapers and via them dictated a statement.

The Princess of Wales feels deeply hurt and angry that Ms Legge-Bourke would behave this way . . . it is idiotic behaviour and clearly shows that she is a bad influence on the boys, as the Princess has been fearing for some time.[16]

The statement dominated the news and Diana realised what she had done. Her private envy had distorted her normal good judgement in media matters. The story threatened to damage her public image. 'Diana's finally lost it', was the reaction of the tabloid editor Piers Morgan.

He noted in his diary:

I heard she was going to issue a statement denying saying anything unpleasant about Tiggy . . . and blaming an employee in her office for speaking without her consent. For God's sake, I heard her in the background giving Michael Gibbins specific adjectives to describe Ms Legge-Bourke. Now she was dumping him in the most disgusting manner . . . Nobody should treat a good guy like this, it's cowardly and horrible.[17]

Lord Carey described a 'dark side' to Diana: 'There was little evidence that she was prepared to make the marriage work . . . (and) . . . there was a streak in Diana's psychological make-up that would not allow her to give in.'[18]

Patrick Jephson was well aware of his employer's dark side. 'However saintly her intentions . . . my boss kept a knife in her handbag. It was jagged and quick.'[19]

I felt that some unconscious childhood memory was being endlessly replayed. The unfairness she felt, although painful, was at least familiar, and if ever its pain showed signs of easing up, she would re-impose it either in her imagination or by deliberate provocation. Like anyone setting out to find a reason to be unhappy or dissatisfied, she had no need to look very far. The people nearest to her (with the notable exception of her children), staff or friends – provided plenty of material.[20]

Through the autumn of 1993 Diana continued with public engagements that went well and enhanced her profile. In November she attended the Remembrance Day service at Enniskillen in Northern Ireland, the scene of a devastating bomb explosion in 1987.

Her staff also noticed that she was beginning to be valued not only for her looks and presence, but for her ideas too. This was certainly venturing onto Prince Charles's territory.

She had meetings with influential figures as diverse as Clive James, Lord Attenborough, Lady Thatcher and Lord Gowrie, noted Patrick Jephson, who observed how these encounters produced high-grade discussions on subjects ranging from international events and world health problems to the possibilities now opening up for her own future occupation. 'The princess contributed well when she could, listened attentively when she could not, and matched such signs of obvious intelligence with well-judged and disarming humour.'[21]

Why then on 3 December of that year did Diana surprise her public with a most unexpected announcement? Speaking at a charity lunch she told an astonished audience that she was withdrawing from public life.

I hope you can find it in your hearts to understand and give me the time and space that has been lacking in recent years. When I started my public life 12 years ago, I understood the media might be interested in what I did . . . but I was not aware of how overwhelming the attention would become.

For a woman who had nurtured and used the press to her own considerable advantage for most of those twelve years it was an astonishing claim. It is true that in the weeks before the press had begun to question her image, but to trigger a complete withdrawal from public life? Hardly.

A month earlier the *Daily Express* had asked, 'Has it all gone wrong for Princess Diana?' and a *Tatler* survey had identified a small minority of participants who believed that she was a 'neurotic manipulator'. But it was not by any stretch of the imagination an avalanche of criticism, such as a politician might encounter in the dying days of a government. She had also been caught off guard and photographed exercising at a gym. She was angered by the intrusion although, as suggested earlier, the pictures did her no disservice. Yet for a while the anger overwhelmed her, and took a bizarre form. Paul Burrell described how she would, when she felt hurt, retire to her bedroom, play requiem masses at high volume and sob. She called it retreating into her shell where no one could hurt her.

Why then did she overreact to media criticism? Had Patrick Jephson, her private secretary, got it right when he noted how Diana often had a need to find a reason to be dissatisfied? If the people nearest to her failed to provide the excuse,

> there was always the diary, stuffed full – at her request – with endless demands on her good nature.

> It became just part of my life that I saw this reality while the world saw the saint it preferred. In the end, the contradictions in her character created unbearable tensions for many who were close to her. These were only magnified by the knowledge that such self-destructiveness was bound to infect the good she was capable of doing. Too many people's hopes rested on a belief that she was as wholesome as she looked. Trying to keep that image alive and at the same time contrive some purpose – even happiness – for her own life eventually became too frustrating.[22]

Whatever her motives, Diana never lacked cunning. Perhaps her announced withdrawal from public life was not an overreaction but evidence that Diana had an intuitive wisdom no professional publicist could ever claim. At the first sign of a turning tide of opinion, she did what no public relations adviser would ever have dared suggest. She did not play safe and make minor adjustments to her image; she played the boldest move possible.

On reflection, her speech has echoes of 'Don't Cry for Me Argentina' and the mawkish and insincere Eva Peron of Tim Rice's lyrics.

In the celebrated song from the musical Eva Peron addresses her fans, the poor of Argentina, from a balcony. Diana addressed her fans via the television cameras. Eva talks about trying to explain how she feels and how she needs the love of the people to support her in her life, and she promises the people that she will never let them down.[23]

'I could not stand here and make this sort of statement without acknowledging the heartfelt support I have been given by the public in general,' said Diana. 'Your kindness and affection have carried me through some of the most difficult periods, and always your love and care have eased the journey.'

And again, 'I would like to reassure the people who love me. I would like to say to them that I will never let them down. That is just as important to me as my children are . . . the people on the streets are particularly important to me.'[24]

And what did Evan Peron do after making her famous declaration of love to the Argentinean masses? Away from the crowds she turned to an officer who had been listening, and said 'Just listen to that, the voice of Argentina. We are adored, we are loved.'

When Princess Diana returned to Kensington Palace, Patrick Jephson noted 'her excited face, flushed with the rapt attention she had received'.[25]

He was too loyal a royal servant to echo the Argentinean officer's riposte to Eva Peron. 'Statesmanship is more than entertaining peasants.'[26]

As an aside, there are many things to be learned about Diana from studying the Eva Peron of mythology. They were both beautiful women who gained power through marriage, they both died young and their deaths provoked immense outpourings of grief. Both have been popularly and post-humously acclaimed as secular saints. Both too referred to themselves as the queens of people's hearts. Beatrix Campbell has written that it was the complexity of Eva Peron, Princess Diana and a third icon Marilyn Monroe, the actress and mistress to the powerful, which fascinates and not their sanctity. 'They suffered shame and excited desire among men and women alike. Their magnetic fields attract both genders – that is part of their potency. Their tangles with politics and popular culture refracted the spirit of our time.'[27]

Eva Peron was more overtly political than the princess. It could be argued that she was also more cynically manipulative and interested in political power in a way that Diana and Marilyn Monroe never were – an important distinction to make. Unlike Diana, Eva also had time to reflect on her own death. She did not die suddenly, but from cancer, and realised shortly before her end how powerful her posthumous legend might become. 'I will return,' she promised, 'and I will be millions.'

After the Princess's speech, which obviously made the news headlines in a very big way, Diana's staff began the thankless task of unravelling her commitments and clearing her diary. Dozens of charities relying on her name and association to raise money had to be disappointed. Yet, astonishingly there were few murmurs against her. Well briefed by the Princess, the *Daily Mail* even produced the headline 'Charles drove her to it'.

Patrick Jephson's reaction was one of reluctant acceptance peppered with cynicism and humour. On her return from making the speech he went to see her carrying a stack of blank papers.

'What have you got for me?' the Princess asked brightly. Her private secretary handed the papers to her. 'Your programme for next year, Ma'am,' he said.

Some of the royal photographers and correspondents were briefly alarmed by Diana's announcement. They feared for their livelihoods. Had they killed the goose that laid their golden egg? Sceptics in Charles's camp wondered why someone so anxious for seclusion should have chosen to stage such a melodramatic exit.

Privately many of Diana's staff hoped that after her big gesture their boss would see sense and take on a reduced, but significant and more focused, workload. Indeed before too long she had rewritten her speech in her own mind. What she had really said, she convinced herself, was that she wished to have a little bit of a break before resuming business as usual. Within two years she was to tell a television audience of millions that in 1993 she had merely 'retreated for a while. With this strategy I confused my enemies.'[28]

At each stage Prince Charles's retinue of public relations advisers appeared outsmarted by Diana. They could not understand how she could appear to cause herself no end of damage and yet come through the scandals and sensations relatively unmarked.

The only weapon they appeared to have at hand was that of gradual exclusion from the royal circle. If the royal magic, which she had acquired through marriage, could somehow be wrested from her, she would be left with no more protection from the vagaries of public opinion than any other celebrity of the day. It was a long-term tactic. 'I was a problem to them,' Diana was to claim later. 'I wasn't allowed to carry on with many of my former duties. Everything changed when we separated. Life became very difficult. My husband and his friends were very active in demoting me.'[29]

But the results from this policy of incremental exclusion were not speedy enough for the Prince's advisers. They noted that Diana's strength was her supposed candidness. She had allowed Andrew Morton to write about her suffering and grievances. Could not the Prince of Wales find a similar sympathetic amanuensis?

Jonathan Dimbleby was chosen, one of the two well-known sons of the late royal commentator Richard Dimbleby, once dubbed 'gold microphone in waiting' for his reverential and loyal coverage of state occasions.

A book and a television documentary were produced. Charles admitted on camera to his adulterous relationship with Camilla which, he wanted viewers to understand, had only restarted once he was certain his marriage with Diana was over.

The press reaction to the admission was unsympathetic. 'Not fit to reign' was the *Daily Mirror* headline and the same day the papers published photographs of Diana in a stunning low-cut outfit at a dinner engagement held the night before and which had coincided with the broadcast. The Dimbleby programme had not worked as Charles had hoped. 'The morale boost it gave her in the public's eyes and in her own was incalculable', Patrick Jephson wrote, and he recalled his employer's reaction: 'There, Patrick, now everybody can see what we've been up against.'[30]

Prince Charles did not see it that way. He wrote to Jonathan Dimbleby following the broadcast praising the interviewer's integrity 'even though I hated having to be asked questions I would never in a thousand years have allowed myself to be asked normally! However, when all is said and done and the dust has settled, I believe that honesty is the best and most appealing course to adopt – if one can.'[31]

In a heart to heart with Prince William shortly after Prince Charles's admission, Diana told her eldest son that she still loved his father, but that they could not live together any more. 'I take fifty per cent of the responsibility for the destruction of the marriage, but no more than this.'[32]

What was to be the next move? The war of the Wales's went underground again. In August 1994, an accusation was leaked to the media that was to suggest that Diana was malicious, vindictive and seriously mentally deranged.

Oliver Hoare, a married London art dealer, was a family friend. Several newspapers were, to quote Patrick Jephson, 'suspiciously', tipped off that a police investigation was being carried out into a series of nuisance phone calls he had been receiving. It was suggested that over a period of time up to twenty silent calls a day had been made to his number.

The calls, it was to emerge, had been traced to a private line at Kensington Palace. It was later suggested that some, but not all, of the calls had been made by a disgruntled schoolboy. The matter was wrongly reported, Diana told Martin Bashir: 'I was meant to be discredited yet again. I then found out that a young man made most of the telephone calls, but they were blamed on me. I phoned Hoare a couple of times.'[33]

'It caused me a lot of damage, didn't it? People thought I was mad.'[34]

Yet, despite her worries, neither the Hoare business nor even the publication of the book about Diana's affair with James Hewitt seemed to dent her image.

The book described in detail the circumstances under which her riding instructor had become her lover. How she spent time with him at his Devon home and fell in love. Anna Pasternak's *Princess in Love* reads like a work of romantic fiction, but had been written with Hewitt's knowledge and cooperation.

> She was going to allow herself to be loved, to be covered in warmth. And here was this quiet, proficient man, brave enough to meet the challenge . . . Diana stood up and without saying a word stretched out her hand and slowly led James to her bedroom . . . Later she lay in his arms and wept. She wept for all the times she had been left feeling deficient and alone, and the times when she had longed for such a union to melt into her husband's bones as she had melted so softly into James's.[35]

For all her anger at being betrayed, there was nothing Diana could do to deny the claim. All she could do was turn the revelation to her advantage, which, of course, she did.

Without telling any of her key advisers, not even her private secretary, she decided to go on television. On 20 November 1995 the BBC devoted an entire edition of its current-affairs programme *Panorama* to an interview with the Princess which involved a cloak-and-dagger operation to record in order to keep its contents secret until the moment of transmission. Not even the BBC chairman knew what the Princess planned to say. In her carefully choreographed performance, interviewer Martin Bashir asked outright, 'James Hewitt admitted to having an affair with you. Is that true?'

Diana replied with a well-rehearsed response. 'He was a very good friend at a difficult time. He was always there and helped me. And I was shattered when this book was published. I trusted him and now he's making money from me. There is a lot of invention in this book. He phoned me ten days beforehand and said that the book was harmless.'

'Did your relationship go beyond a close friendship?' Bashir asked.

'Yes, it did,' the Princess replied.

'Were you unfaithful?'

'Yes, I loved him and I idolised him. I was in a very bad way.'

'Now you live alone.'

'That doesn't bother me. I don't believe that one needs a man.'

Her final reply went unchallenged. With hindsight it can be seen as downright dishonest. Was Diana trying to delude herself as much as the viewers? Her list of lovers was so long that she and her butler joked about the difficulties they had keeping tabs on them all. They devised what they called the trap system as if the men in her life were lining up at the start of a race. There were up to eight at a time including a musician, a well-known politician, a novelist and a leading sportsman. How many she slept with is uncertain.

One thing Diana made certain of was that the *Panorama* interview left her with no blame for having initiated the breakdown of her marriage. She was fed questions about Charles and Camilla and replied that the effect on her of knowing her husband had a mistress was 'shattering'. She described how there were 'three of us in this marriage. And there was one person too many.'

But I simply couldn't do anything about it. I had tips from differing people who cared about our marriage . . . I had the feeling that I was not worth anything anymore. Without hope, a failure. With a husband who loved another. The change in his behaviour made me certain. A woman senses these things. My husband's friends said that I was unstable again and should be placed in a clinic. I was, as it were, an embarrassment to him. A perfect tactical way to isolate a person.

Her decision to record the interview was, she believed, vindicated when she read the newspapers the next morning. There was almost universal sympathy, although in private several observers noted the potential long-term damage. 'Went to my room at the Commons and watched the Princess Diana interview,' Tony Benn recorded in his diary. 'She is a very disturbed person. She absolutely destroyed the Prince of Wales by what she said. She also admitted that she had had an affair with James Hewitt. The interview was full of self-pity and harassment. She did great damage to the monarchy . . . I think she will just soar to the top of the popularity poll.'[36]

The Diana edition of *Panorama* attracted 23 million viewers, the most watched single programme in British television history. Her advisers were not so amused, especially as most of them had been unaware of her plans until the very last moment. They all realised what Diana did not wish to admit to herself – that a broadcast of this nature could only hasten the inevitable divorce.

Two sections in particular would have sealed her fate. The one in which she suggested Charles would never sit on the throne:

To be king is yet another huge challenge. I know his character and his personality and I believe that becoming king would be an immense strain for him as he would lose his freedom. And I don't know whether he would be in the position to allow himself to give so much up.

And the other section in which she took upon herself a new and greater royal position. No longer was she merely royal by marriage, she was now royal by popular acclaim and self-promulgation. Asked if she would ever be Queen she said: 'No, I don't believe so. I would like to become the queen of peoples' hearts.' Her observation that someone has to show love to the people was a clearly implied criticism of the cold, impersonal style of the Queen and her family.

In coining the simple phrase 'queen of people's hearts', Diana was securing her place in legend. The irony never struck her, nor has it subsequently occurred to the Dianaphiles, that the original Queen of Hearts was a character from a nursery rhyme that was turned into a caricature of royalty by Lewis Carroll in *Alice in Wonderland*.

Patrick Jephson, who had not been kept in the loop when the secret plans had been made to record and broadcast the interview, was however close at hand to observe the consequences.

She had made no plans for what to do with the deluge she had released. She had not thought further ahead than the newspaper headlines the next day. 'The aftermath was an anticlimax,' Patrick Jephson later recalled. 'She had taken the biggest possible injection of her favourite drug, and now she felt even worse.'[37]

A friend of Prince Charles, government minister Nicholas Soames, said of Diana's performance that she seemed 'on the edge of paranoia'.

6

A TIMELY DEATH

After the broadcast of the *Panorama* interview there was no way back. For the Queen and Prince Philip enough was enough and in letters sent shortly after the programme was transmitted, they told their son and daughter-in-law to move from a separation to a divorce. By that time the Queen was used to marriage breakdown in the family. At the start of her reign divorce had been considered a form of social suicide, by the late 1990s, the royal family was leading the way. The Queen's sister and three of the Queen's children have ended their marriages in the divorce courts.

The letter began, 'Dearest Diana' and ended 'With love from Mama', but in between the words were those of Diana's Queen as well as her mother-in-law. The letter was a royal command.

As the constitution requires, the Queen had consulted Prime Minister John Major. She also told Diana that she had conferred with the Archbishop of Canterbury. This news infuriated Diana who felt naively that her marriage was her business and not a matter of public property or state concern. The tone of the letter, says Paul Burrell, with whom Diana shared its contents, was 'sympathetic, delicate, devoid of anger, but it did smack of a mother-in-law frustrated with the behaviour of both parties, emphasising that a divorce could not inflict further damage on the two sons who had suffered enough over the previous years.'[1]

Diana replied immediately to say she needed time to consider the next stage, but the very next day received a letter from Prince Charles asking for a divorce. He described the breakdown of the marriage as a personal and national tragedy. For a while she attempted to resist the inevitable, but it was only a gesture of defiance. She did not want it to appear that she had been forced out of the royal family. She had a cordial, even warm, but nevertheless formal meeting with the Queen, but to no avail.

To help her cope emotionally with the situation she increasingly fell back on her official and her impromptu 'missions of mercy' to hospitals and care centres.

> She went out and sucked up grief, pain, plight and suffering on her visits to the homeless, the sick, the dying and the poor, and returned to Kensington Palace burdened with it but satisfied that, in a day's work, she had showered love and affection on the people who mattered. Put that with her own insecurities, fears and problems, and emotional overload was the result.[2]

For a while Diana started to behave increasingly strangely. She became convinced her home was being bugged and that even her own staff were turning against her. It was around this time that Diana expressed her fears that her life was in danger and she might be killed in a car accident.

Diana described Wednesday 28 February 1996 as the saddest day of her life. It was the day she realised she had no option but to pre-empt defeat and issue a statement of her own that she had agreed to end the marriage.

The lawyers began to draw up heads of agreement. What title would Diana have after the marriage was over? What financial settlement would be offered? Would she continue to have any sort of royal role as mother of the future King? Would she have an office and if so who would fund it?

On 15 July 1996 the divorce was presented before the High Court and on 28 August at 10.27 a.m. the marriage was ended.

Under the divorce settlement, Diana retained the title Princess of Wales but lost her royal status as 'Her Royal Highness'. She also received a lump sum payment of £17 million and was asked to return to Prince Charles a number of small family items. The loss of the prefix HRH might seem a minor matter, but to members of the royal family the title looms large. It determines, for instance, who curtsies to whom. Deprived of her HRH status, Diana would now be expected to curtsy to Princess Michael of Kent, although Princess Michael wrote to Diana immediately saying she would expect no such deference. It was a spiteful move to downgrade her, Diana thought, although Prince William reassured her it would be restored once he was King.

In his funeral oration her brother Earl Spencer was to make reference to this perceived royal slight. Diana, he declared, was 'someone with a natural nobility who was classless and proved in the last year that she needed no royal title to continue to generate her particular brand of magic'.[3]

Interestingly Patrick Jephson, by then her former private secretary, wondered if the loss of her HRH title was due to a clerical error rather than a calculated snub. In her rush to get her statement into the public domain before the Buckingham Palace statement, her own staff had inadvertently omitted the all important three letters 'HRH' and the Palace took no steps to correct the mistake.

Strangely the finality of the proceedings lightened the relationship between Charles and Diana. On 1 July, Diana's thirty-fifth birthday, just a fortnight before the divorce went to the High Court, the Princess had an unexpected visitor – the Prince. They greeted each other with a kiss. Diana joked 'I suppose you've come to take the furniture way,' and they both laughed together for the first time in years.

The rapprochement was witnessed by Paul Burrell. 'It was a bizarre scene and also sad: I detected a surge of excitement in the princess . . . it was all very cordial, relaxed and civil.'[4]

When the divorce was finalised Diana set about reorganising her office. She moved offices from St James's to Kensington Palace. As at the time of the separation, she saw the ending of the marriage as the beginning of a new chapter. With her new-found wealth she raised staff salaries. The 28 August, her first day as a single woman for fifteen years, was also a day of reflection.

> Fifteen years have now been signed off. I never wanted a divorce and always dreamed of a happy marriage with loving support from Charles. Although that was never meant to be, we do have two wonderful boys who are deeply loved by their parents. A part of me will always love Charles, but how I wish he'd looked after me and been proud of my work . . . I want to become Charles's best friend.[5]

Diana had one more year to live, but in obvious ignorance of what lay ahead, she began planning the rest of her life. First there came a typical Diana grand gesture. She decided to sell her huge wardrobe of dresses. Each one, she said is a memory and an old friend, but now is the time to sell. A charity auction was the obvious solution. Seventy-nine dresses raised £1.85 million for AIDS and other charities.

In one way the divorce did not change her lifestyle. She continued to divide her time between her public duties, her unofficial role as a carer and her expensive pleasures. But she began increasingly to negotiate a dangerous path through life and neither the royal family nor the government had any means of restraining her. The causes she backed with her considerable media pulling power became increasingly political. 'I would like to be an ambassador for this country, I would like to represent this country and her good qualities abroad,'[6] was how she had articulated her future plans less than a year earlier. Yet once the divorce was absolute she became widely identified with a single controversial issue – landmines – about which Britain, along with other weapons' exporting countries, had reason to feel shame.

Her sources of pleasure became, in establishment eyes, increasingly unsuitable and undignified. She accepted free holidays from multi-millionaires and was seen leading a hedonistic lifestyle. 'How I longed for the legions of good people who made up the forgotten armies of her charities to feel that their patron had turned her back on at least some of the glamour which now tempted her in order to strengthen them,'[7] Patrick Jephson reflected.

Diana had no structured plans for her life after the divorce. Had she decided to spend some time focusing on her humanitarian work and demonstrating some form of public reconciliation with her husband, it might have been a wise strategy. The few thoughts she allowed herself to entertain about what the middle- or long-term future might bring, were focused not on herself but on her children.

In her *Panorama* interview she had allowed speculation that Prince William might succeed to the throne, bypassing his father. 'William is still very young,' she replied carefully. 'Should he now already carry such a burden around his shoulders? I cannot answer this question.'

Diana was asked, 'Would it be your wish that Prince William follows the Queen when he is of age?'

'My wish is for my husband to find his inner peace,' she replied. 'That is important, and the rest will result from this.'

'Are you guilty for the unstable condition of the monarchy at the moment?' Martin Bashir wanted to know.

'No, I don't believe so. I don't want to destroy my children's future. I believe, what is most important to me when discussing the monarchy, is that the people don't become indifferent and apathetic. It is a problem. My children must change the monarchy one day . . . I visit the homeless and people who are dying from AIDS with the children. I take them everywhere with me. I give them knowledge and experience, as knowledge is power. I would like them to be understanding. So they can learn about desperation, hope and dreams.'

'What type of monarchy do you expect?'

'One that cared for a close contact to the population.'[8]

Whatever her dreams and goals might have been, Diana was not one for making careful plans and sticking to them. She talked wildly about emigrating. Would it be America or Australia? She explored changing religion and on a visit to Pakistan asked questions about Islam. 'There is no doubt she was looking for a new direction in her life,' her brother said at her funeral. 'She talked endlessly about getting away from England.'

At least when she was within the royal circle she had solid advice on which to fall back, however much she might have railed against what the men in grey suits suggested she do. On her own she was rudderless. Her lifelong habit of cutting friends and family out of her life meant that she had fewer trusted confidantes.

When Diana harboured a grudge there was no telling how long it would be before she decided to resume contact, if at all. Rosa Monkton, one of her closest friends, found herself out of favour after offering some advice that Diana did not wish to hear. On that occasion Diana ended her feud after four months by phoning out of the blue as if nothing had happened.

It was Diana's way throughout her life to take people up and then drop them at whim. It happened to friends, staff, family and many others who were well placed to offer her wise well-intentioned guidance from their own experience. Lord Palumbo was one who discovered what it was like suddenly, and unaccountably, to become an ex-friend of the Princess of Wales. He expressed the opinion in May 1996 that she was totally self-obsessed, deserted by her mother and her husband and by everybody, just thinking about herself.[9]

She never made it up with her mother having fallen out in May 1997. What happened was that Frances gave an interview to *Hello!* magazine. It was a rare event as Frances was normally highly distrustful of the press. In the interview Frances tried to put a positive spin on Diana's new status as Princess of Wales, minus the title Her Royal Highness. When asked for her views on the courtesy title being lost she said, 'I thought it was absolutely wonderful. At last she was able to be herself, use her own name and find her own identity. It's a very personal thing and I don't understand why it became so important to so many people.'[10]

Diana took her mother's words the wrong way and was reportedly furious about her comments on the loss of her HRH title. She did not assume that her mother had meant well and had perhaps expressed herself badly; she took the words as a slight. She petulantly cut off all contact with her mother. Hearing how Diana had reacted, the magazine sent her an advance copy of the second episode of her mother's interview. Diana refused to read it. A conciliatory letter from Frances was returned unopened. Frances tried to phone her, but was told Diana was not available. All she could do was to wait until Diana's mood had changed and she would receive a perky phone call as if nothing had happened.

One royal observer has gone so far as to say that towards the middle of 1997 Diana

> . . . began to spiral into a form of dangerous chaos. Shunned by the establishment, she came to rely on the kindness of tycoons, and eventually fell into the camp of Mohamed Al Fayed, the controversial owner of Harrods, accepting a summer holiday in the south of France with him, and later consorting with his playboy son Dodi. To the first holiday she took her sons but they refused to go again. She went for a series of further holidays on the newly acquired Fayed yacht, openly disporting herself with Dodi.[11]

'I wondered how she would ever find peace of mind,' Patrick Jephson reflected, 'if the means of achieving it were controlled by people who would always want something back from her in return for their support, be it jet, yacht, holiday, pet project or even love.'[12] He had long noted a self-destructive pattern in Diana's behaviour. He called it her death wish. 'I could think of no other explanation . . . and it was inextricably linked with a craving to be noticed.'[13]

He had often observed her in crowds or when pressed by photographers. She suffered the inconvenience and occasional alarm as if they were the wounds of martyrdom. 'The experience was painful but somehow holy, and suffered in the cause of reminding the world not only that she was there but also that she was defenceless and occasionally at least potentially in danger.'[14]

Diana also began to brood on the past and on what might have been. While her relationship with Charles had improved, she could still not get Camilla out of her mind. Would they marry one day? She wondered. How would she feel about that and how would the boys react? To get away from England in the summer of 1997 when Prince Charles was planning a fiftieth birthday party for Camilla, Diana accepted an invitation from Mohamed Al Fayed, to join him in the south of France.

She could not of course shake off the media attention and the paparazzi of Europe followed every move through their long lenses. She took advantage of the opportunity. On the day of the birthday party, Diana cavorted in a leopard-skin swimsuit in front of the cameras, supplying the press flotilla with 'amazingly sexy photos'. 'The message was obvious: "Happy Birthday Camilla",' observed Piers Morgan, 'Nobody's going to stick the party pics on page one now: it will be Diana looking sensational.'[15]

The British media was not enraptured by the idea that she should holiday with such a controversial personality. It was Al Fayed who claimed to have bribed Conservative MPs with brown envelopes stuffed with cash, an image of petty corruption that came to epitomise the era of Tory sleaze. His son was reputedly a cocaine user. He had no profession or business and relied on his father's wealth to pursue his high life. He had been involved in film production, but it was said he had to be warned off the set of one production after trying to interest the cast in cocaine.

What raised the stakes were the hints that Diana and Dodi Al Fayed had begun a close relationship. Mohamed Al Fayed did nothing to dampen down the speculation. 'I'm like a father to Diana,' he told journalists. Some supporters later tried to claim that her real interest in befriending Dodi was to try and wean him off his drug dependence.

When Dodi appeared to call off his engagement to Kelly Fisher and Diana accepted a second invitation to holiday on the Fayed yacht in the Mediterranean without the two Princes, the tabloid press pack sensed a major story unfolding. Diana added to the speculation by hinting that shortly she had an important announcement to make, an announcement which in the event was never made.

In one sense, her death, when it came, was a timely affair. Her brother went as far as to say at her funeral that God was to be thanked for a small mercy 'at this dreadful time. For taking Diana at her most beautiful and radiant.'[16]

For at the moment of her death, Diana's reputation, which had survived so many onslaughts from her former husband's supporters, was just beginning to crumble. The British public was beginning to feel uneasy about her playgirl life enjoyed on the yacht of an Egyptian tycoon. That unease was described in the bluntest terms by Julie Burchill two days after Diana's death. She was speculating about what Diana's future might have been as the merry divorcee.

Burchill envisaged a sleazy future of indulgence, neglect and the ultimate abandonment of Lady Diana Al Fayed, 'an Arab merchant's bit of posh, endlessly sunning herself on the deck of some gin palace hooked up in the Med, toasting herself until her skin lost its bloom and she lost her husband to a newer model'.[17]

An element of racism was undoubtedly involved. Graffiti in Paris at Place D'Alma where she and Dodi died expressed a commonly held view, 'It was not an accident because the imperial family will not permit to halfbreed children.'

It was not surprising that when Diana died many Muslims latched onto conspiracy theories. Within hours of her death stories were circulating that she had been killed by the British establishment because she was getting too near to being married to a Muslim and that she might convert to Islam herself.

In the weeks before her death not even Diana's identification with the landmine issue appeared as it once had – a powerful symbol of the Princess's independence and determination. With a change of government in May, and the election of New Labour, she no longer had a case to make. The government agreed with her that landmines were evil. What had once been a bold and controversial political stance had become transformed at a stroke into a statement of mainstream policy.

The election coincided with Diana's slide from grace. Up until that point, it had done the Princess's cause no harm that there had been a tired Conservative government in power. Her self-projected image of empathy and compassion contrasted with that of the government. The Major government was surviving on the legacy of Margaret Thatcher – a woman who was the complete opposite to Diana. In her battles with the establishment Diana's case was boosted by a general feeling in British society that political change was due. In the same way that it was time for the Conservatives to be replaced by New Labour, so it was ripe for Old Monarchy, as represented by Prince Charles, to be replaced by New Monarchy, as personified by Princess Diana.

At the time of her funeral one American observer described the outpouring of sentiment over the death of Princess Diana as a political moment which, along with the New Labour electoral landslide of four months earlier, was helping to define the future of Great Britain.

119

Dan Balz of the *Washington Post* noted how Tony Blair had attempted to imitate Diana's embodiment of Britain. New Labour's mastery of the dark arts of spin-doctoring appeared to owe much to a study of Diana's intuitive media skills.

'The combination of the Labour Party's huge victory last May, which swept the Tories out of power after 18 years, and the impact of Diana's death represent the intermingling of political and cultural change that are giving voice to a new Britain,'[18] Dan Balz maintained.

He cited the view that the fundamental cultural crisis in Britain over the preceding years had been the chasm between the institutions of government – Westminster, Whitehall, the Judiciary, Buckingham Palace – and their dominant culture, which was essentially bound by tradition, habit and formality, and, on the other hand, the new culture of the people, which was born in the 1960s and now encompassed almost everyone.

It was not solely the old establishment order that Diana and New Labour challenged. The old mindset of the left was also on its way out. Back in the 1980s when she was at her lowest with bulimia and post-natal depression, Diana was largely unaware of the economic and social upheavals engulfing Britain. The miners' strike would have only been in her peripheral vision of the world. Yet in due course she was to provide one stalwart left-wing campaigner with definitive proof that the battles of the left had been lost. Tony Benn recorded this observation after watching Diana's *Panorama* interview: 'I think it is the end of politics. We have seen socialism killed; we have seen Parliament diminished in public esteem; we have seen democracy undermined. And now we have seen the end of all politics, I think. Just back to a gossiping nation wondering what will happen to the royal princes and princesses.'[19]

If the election demonstrated a public wish for change, the reaction to Diana's death showed how strongly that desire was felt by a sizeable minority. Two million people were drawn to London in the week following her death. The clamour for the Queen to break with protocol and show emotion was the nearest thing to a republican revolution the nation had ever experienced.

In all of this timing was crucial. If Diana had died a year later the reaction might have been far less intense and memorable, for once New Labour had triumphed at the polls, Diana's position was weakened. She represented, along with Tony Blair, a mood of hope in Britain – that things could change and be different.

The inevitable reality of politics is that from the moment a new government is elected it is destined to disappoint and Tony Blair's halo slowly began to tarnish from day one.

Within weeks he was on the slippery slope of his own self-destruction, a descent which would inevitably and inexorably lead to the total dissipation of that hope. From what came to be seen as the folly of the Millennium Dome and the early decision to offer political favours to New Labour's party funders, his route downhill was to take him to the Iraq war and allegations of lying to the country over weapons of mass destruction.

As the years of New Labour government passed, respect drained away from it and its leader. Over the years, the hope and moral courage it once appeared to embody were increasingly regarded as little more than image and spin.

From the summer of 1997, Diana was poised at the top of her own Cresta Run of self-immolation.

Her behaviour in the summer of 1997 did nothing to enhance her reputation as the carer, the outsider, the wounded healer, the empathiser or the fellow-sufferer.

When the newspapers caught her out in May 1997 lying about her involvement in issuing the statement accusing Tiggy Legge-Bourke of setting a bad example to her sons, she was not spared. 'Queen of Fibs' said the *Daily Mirror*. 'Diana's got to learn you can't behave like this,' Piers Morgan, the editor, wrote in his diary on 30 May.

Five weeks before Diana's death Nigel Fountain in the *Observer* had savaged Diana and everything she represented under the heading, 'A trash icon for our times'. His article was a reaction to the pictures widely published of Princess Diana comforting Elton John at the funeral of their mutual friend the designer Gianni Versace.

The image was described as 'Tragedy Lite'. 'The Queen of England manqué . . . consoling a weeping, defunct, re-haired Seventies glam rocker about the murder of an Italian porno-frock-designing bondage freak by a gay hustler serial killer and/or Mafia hit person.'[20]

He continued in similar relentless vein to describe Diana and Elton John, who he referred to by his original name of Reg Dwight, as 'a much loved quality British double act for the Nineties, icons for display in that global gallery of people whose native land is the airport. Time does not pass, locked in Groundhog Day, is endlessly recycled liked fugged air in a submarine.'

Nigel Fountain made repeated references to Hollywood in order to, in the view of Rosalind Brunt of Sheffield Hallam University, 'reinforce the hollowness of the scenario' and imply a more sinister suggestion that behind Diana's popularity lay 'the Hollywood-horror of madness'.[21]

> After a while I figured out where I had seen Di's comforting expression before. It was Kathy Bates, the crazed fan/kidnapper of pulp writer James Caan in Stephen King's *Misery*, round the time she realises he isn't happy with her favoured plot outline and gets serious about cracking his legs.[22]

By the end of July 1997, Rosalind Brunt noted, Diana was being portrayed as 'the flash-trash, mad-bad emblem of a superficial, amoral and emptily post-modern' decade. Just over a month later she was being described as a symbol of the 'caring' feminised nineties.

You can fool some of the people all of the time, and all of the people some of the time, goes the old adage of public life, but you cannot fool all of the people all of the time. Had time been running out for Diana? She was not what she claimed to be, and certainly not unique or modern. She was of a type long ago identified through history as the Lady Folly. In the words of Professor Richard Fenn, she was acting out a part 'once described by Erasmus that is actually a composite of roles: court jester, fool, saint, masker, actor, carnival-goer, ecstatic and lover of souls'.[23]

What might Diana have grown to be like had she lived? Imagine the figure of Diana as she might have appeared at the coronation of her son. She is invited as the mother of the King, yet excluded from the royal family, which is by then presided over by the matriarchal Camilla. She is accompanied by the children of her second marriage. Her glow of beauty has been cruelly transformed by Mediterranean sunshine and the passage of time into stark, hard, lined features. A woman with few true friends to whom she remained loyal. A woman who, although she was not a drinker in her youth, nevertheless had a self-confessed addictive personality. Might she perhaps, like her mother, have taken to alcohol as her consolation? A sad figure, a lonely figure, a fallen angel who had turned her back on good works to live a life of blue sky luxury on board the yachts of the international nouveau riche.

If acquiring a glowing, posthumous reputation is all important, then Diana's death was perfectly timed.

7

'MINES KILL CHILDREN, DON'T THEY MUMMY?'

In the year before her death, what upheld Princess Diana's serious, as opposed to frivolous, public profile was her involvement in a campaign whose purpose was to shame governments across the world, so that they would outlaw the use of anti-personnel mines as weapons of war. For her so conspicuously to embrace the landmine issue involved a marked change of direction. It took her in a decidedly political direction and it made her enemies. Landmine manufacture is a multi-million pound business.

Landmines differ from other forms of munitions in that they are planted as tactical devices during armed conflict and then remain hidden and lethal for long periods after those conflicts have been resolved. There were daily instances of children around the world being killed or seriously injured by accidentally treading on uncharted and long-forgotten mines. They strike indiscriminately.

Diana was introduced to the issue by the British Red Cross,

a charity with which she had a long-standing relationship. At the outset, it was a subject about which she knew very little, but she quickly grasped how her involvement could rapidly put the issue at the forefront of world opinion. She was shown graphic videos, reports and photographs on the subject and was much moved. She shared her new concerns with her sons and showed them some of the images of maimed children. Prince Harry is said to have responded with the words, 'Mines kill children, don't they Mummy?'

In the last year of her life Diana was to give many speeches on the subject and take an active role in the worldwide lobby calling on governments for a global ban on landmines. In between her widely reported love affairs she took on the landmine issue with considerable dedication.

In January 1997, she visited Angola as part of her campaign. In June, she spoke at the landmines conference at the Royal Geographical Society in London. From there she went to the USA to promote the American Red Cross's landmines campaign. Her last public engagements were in Bosnia between 7 and 10 August. She broke from her summer of luxury and romance with Dodi Fayed to visit landmine projects in Sarajevo, Travnic and Zenezica. In publicity terms her efforts were somewhat overshadowed by press delight in having secured the photograph the paparazzi had been striving for. As Diana stepped off the plane from Bosnia, a British tabloid newspaper published a front page colour photograph of Dodi and the Princess kissing.

On her first trip as an International Red Cross VIP volunteer, in January 1997, Princess Diana met landmine survivors in hospitals and was shown projects run by The HALO Trust that was involved in searching for mines and rendering them harmless.'

Paul Burrell, who accompanied her, recalls a visit to a hospital where Diana had met a young girl who had been out fetching water for the family when she stepped on a mine. In her abdomen was a gaping wound. Her entrails were clearly visible.

The Princess forced herself to focus on the girl's eyes. She didn't want this young patient to think she was unbearable to look at, even though she was beyond help. The Princess placed her hand in the girl's hand. The Princess bit her lip to stop herself crying. Then she pulled the sheet up to the girl's neck, turned to the press and said: 'Please, no more.' The camera lights flicked off.[1]

The media pack accompanying her included royal reporters and those familiar with covering areas of conflict. Angola had become infested with mines following a long and bloody civil war. The veteran correspondent W. F. Deedes described the scene that faced the Princess and her entourage: 'Luanda appeared to have lost its heart and all self respect. Garbage accumulated on the street corners, the hot weather rendered the stink unendurable.'[2]

The pictures which came to sum up her work were of two kinds: the familiar pictures of the Princess embracing children; and those showing her in protective clothing standing alone beside the minefields themselves. Normally the Princess allowed the pictures to convey the message she wished to share with her audience; on the landmine issue her growing confidence as a public speaker enabled her to speak out forcefully as well.

The mine is a stealthy killer. Long after conflict is ended, its innocent victims die or are wounded singly, in countries of which we hear little. Their lonely fate is never reported. The world, with its many other preoccupations, remains largely unmoved by a death roll of something like 800 people every month – many of them women and children. Those who are not killed outright – and they number another 1,200 a month – suffer terrible injuries and are handicapped for life. I was in Angola in January with the British Red Cross – a country where there are 15 million landmines in a population, Ladies and Gentlemen, of 10 million – with

126

the desire of drawing world attention to this vital, but hitherto largely neglected issue.[3]

But as the old saying goes, one picture is worth a thousand words. The photograph of Diana wearing the uniform of The HALO Trust has become one of the iconographic images of her life.

Inevitably, and perhaps deliberately, Princess Diana's high-profile trip took her across the fine dividing line between expressing humanitarian concern and entering the political arena.

Her trip to Angola did not please members of the Conservative government. Her call for an international ban on landmines was perceived as being out of step with government policy. The Junior Defence Minister, Earl Howe, called the Princess a 'loose cannon', talked of her political interference, saying that she was ill, informed on the issue.

BBC News quoted Peter Viggers, a Conservative member of the Defence Select Committee:

We all know landmines and other weapons are vicious and nasty. The question is how best to negotiate so they are not used in future. The government's policy on this has been an extremely careful one and the statements made by the Princess of Wales have not been in line with that policy.

The government, said the BBC, was involved in international negotiations for a worldwide ban on landmines, but in the meantime the army was still using them.

Labour has welcomed the intervention by the Princess. It is backing calls for an international moratorium on the use of anti-personnel mines.

Shadow defence spokesman, David Clark, said: 'I think we should all welcome the fact she has gone to Angola and she has tried to warn the world of the dangers of these terrible weapons. I think we should be applauding what she's doing.'[4]

'Diana's visit to Angola had caused a modest stir,' W. F. Deedes observed. 'If it was causing offence to the Tory government that doubled its news value.'[5]

Word of the government's discomfiture reached Angola overnight.

'We had flown to Huambo and were standing in a disconsolate group near a minefield,' recalls W. F. Deedes. 'Diana approached me. "A disturbing night," I said to her softly. "Idiot minister," she replied succinctly.'[6]

'Some people chose to interpret my visit as a political statement. But it was not. I am not a political figure,' she told the conference in June.

As I said at the time, and I'd like to reiterate now, my interests are humanitarian. That is why I felt drawn to this human tragedy. This is why I wanted to play down my part in working towards a world-wide ban on these weapons. During my days in Angola, I saw at first hand three aspects of this scourge. In the hospitals of Luanda, the capital, and Huambo, scene of bitter fighting not long ago, I visited some of the mine victims who had survived, and saw their injuries. I am not going to describe them, because in my experience it turns too many people away from the subject. Suffice to say, that when you look at the mangled bodies, some of them children, caught by these mines, you marvel at their survival. What is so cruel about these injuries is that they are almost invariably suffered, where medical resources are scarce.[7]

As much as she claimed to be apolitical, her words inevitably were interpreted as politically partisan.

One of my objectives in visiting Angola was to forward the cause of those, like the Red Cross, striving in the name of humanity to secure an international ban on these weapons. Since then, we are glad to see some real progress has been made. There are signs of a change of heart – at least in some parts of the world. For that we should be cautiously grateful. If an international ban on mines can be secured it means, looking far ahead, that the world may be a safer place for this generation's grandchildren.

But for this generation in much of the developing world, there will be no relief, no relaxation . . . . The toll of deaths and injuries caused by mines already there, will continue.[8]

When the New Labour government was elected in 1997 Tony Blair made a point of backing the Princess's campaign. In some ways, as suggested earlier, this detracted from the image she wished to project of being anti-establishment and by implication the champion of ordinary people. The Prime Minister told the *Daily Mirror* editor Piers Morgan, 'It's important she is allowed to carry on the work that she is doing. She earns a lot of respect around the world for her work on landmines and I want that to continue.'[9]

The *Mirror* headlined the remarks 'Blair: I back Diana'. At his next meeting with the Queen, Morgan claims, the new Prime Minister had an uncomfortable session, with Her Majesty making it clear that she was not happy with what he had said. She did not approve of any member of the royal family, even one under exclusion, being used as a party-political pawn.

Diana made other trips to former war zones. W. F. Deedes accompanied her again on her Bosnia trip of August 1997.

We sat alone with a young widow whose husband had been killed by a mine while fishing. With no interpreter present very little could be said. What passed between them is beyond reckoning. All this in the middle of a fling with Dodi Fayed.[10]

By the end of the month Diana was dead. In the days that followed the Paris crash many references were made to Diana's involvement in the landmine campaign. It was the most recent high-profile interest that she had embraced and it had hinted at a more serious and controversial future. It was fine for Diana to use her fame and iconographic appeal to draw attention to charitable causes, but when these causes strayed over into the realm of politics it was an altogether more serious matter. Manufacturing and trading anti-personnel mines is an important business and one in which British arms manufacturers are actively involved. Profits were at stake. It was not surprising that those who saw conspiracy behind her death added her landmine campaign to the list of possible motives and the arms traders to the list of possible assassins.

The publicity created by Diana's work and the fact that it was cut off in mid-stream by her death, gave an important fillip to the efforts of the many people dedicated both to clearing old minefields and outlawing the weapon in future.

Over a hundred charities and non-governmental organisations have been involved in the International Campaign to Ban Landmines. Four months after Diana's death, 122 governments signed the Mine Ban Treaty in Ottawa, Canada. The International Campaign to Ban Landmines and the campaign coordinator were awarded the Nobel Prize for Peace.

There is still, however, much work to be done in clearing minefields and helping victims. One of the aims of the Diana, Princess of Wales Fund is to promote a continuation of her work by making grants to help the poor and dispossessed in the United Kingdom and abroad, including those affected by landmines.

The HALO Trust that Diana conspicuously promoted

continues its work to remove what it describes as the debris of war.

It has over 5500 mine-clearers in nine countries and in June 2002 celebrated clearing its first million landmines and other unexploded ordnance. By early 2004 the total figure had exceeded 1,600,000.

Without detracting from some immense achievements, there are commentators who say that while Diana helped win a battle, the war against landmines is far from over.

'One of Diana, Princess of Wales', most notable achievements in life and death was the role she played in securing a ban on anti-personnel landmines', wrote Paul Donovan on the fifth anniversary of her death.

> Her involvement effectively secured millions of pounds of free publicity for the campaign seeking a ban on the weapon. Ironically, Diana's death put the icing on the cake, acting as a catalyst to propel the British Government and others forward toward signing the Ottawa Treaty banning the weapon in December 1997.[11]

However, he suggested that, five years on, this legacy had been wasted. He accused governments of failing to fund landmine clearance, he claimed that a number of arms companies had been caught trying to sell banned weapons in the UK and that other arms companies were actively seeking ways of getting round the treaty.

> While the British Government signed the Ottawa Treaty, there remain serious questions over its willingness to police it properly. Anti-vehicle mines are not banned under the Ottawa Treaty and provide a convenient way of getting round the law.

> In terms of usage, one in every five landmines lying dormant in two of the worst effected countries, Angola and Ethiopia, is of the anti-vehicle variety.

While the Blair government did much to spin its early ethical credentials on the back of signing and ratifying the Ottawa Treaty in 1997, its actions since suggest something less than commitment to this cause. In addition to the failure to police the treaty effectively, it has taken a miserly approach to funding clearance.

So overall the British government's commitment . . . is highly suspect. The law enshrining the ban in UK domestic law has so far proved ineffectual while the amount given for clearance is derisory and misdirected. Not a great legacy for a Princess.[12]

Indeed in subsequent conflicts the British government has continued to condone the use of weapons that in ethical and moral terms differ little from landmines. A report published in November 2005 by Landmine Action and the Diana, Princess of Wales Memorial Fund called for a moratorium on the use of cluster munitions until proper research has been undertaken into their effects and new international law governing their use has been agreed.

The report described how when cluster munitions are used they have a high failure rate. Unexploded duds kill and injure long after conflicts have ended. They have caused significant civilian casualties in Kosovo, Afghanistan and Iraq.

Britain has confirmed that during the 2003 Iraq conflict it employed 2000 artillery shells each containing 49 sub-munition bomblets plus 70 air-dropped bombs each containing 147 sub-munition bomblets. A total of over 108,000 bomblets. Experienced clearance operators estimate that up to 30 per cent of these bomblets fail to explode and are left in a highly dangerous condition on the ground. In March the British government publicly acknowledged that its RBL755 cluster munitions, the main cluster weapon dropped during the Iraq campaign, has an 'unacceptably high failure rate'.

Astrid Honeyman, Chief Executive of the Fund, added Princess Diana's posthumous support to the report calling for a moratorium on the use of cluster munitions until such time as the British government could show it had investigated the true potential impact of such weapons on civilian populations.

Or to quote Diana herself, 'Even if the world decided tomorrow to ban these weapons, this terrible legacy of mines already in the earth would continue to plague the poor nations of the Globe. The evil that men do, lives after them . . .'[13]

8

WITH THE ANGELS

The news broke in the early hours of the morning on 31 August 1997. It was sudden and shocking and as dawn broke on the Sunday morning the full horror of the night's tragic events began to emerge. In Britain, many of the first to know the news were children who had turned on the television to watch the morning cartoons and instead found themselves watching sombre news reports from Paris and London.

That morning's news was simple and stark. A car in which Diana, Dodi Fayed, their bodyguard, Trevor Rees-Jones and driver, Henri Paul, had been travelling through Paris had smashed at speed into a pillar in an underpass at the Place D'Alma. Bit by bit other details emerged. The paparazzi, from which it is said the car was fleeing, arrived very quickly afterwards to find the wreckage. They swarmed around it taking photographs. Diana was at that stage still alive. By chance a doctor was passing and he rendered first aid without realising who his patient was. The emergency ambulance took Diana to the Pitié Salpetrière Hospital where she was pronounced dead. The length of time it took to travel with the dying Princess from the scene of the accident to the hospital has been subject of much debate.

It is unlikely that the full facts of what happened that day in Paris will ever be known. The enquiry by the French authorities is being replicated by an English coroner's court. The French blamed the driver Henri Paul. It was alleged that he was massively over the legal alcohol limit. Plausible claims have surfaced that the blood samples from which the French investigators worked were not those taken from Paul.

Attempts to use the British Freedom of Information Act have only confused the matter.

For instance, Cabinet Office documents written after Princess Diana's death give differing reasons why she was in the car in which she died.

One memo addressed to the Prime Minister said Diana and Dodi Al Fayed switched cars as they left the Ritz hotel in Paris to divert paparazzi.

But another memo addressed to the Foreign Secretary suggested it was simply because their first car failed to start that a last minute switch of vehicles was made. Whatever the causes, which will no doubt be debated for years to come, the consequences of the crash were astonishing.

There followed one of the most extraordinary weeks in British social history. More than that, the reaction to Diana's death became a global phenomenon in a way few other single events had ever been before. The leaving of flowers, the erecting of shrines, the public displays of grief were noted from countries all around the world.

It was not just Kensington Palace, Althorp and other places where Diana had lived that became foci of grief. Anywhere with any remote Diana-connection became a local focus. Birmingham Cathedral, which normally has around a thousand visitors a week reported 40,000 visitors during the week of mourning. Twenty-five thousand candles were lit and an oak tree planted in the grounds by Diana in 1995 became a special place of mourning.

In Britain, for two Sundays there was a marked increase in church attendance. When people have spiritual needs, they still turn to the established churches, however unchurched and unaware of church practice, doctrine and belief many of them might be.

The thousands of messages left with flowers and gifts at the many makeshift Diana shrines fell into two main categories. There were first those focused on the meaning of death and the hope of life to come, and second those expressing contrition. Typical of the first category were these three messages.

Thank you for the love you gave the poor, may the Lord make you a saint.

Dear God, please keep her safe and let her rest with the angels.

The good on earth are always snatched the earliest.

And this contrite note was one attached to a bouquet of flowers and left outside Buckingham Palace:

I killed her, I hounded her
To the death. I followed her
Every movement.
I gave her no peace. For I bought the papers. I read the
Stories and
I looked at the photographs.
They did this for me.
How can I live with that?

From the first hours the media was being blamed for Diana's death. The French authorities arrested the press pack which had been following the car and the implication was obvious. Diana had been hounded to death by the paparazzi. The image of the shamed photographers being taken away in a French police van served to reinforce the idea.

As the week went by new scapegoats were identified. Very quickly it was suggested that the driver had been well over the alcohol limit. The press was glad to divert attention from its own implied responsibility. Then, in its quest for something or someone to blame, the public focused on the royal family. By staying in Scotland and refusing to allow the Buckingham Palace flag to fly at half mast, the Queen was seen as cold and insensitive. A rumour later spread that one of the Queen's first reactions on hearing of the death was to instruct officials to contact the hospital to make sure any royal jewellery the Princess might have been wearing was accounted for and returned. If that rumour had surfaced within the first week, the public mood might have turned very hostile. Had there been any request for the return of the jewels it would not so much have been a sign of indifference, more a symptom of confusion and a failure to cope. Palace officials, unable to appreciate the wider picture, became much bothered with irrelevant details and, as Diana's body lay in the Paris hospital, they made insensitive phone calls about Crown possessions.

In his funeral oration Earl Spencer took aim at both estates – monarchy and media.

Psychologists talk of flashbulb memory. The majority of people can recall where they were when they first heard an item of devastating worldwide news: the assassination of President Kennedy, the attack of 11 September, the death of Diana. Something happens in the brain at the moment the news is received which imprints it, and the circumstances of hearing the news, in the memory.

Prince Charles was staying at Balmoral and was woken sometime after midnight with the first news of the accident. It was not known initially how serious it was. By 3.30 a.m. a phone call to Paris had confirmed the worst. The Prince was genuinely and deeply distraught. He wept. The Queen did not display her feelings. The young Princes were told of the news by their father as soon as they woke around 7 a.m. At the centre of discussions as to what to do was Sir Robert Fellowes, the Queen's private secretary and as husband to Lady Jane, Diana's brother-in-law.

Diana's mother heard the news from Jane. At first Frances was told that Diana had survived the accident, but quickly that bulletin was updated and corrected. Even at that time royal protocol ruled and she was told to tell no-one of the news for an hour, giving the royal family time to tell other heads of state.

Not that protocol was straightforward. This was an unprecedented event – the divorced wife of a member of the royal family dying on foreign soil. Frances waited and waited for news as to what she should do. There were difficult discussions at Balmoral. Should one of the royal aircraft be sent to reclaim Diana's body? Protocol suggested no, compassion and common sense suggested yes. In the end an aircraft from the Queen's Flight was used.

Paul Burrell heard the news via a friend of the Princess who was in America. She telephoned on hearing of the accident through a contact at the White House. He went immediately to Kensington Palace, where other members of her staff had gathered, waiting for news. When her death was confirmed he took the first flight he could book to Paris.

It was not in the Queen's nature to break with royal tradition on the morning of Diana's death. The best way of protecting the young Princes, she considered, was to proceed with the day as planned. As it was a Sunday they attended the local parish church. Acting on advice from the royal family, the minister made no mention of the news from France during the service. The Queen took comfort from familiar hymns and long-established custom. As Charles flew with Diana's sisters to Paris, the Princes and the Queen stayed out of sight at Balmoral.

At Birkhall, the Queen Mother's Scottish home, once news of Diana's death was relayed no further mention of the Princess was made, although the ninety-seven-year-old Queen Mother wore black to the morning service at Crathie Church.

The royal family was still in Scotland on the Wednesday when Frances left her home on the Scottish island of Seil to travel to London. By that time the plans for the funeral were well underway. Initially the Queen had wanted the funeral to be a small scale, private family one at Windsor. Both Charles and the new Prime Minister Tony Blair realised this would be highly inappropriate. Within twenty-four hours of Diana's death, it was obvious to everyone outside Balmoral that the public was demanding a major royal occasion. Westminster Abbey was booked. It took several days and hours of heated debate for the royal court to realise the magnitude of what had happened.

The extraordinary and worldwide public displays of grief took the Queen and her advisers by surprise.

> Her instinct and upbringing had taught her that you keep tears for the pillow. Crying in public was not something the Queen would allow of herself, or expect of her children and grandchildren. It is not the royal way. It is neither dignified nor necessary or helpful. But, on television, in the first week of September 1997, it seemed the whole world was openly weeping and wailing, and baying for Her Majesty to shed some tears too.[1]

In Britain people heard the news as they awoke in the morning and listened to the radio and television news bulletins. In America, thanks to the time difference, news arrived late in the evening. In Australia it was the afternoon.

Those working in the news media were among the first to hear, but to begin with they only had rumours of an accident to go on. Piers Morgan, editor of the *Daily Mirror*, was phoned by his news desk at 12.30 a.m. to be told of 'a run in with photographers . . . It didn't sound too serious.'[2]

Initially the news media, like the court officials, did not know how to respond. 'This was the single most dramatic news story of my career. Diana, the great icon of our times, was gone,'[3] Piers Morgan recalled in his diary.

It was a big story, indeed so big that few in the media quite knew what to do. There was news to convey and obituaries to pull together, but how were journalists to prepare for what was to come? Within hours of confirmation of her death and totally unprompted by the media, Londoners began to leave flowers at the royal palaces. A few wrapped bouquets turned into huge oceans of colour as the day passed and thousands of people came to London, wanting to do something. No-one who was in London in the days following the death of Diana can forget the sight. Thousands of people milled around Kensington, St James's and Buckingham Palaces – drawn to the capital to pay their respects to Diana: they formed long, orderly queues to sign books of condolence; laid flowers; left cards and letters; sat silently; wept; lit candles. All the royal parks were seas of flowers. The cynics scoffed, what a lot of fuss about an air-headed royal! But they failed to understand what was happening. On the day of the funeral the world watched the two young Princes, their father, uncle and grandfather walking behind the cortège. The television audience was the largest ever recorded for a single event, far outstripping the massive numbers who had watched the wedding sixteen years before.

> Even the more notoriously sceptical journalists in the United Kingdom had to give in to the evidence: the public's reaction to the death of Diana, Princess of Wales, was as momentous a watershed as the British are capable of, considering their historical aversion to actual revolutions.[4]

The reason why the death of Diana provoked such a response has been the subject of much speculation. It has been debated in newspapers, weekly magazines and academic papers to the extent that hundreds of thousands of words have been written.

The answers arrived at depended on the writers' own preconceived ideas. Those with a spiritual agenda tended to find only spiritual explanations. Those taking an anthropological or political stance analysed the events according to those disciplines.

A point overlooked by several observers was a simple one. While millions watched the events unfold on television and thousands travelled to London and other centres to leave their tributes, millions did nothing. They looked on from the sidelines bemused. Why was this? Why were millions unmoved, indeed some rather irritated by the attention given to the death of one young woman? What, if anything distinguishes those who were interested from those who were uninterested?

It was the observers who approached the subject from a social, as opposed to spiritual, viewpoint who noticed the fact that the overwhelming majority of British people who took to the streets and laid flowers were

> . . . young women, gays and people of colour. The excluded or marginal social subjects, those whom Thatcherism had forgotten or swept aside, bounced back onto the political arena with a vengeance. It was the return of the repressed, not with a bang but a whimper . . . a gesture of civil disobedience: the public outpour of grief is also a sort of 'emotional Gandhism', which expresses the need for in-depth and structural reforms not only of the British political system but also the Constitution.[5]

As noted earlier, the death of Diana came at the end of a summer that had started with a British general election in which New Labour ousted the old Tory government in a major landslide. The election had produced not only a new Prime Minister and government, but a widespread sense of hope. Although that hope has since been dashed, it was still there in August 1997. There was a feeling that those who had been excluded from the economic prosperity of the Thatcher years would enjoy a better deal.

Thus the timing of Diana's death was significant. A new political spirit was in the air. For those looking for spiritual explanations the date was also important. It was the run up to the new millennium – a time when people were especially susceptible to all things apocalyptic and supernormal.

Hers was a timely death, if such a thing can ever be said about a young woman dying in such tragic circumstances. She died as a beautiful woman and at a time when she still retained the title and trappings of royalty. Her end also came while she still represented the magic of royalty in people's minds. She had not done herself sufficient damage that summer for her work as a campaigner against landmines, and her image as a healer and comforter of the sick, to have been overshadowed.

Despite the early signs that the tide of public opinion had turned, a largely unblemished Diana was the one fresh in people's minds. Had she married into the Fayed family there might have been a groundswell of disapproval. Was it right that the mother of a future King should marry the playboy son of the owner of Harrods? Would her appeal have survived the ageing process as she appeared less and less in print as an iconic beauty and more and more as a middle-aged curiosity?

Such speculation is idle. At the moment of her death those were not the questions being asked by the overwhelming majority of people who heard the news.

The questions being posed were angry and uncomfortable. Who caused her death? Was it the paparazzi? Why did the Queen appear to be so isolated and indifferent? Why did she stay hidden away in Scotland? Should she not be with her people? And symbolic of the whole undercurrent of feeling, why did the Queen not order a Union Jack to be flown on the Buckingham Palace flag-pole at half mast?

All around the country flags were at half mast as a universally accepted sign of respect and mourning – all that is bar the one flag at the heart of the capital city, on the Queen's London home. The argument that it was not traditional or in accordance with royal protocol to fly the flag at half mast cut no ice.

'Show us you care', was one tabloid headline, and it spoke for the entire media.

Her Majesty, pressed from all sides: from family, friends and Tony Blair, took notice and, biting the inside of her bottom lip, did as she was counselled. She broke with all precedent and commanded that the Union flag be flown above her palace at half mast. She returned to London. With Philip at her side, she got out of the car and inspected the tributes, the single flowers, the bouquets, the poems, the teddy bears, left in their thousands in remembrance of her ex-daughter-in-law. On Friday night, on the eve of the funeral, the Queen gave a live broadcast that changed the national mood.[6]

She spoke as a grandmother and of Diana's exceptional gifts and how there were lessons to be learned.

As well as the royal family, the public also turned on the press. Press photographers were physically attacked in London and newspaper editors received threatening letters.

As Diana's death had thrown Palace officials into a state of confusion, they lived by protocol and precedent and nothing like this had ever happened before, it was not too difficult for the spin-doctors of Downing Street to take control. They sensed a huge and unexpected political opportunity. Instead of crafting a formal address to the nation to deliver from the cabinet room at Downing Street, Tony Blair paid an informal and highly effective and emotional tribute on the morning of Diana's death.

She was 'the People's Princess' he said, in the memorable phrase reputedly coined by his press adviser Alastair Campbell. It was a masterly reinforcement of the Diana brand.

Tony Blair was in his parliamentary constituency at Sedgefield in the north east of England. He spoke to reporters at around 10.30 a.m.

We are today a nation in a state of shock, in mourning, in grief that is so deeply painful for us.

143

She was a wonderful and warm human being, though her own life was often sadly touched by tragedy. She touched the lives of so many throughout the world with joy and comfort. How many times shall we remember her in how many different ways, with the sick, the dying, with children, with the needy. With just a look or a gesture that spoke so much more than words, she would reveal to all of us the depth of her compassion and humanity.

Sensing perhaps how her halo might have been slipping in the months since the election of New Labour, he sought to reinforce the public perception of Diana, freezing her in time, as she had been some four months earlier. His words helped eradicate any images the public might have retained of the last hedonistic months. 'People everywhere kept faith with Princess Diana. They liked her, they loved her, they regarded her as one of the people. She was The People's Princess, and that's how she will stay, how she will remain, in our hearts and memories for ever.'

In the early days of the New Labour government, Peter Mandelson was also right at the centre of events. As a strong monarchist he was concerned to stem the tide of antipathy towards the royal family.

Thus Tony Blair's purpose in advising the royal family was twofold: to squeeze the maximum political advantage out of the unexpected turn of events, and also to ease the royal family through a period of challenge and upheaval. It was not in New Labour's long-term interest to do anything that might lead to the demise of the monarchy.

Both the Queen and Prince Charles sought advice from Downing Street. It was Tony Blair who persuaded the royal family to emerge from its seclusion, meet with the crowds outside Buckingham Palace and to address the nation.

During the live broadcast she spoke from 'my heart', she said, both as Queen and as a grandmother to the two Princes who had to cope with the 'devastating loss':

I want to pay tribute to Diana myself. She was an exceptional and gifted human being. In good times and bad, she never lost her capacity to smile and laugh, to inspire others with her warmth and kindness. I admired and respected her for her energy and commitment to others.

And veteran Labour MP Tony Benn noted at the end of the week, 'Tony Blair has come out of it very well because he is supposed to have told the Palace how to handle it.'[7]

The week had started with the Princess's body being brought back to England by Prince Charles, Diana's two sisters and Paul Burrell. The haste with which it was returned and the suggestion that French procedures concerning embalming and repatriation of remains were short-circuited have been issues which have subsequently fuelled the conspiracy theories.

There was much debate as to where the body should rest before the funeral. Palace officials at first suggested a public mortuary, as the Princess had no claim to royal status. In the event the chapel of St James's Palace was thought the most appropriate place.

It is remarkable on reflection that the arrangements for the return of Diana's remains and the funeral service seem with hindsight so appropriate. At the time the arrangements were made there was a three-way tussle for control. The royal family, the New Labour government and the Spencer family being the three contesting parties.

Diana's mother Frances Shand Kydd later said that the Spencer family almost boycotted the service. The problem, the Spencers claimed, was with the abbey clergy adhering to protocol. Diana's sister Lady Sarah was initially instructed to arrive at the abbey thirty-six minutes ahead of the royal party and wait for them in the abbey.

It was a tricky time and Tony Blair did not want matters to degenerate into an unseemly public row. Government documents released under the Freedom of Information Act indicate that during the days following Diana's death, Tony Blair warned government ministers not to engage in any activities that 'could result in political controversy'. As ever New Labour was warned to stay 'on message'.

One debate concerned cost. Who was to pay for the unexpected expenses of holding and policing the funeral? One unsigned memo noted how 'the Treasury have been pretty good so far, but the bill, which stands at around £3m, is mounting'. However, the author added: 'I suspect something around £5m will be the final figure – scarcely a deck on the Royal Yacht.'[8]

However, on the same day, Hayden Philips, Permanent Secretary at the Department of Culture, Media and Sport, said in a separate document that the department had 'no financial cover' for the event.

He said it was 'extremely difficult' to detail what the eventual cost would be, and that the department had been 'exercising all the restraint we can, but estimated it would be around £4m to £5m'.

Mohamed Al Fayed meanwhile was focused on his own grief and the burial of his son Dodi. As a Muslim it was the family's duty to hold the funeral within twenty-four hours of death. And in his sorrow Al Fayed began to see plot and conspiracy. He began discovering, some say imagining, and subsequently believing, controversial accounts of the events of the night. Today he is convinced that the car crash was not a simple accident, but a sinister conspiracy authorised at the highest level to prevent Diana from marrying his son.

Just two people, Paul Burrell and the Bishop of London, stayed with Diana's body the night before the funeral. As in life, so in death, one moment she was almost alone and the next on show and adored by billions. The funeral itself was watched by the largest global audience ever. Some estimates suggest it was, at three billion, four times greater than the audience that had witnessed the wedding of the Prince and Princess. It began with the appearance of the cortège followed by the young Princes walking in line with their father, uncle and grandfather. Crowds numbering hundreds of thousands lined the streets, silently watching. Some bowed, others genuflected as the coffin passed them by. The ceremony was a masterpiece of organisation, blending old and new and representing all that had been best in Diana's life. It included Earl Spencer's combative address, but most significantly it was an occasion which tapped into a collective reservoir of human spirituality.

It might have been a very different and possibly less memorable occasion if the Archbishop of Canterbury's advice had been heeded. He thought it was a mistake to invite Earl Spencer to give the address. When he found he could not influence the matter, as the abbey is a Royal Peculiar and outside his jurisdiction, he telephoned Diana's brother offering to help him to write the address to bring out the 'Christian message of hope and life evermore in God'.[9]

Archbishop Carey sent his first draft of the prayers he proposed to the Dean of Westminster. He was taken aback to hear that the Spencer family did not want any mention of the royal family, and that Buckingham Palace wanted all use of the phrase 'People's Princess' removed. 'It was a time of exceptional bewilderment and the strain was affecting everybody', Dr Carey later observed.[10]

The funeral in the form that finally emerged from the discussions and heated disagreements served to secure the myth of Diana and seemingly authenticate her elevation to sainthood by popular acclaim.

> Although a princess, she was someone for whom, from afar, we dared to feel affection, and by whom we were all intrigued. She kept company with kings and queens, with princes and presidents, but we especially remember her humane concerns and how she met individuals and made them feel significant.[11]

Her royal status was exalted by the place – Westminster Abbey – where kings and queens are crowned and anointed.

Her celebrity status was confirmed by Elton John's new version of his elegy 'Candle in the Wind' which had originally been written by the singer's long-time collaborator and lyric writer, Bernie Taupin, for the film star Marilyn Monroe, who, like Diana, had also died in her thirties and just at the point when her beauty and fame were beginning to decline. In it he bade farewell to the princess, describing her as 'England's Rose'. The country would be 'lost without her', he suggested. It would be her compassion that would be missed.

Her spiritual status was elevated by the choir's singing of a John Taverner anthem as Diana's coffin was carried out of the abbey to the waiting people.

Alleluia. May flights of Angels sing thee to thy rest.
Remember me O Lord, when you come into your kingdom.
Give rest O Lord to your handmaid, who has fallen asleep.
The choir of saints have found the well-spring of life, and door of Paradise.
Life: a shadow and a dream.
Weeping at the grave creates the song:
Alleluia. Come, enjoy rewards and crowns I have prepared for you.

For it was at that moment that what can only be described as an astonishing spiritual event seemed to take place. A silence fell over the land. All traffic stopped within hearing of the abbey. Around the world people broke off from their conversations to focus their attention on the small screen. There was silence in Paris and in towns and villages across Europe. The silence reached across time zones to America and Australia, Africa and Asia. The silence that had descended over the world was only broken by the ringing of bells. Following an English traditional form of mourning and respect, a peal of bells was rung from the abbey tower with each descent of the scale being echoed by a muffled repeat. A sound of hope being echoed by a distant peal of sorrow.

And right at the heart of the funeral service there was an oration that has gone down in history. It was given by Diana's brother and as he descended from the pulpit applause was heard outside the abbey, which was slowly echoed by those inside. The first impact of Earl Spencer's words revolved around his implied, and sometimes direct, criticism of the royal family. In retrospect the address can be seen to have cemented many aspects of the Diana myth in people's minds. He articulated what millions felt about her. Even though he had known Diana as a real person, he also recognised the legendary princess who had been his sister and deliberately reinforced the legends.

There is a temptation to rush to canonise your memory; there is no need to do so. You stand tall enough as a human being of unique qualities not to be seen as a saint.

Your greatest gift was your intuition and it was a gift you used wisely.

Without your God-given sensitivity we would be immersed in greater ignorance at the anguish of AIDS and HIV sufferers, the plight of the homeless, the isolation of lepers, the random destruction of landmines. Diana explained to me that it was her innermost feelings of suffering that made it possible for her to connect with her constituency of the rejected . . . Diana remained throughout a very insecure person at heart, almost childlike in her desire to do good for others so she could release herself from deep feelings of unworthiness.

Of all the ironies about Diana, perhaps the greatest was this – a girl given the name of the ancient goddess of hunting was, in the end, the most hunted person of the modern age.[12]

In a few carefully crafted sentences he reinforced Diana's ancient mystical pedigree, her God-given, or charismatic, qualities and suggested, although felt required to deprecate, that she might be worthy of canonisation. Later, his choice of burial place for the Princess, on an island in the middle of a lake, reinforced the mystical and romantic aspects of the growing Diana legend.

Until recently it would not have been possible for millions of people to have united in a single spiritual moment. The technology of television did not exist. And even now in the television age it may not be for many years that a comparable event will happen again, for it required a unique combination of grief, sacred music, poetry, mythology and image to create the effect.

As the hearse carrying Diana made its way slowly from Westminster to Althorp for the burial, flowers were strewn in its way. All through the streets of London, even on the motorway bridges there were people standing waiting for just a short glimpse.

Balloons floated towards the sky to symbolise Diana's journey to heaven and one bystander released a white dove.

At one level the reaction to Diana's death was that of grief at the tragic loss of a young life, and sorrow that two boys had lost their mother. Some people perhaps felt guilt that they had been complicit in her death through their own appetite for gossip and news concerning the Princess and the royal family.

Yet the intensity of the emotions expressed suggests more. Through grieving for Diana many people admitted they were also mourning their own friends and members of their own families who had died. It was as if the collective act of sorrow was enabling emotions to surface that had lain suppressed for many years.

A study published three years after the event noted that the suicide rate in England and Wales rose by 17 per cent in the four weeks after her funeral, compared with the average reported for that period in the four previous years.[13]

The increase in suicide rate was most marked among women, especially those around the same age as the Princess.

In the month following Diana's death the female suicide rate increased by 34 per cent and among women in the 25-to-44 age group the rate rose by over 45 per cent. The researchers from the University of Oxford Centre for Suicide Research suggested that the people who most identified with the Princess were those most affected by her death.

Reviewing the findings the psychiatrist Dr Raj Persaud suggested that it might be that women close to her in age and 'who identified with her relationship and psychological difficulties became more pessimistic about their own ability to conquer similar problems, leading to depression and hopelessness, so paving the way to suicidal thoughts'.[14]

Particularly intriguing, Dr Persaud noted, were the findings from the national confidential inquiry into suicide and homicide by people with mental illness that there was no change during this period in the proportion of suicides known to mental health professionals. This suggests that many people affected by Diana's death were not those who would traditionally be classified as 'vulnerable', as they were not known to mental health professionals.

The same research project also found that deliberate instances of self-harm, as seen and monitored by a major general hospital, increased by 44 per cent in the week after the death of the Princess, especially in women. A review of these patients' case notes suggested that the influence of her death was largely through 'amplification of personal losses and exacerbation of existing distress'.

There were anecdotal reports of a significant increase in calls to the Samaritans.

Another explanation, which has been floated for the extraordinary collective act of grieving, expands on Dr Persaud's observation. Thousands of people had all but convinced themselves that they somehow knew Diana. They had known her as a member of the royal family, in which millions take a vicarious interest. They had identified with her through her admissions of weakness and unhappiness. She was a fellow victim, sufferer or sinner. Then there were AIDS patients, landmine victims, betrayed wives, sufferers from bulimia who all felt a personal connection with Diana.

'She acknowledged the pain of being,' was how the writer Jeremy Seabrook put it, 'and there is no outlet for that in the hedonistic, high-consuming environment of the late twentieth century.'[15]

But explanations go back further and pre-date the twentieth century by many generations. As was suggested earlier Diana embodied three of the classical archetypes that have shaped human thought. She was a Cinderella figure, the virgin bride destined to be the mother of the future king-redeemer and she was the woman of sorrows, the wronged, betrayed and cheated wife.

Other archetypes can be added to the list. All names have meaning, even if they only imply modern stereotypes. A Wayne, Sharon, Cyril, Florence or Tarquin can be seen instantly in the mind's eye. Some names have ancient archetypal roots and Diana is one of them. Diana was a goddess and a hunter. Her festal day was celebrated in August with followers gathering in her wooded grove to light torches in her honour. It was curiously appropriate that one of the abiding images of the week following Princess Diana's death was that of a multitude of candles being lit beneath the trees of the London parks. Earl Spencer, in his funeral oration, turned the huntress image on its head and described Diana as the quarry, hunted and hounded by the press to her death. The hunt too is an archetypal image, based as it is on what was once a primitive necessity, the hunt for food. The spectral wild hunt is one of paganism's most telling incubi, conjuring up disturbing images of lost souls caught in a no-man's-land between life and death.

Princess Diana had also come to represent the archetype of the wounded healer, the one who offered healing through his or her own suffering. More darkly, she was the blood sacrifice for the age, or the Faustian figure who had wealth and beauty in life, but in death was destined to pay the price. As will be seen, this darker collection of archetypes assumed greater importance in the years following Diana's death as the legend of the Princess evolved.

She was also the penitent one. She confessed her faults in public to seek the forgiveness of the people. John Taverner hinted at this by quoting the words of the penitent thief who was crucified with Christ, 'Remember me O Lord, when you come into your kingdom.' Normally the royal family kept its secrets to itself. Diana sensed that to admit her weaknesses was to enhance and not diminish the magic of royalty. Light needs darkness in order to shine; strength requires weakness with which it can be compared.

The motifs associated with Diana were also full of ancient meaning, particularly the heart and the rose. The heart is a symbol of life and love that goes back to prehistoric times when hunters saw that organ as the fount of life. An animal only died when its heart stopped beating. In human terms, a living heart came to represent the emotions. It was where the essence of life and an individual's personality resided. The heart continues as the metaphor for romantic love long after medical science has downgraded the organ to that of a muscular blood pump. Valentine cards always have hearts on them and crooners 'lose' their hearts in love. The English language is full of non-anatomical references to the heart. Jilted lovers have broken hearts. Mourners are offered heart-felt sympathy. Some people set about their work in a half-hearted manner, others laugh heartily or show heartless indifference.

In some cultures the belief in the supreme importance of the heart was taken to gruesome extremes. The ancient Mexicans who worshipped the God of the Sun gouged the pumping hearts from their sacrificial victims as the ultimate oblation to the divine.

The rose symbolises beauty and fragility and its perfume

sanctity. It is the bloom's delicacy and transience that have attracted poets. It has been called the queen of flowers and its symmetry represents perfection, elegance, romance and love. In one of his best-known glass engravings, the artist Laurence Whistler depicted a rose and a yew tree and with T. S. Eliot's words expressed the thought that:

> We die with the dying
> See they depart and we go with them
> We are born with the dead.
> See they return and bring us with them.
> The moment of the rose and the moment of the yew tree
> Are of equal duration.[16]

The rose is also protected by sharp thorns. In one classical legend the goddess Aphrodite steps on a bush of white roses and the thorns draw blood. The blood then turns the roses red. In Christian mystical writing the rose was placed at the foot of the cross to catch the blood of Christ.

In a few lines, Elton John's contribution to Diana's funeral made mention of almost every ancient emotional trigger. The heart, the rose, the stars of heaven, the candle in the wind. Some would say he did not so much touch deep mystical chords as pull every sentimental lever. Under most circumstances his song would have been dismissed as kitsch and tacky. Yet it fitted the occasion and worked as a vehicle on which the emotions could be transported to a higher plain. Even in this attention-deficit, sound-bite age, the heart is still understood to represent life, the rose to symbolise beauty, the stars of heaven refer to the infinite, candles tell of light and wind is the breath of God.

These simple images cross boundaries of culture and generation.

9

THE MYTH SPREADS

Through the autumn of 1997, the House of Windsor, despite being saddened and shaken by events surrounding the death of Diana, attempted to return life to normal.

It took some persuasion for Tony Blair to convince Prince Charles that he should not pretend that the death and funeral had never happened and carry on his public life regardless. The Prime Minister considered that at least one last exhibition of grief was appropriate following the funeral. The public needed to be convinced that the royal family was truly grieving.

The Prince's first public speech following the funeral was scheduled for 19 September. Peter Mandelson and Alastair Campbell were of the view that he could not simply ignore the events of the previous three weeks as if nothing that had taken place had anything to do with him.

With their help he scripted a speech that included the following:

I am unbelievably proud of my children. They have been quite remarkable and I think have handled an extra-ordinarily difficult time, as I am sure you can all imagine, with quite enormous courage and the greatest possible dignity.

They are coping extraordinarily well but obviously Diana's death has been an enormous loss as far as they are concerned and I will always feel that loss.

Like the Queen in her address to the nation on the eve of the funeral, Prince Charles thought it best to focus on the Princes' grief rather than his own.

To all outward appearances the routine of the royal household continued as before, moving from one grand house to another depending on the season of the year. The family 'firm' had its duties to perform and its private pleasures to pursue. The State Opening of Parliament, the distribution of the Royal Maundy, Trooping the Colour, Royal Ascot, grouse shooting and deer stalking at Balmoral, plus other events as determined by the news and the politicians of the day. Ahead too were other milestone events to prepare for, ones which were reassuringly predictable. There was the coming of the new millennium, the Queen Mother's one-hundredth birthday, the Golden Jubilee, the fiftieth anniversary of the Coronation, the Queen's eightieth birthday, the sixtieth anniversary of the ending of the Second World War.

In one sense the decisions concerning the future of the two Princes were made easier by the death of Diana. They could be prepared for their future duties and totally absorbed into the Windsor scheme of things without any fear of interference. From an early age Diana had had strong views on how her sons were to be raised, views which often conflicted with those of the royal family. After the divorce it was acknowledged that both she and their father shared responsibility for their upbringing. Despite the rhetoric of his funeral address in the abbey, Earl Spencer knew that he could exercise little practical influence.

We, your blood family, will do all we can to continue the imaginative way in which you were steering these two exceptional young men so that their souls are not simply immersed by duty and tradition but can sing openly as you planned.

As his words were applauded he must have known that the promise he had made so publicly to his dead sister could never be kept. He admitted as much several years later in a conversation with the writer and former MP Gyles Brandreth. How much hands-on involvement had he had in the rearing of his nephews? 'Not a lot.' He was quick to add however that this involvement had not been necessary as Prince Charles was a good father. 'The boys are doing well. I think Diana would be very happy with the way they have grown up. She'd be very proud of them.'[1]

The Windsor family was acutely aware that even from beyond the grave Diana could still pose problems. Had she kept incriminating tapes or other material that might one day come into the public domain? How were the rumours that her death was not an accident to be controlled and eventually laid to rest? How was she to be officially remembered – by a statue perhaps or a trust? How was the public expression of that memory to be kept in proportion?

It was felt within government and royal circles that Diana should be remembered and celebrated with dignity. The popular expressions of grief exhibited at the time of her funeral included many things that were, to the traditionalists, 'pop' and 'inappropriate'. Her image and likeness, it was thought, should not become public property available to manufacturers of tacky souvenirs to exploit. This desire to control the image and memory of Diana was to result in two unfortunate trains of events. One involved a highly expensive legal battle to protect Diana's likeness from commercial exploitation and the other the prosecution, and dramatic acquittal of Diana's former butler Paul Burrell, accused of stealing his former employer's property.

Prince Charles had a further agenda never far from his mind following his former wife's death. He was now a widower and not a divorcee. When might it be appropriate for him to introduce Camilla Parker Bowles to the public as his official partner? Might it be possible one day to marry her?

There were many things that in the aftermath to her death the Windsor family could hope or at least attempt to control. Some things however were beyond the control of even the practised Palace spin-doctors. The mass media could be manipulated to a certain extent and reporters and editors flattered or cajoled into taking an approved line. The internet however was beyond such control and was an unpredictable and often bizarre rumour-mill.

The rumours have been of two main kinds: those relating to Diana's death, conspiracy theories in particular; and those relating to her ethereal and spiritual significance. A third set of rumours have combined these two categories by suggesting that because Diana was a figure of huge spiritual, religious and apocalyptic significance, she had to be killed by the 'establishment'.

Very shortly after her death claims began to surface that Diana's death had been predicted. Some of these predictions were interpreted as being of sinister or cosmic significance. The works of Nostradamus were closely examined and, not surprisingly, it was announced that the sixteenth-century seer had foretold the events of 1997.

Le tant d'argent de Diane & Mercure
Les simulachres au lac seront trouvez :
Le figulier cherchant argille neufue
Luy & les siens d'or seront abbreuuez.
(So much silver of Diana and Mercury,
The images will be found in the lake:
The sculptor looking for new clay,
He and his followers will be steeped in gold.)[2]

This was taken to be a reference to Earl Spencer's subsequent opening of Althorp. The Spencer family home now contains Diana's burial place on an island in a lake and a Diana museum, which visitors can pay to visit.

Although this next quatrain, given the involvement of the son of a certain Mohamed, might appear to be more immediately apt:

Le penultiesme du surnom du Prophete,
Prendra Diane pour son iour & repos:
Loing vaguera par frenetique teste,
En deliurant un grand peuple d'impos.
(The penultimate of the surname of the Prophet
Will take Diana for his day and rest:
He will wander far because of a frantic head,
And delivering a great people from subjection.)[3]

Some contemporary 'prophets' resorted to self-publicity, and an American numerologist styled Sollog brashly claims on his website that documents previously lodged in an American court contained a prophecy that Diana would die on the thirty-first day of a month sometime in the unspecified future. Later he was also to claim to have foretold the 11 September terrorist attack.

It might seem strange to explore and give space to some of the more improbable ideas that have evolved since the death of Diana, perhaps even unwise in case it appears to lend them credence. Yet to examine the aftermath of the princess's death without mentioning a representative sample of some of the ideas in circulation would be to ignore important evidence. Perhaps G. K. Chesterton's much quoted observation is true, that when people cease to believe in God they will believe in anything. Certainly many upholders of traditional belief will be staggered by the breadth of what they would consider the gullibility of the internet generation. The traditionalists may argue that there have always been 'crackpots', but the internet uniquely provides instant access to hundreds of highly imaginative and untested theories. These theories encompass both the ancient world, that of southsayers and ancient writings, and the modern world of popular culture and rock music.

Retrospective wisdom abounds after major events and fans of the musician Morrissey began to read previously unrealised significance into the words of the album 'The Queen is Dead'.

There was however a certain common resonance between the news events and the words of one of the tracks on the album called 'There is a light that never goes out':

There is a reference to being taken out one night and being driven in a car and never wanting to go home. And then there is a crash and talk of a darkened underpass and two people who die side by side. Yet afterwards it is said that the light never goes out.[4]

The effect of the music and the weirdness of the apparent coincidences of phrase and history enable those wanting to find strange meaning to find it.

Yet, many of the supposed coincidences highlighted were very thin. For instance, the man photographed on the album cover was a frenchman called Alain. The first public announcement of Princess Diana's death was, it is claimed, made by a Frenchman named Alain.[5]

The prophecy that excited most interest at the time was one that graduated from the internet to the mainstream media.

It involved the member of a Baptist Church in Sheffield who in May 1997 presented this prophecy to her church. It is significant to note the religious climate of the time within Christian Evangelical circles. There was a mood of excitement and talk of a new 'revival' being underway.

I am at work in the heart and the spirit of the people of this nation. I am doing a work which at the moment is very, very unseen. But it is happening quicker than you think. Things are happening much more quickly than you think. And as a sign, this shall be a sign, that there will be a day very soon when the whole nation will mourn. And the whole nation will put flowers in their cities.

When that day happens the sign is this: the speed at which the heart and spirit of the people of this nation can be affected, that is the speed at which I will work among this nation. Do not think that what you see and hear are small, insignificant happenings. Do not despise the day of small things. For I tell you, when you see this sign, I am on the move, says the Lord.

In Christian terms, prophecy is less about foretelling events than discerning the meanings behind them. If they do contain elements of precognition, they exist as warnings. The ancient prophets of the Old Testament warned the Israelites to modify their behaviour, or experience the consequences.

In New Age, and what might be loosely described as post-modern patterns of spiritual thinking, prophecy and inter-pretation fulfil a subtly different function. Prophecies occur when seers or channellers are enabled to glimpse a pre-destined course of events. Millennial prophecies focused on 'end-time' scenarios. Nothing in them suggested ways by which the inevitable course of preordained events could be averted. Alternatively seers were enabled to explain events within a wider cosmic framework, but again no suggestions were made as to how to alter the status quo.

Sedona in Arizona, USA is one of the centres of the American New Age movement. The strange, yet imposing landscape where mountain meets desert, stirs the imagina-tion. In the years leading up to the new millennium there were few New Age theories, prophecies and interpretations not represented there. The town lends its name to the magazine of the New Age that published this channelled message in November 1997:

Diana, Princess of Wales . . . in her origin, is not native to your world. Rather, she is from a dimensional reality of which you are generally unaware but which shares Earth space with you. Let us explain. The one who came to be known amongst you as Diana, Princess of Wales, entered your dimensional reality through a portal that opened within a standing stone circle on the Orkney Isles. On the other side of this portal, before her emergence into your vibration, she sat on a majestic throne governing as queen within the dimensional reality to which you refer as the realm of faerie.

The question is, why did this queen of faerie choose to incarnate amongst you of the human kind? In a word, because of planetary evolution . . . With the increase in planetary vibration and the resultant progression in the unification of the fields of consciousness that share space and reality on the Earth plane, the traditional pattern of interaction between faerie and human is undergoing a profound alteration. Diana played a key role in the creation of this new pattern. As an ambassador from faerie to the human world, she injected into the human vibrational field an intense energy frequency direct from the faerie realm.[6]

Thus, for some, Diana could be understood as coming from the faerie realm. Others have looked to the heavens for meaning. Elton John's choice of the celestial option in his tribute sung at Diana's funeral helped authenticate the Princess's cosmic destiny in the minds of those prone to believe.

He sang of how Diana belonged to heaven and her name was spelt out by the stars. Whether visually or astrologically was unclear – but poetically, certainly.

But the song also included other references, more rooted in earth mystery. With a line, describing how her footsteps will always fall along England's greenest hills he tapped into the ethereal world of William Blake, whose hymn 'Jerusalem' was inspired by the Glastonbury legend that Christ had once set foot in England.

> And did those feet in ancient times,
> Walk upon England's mountains green?
> And was the holy Lamb of God,
> On England's pleasant pastures seen?

Glastonbury, where Christ is said to have landed, became in medieval times the Arthurian shrine. It became identified with Camelot and Avalon.

> Whether by intention or design Elton John's song sets Diana not only in the heavens, but also in Blake's Albion, in, that is, a spiritualized England, whose royalty is Arthurian, whose rightful king is the Pendragon, whose tone is Celtic and whose centre lies at Glastonbury. And already – with the Arthurian reference, with the sacral kingship of the 'once and future' king, we are in the heart of the poetic Matter of Britain, and of myth.[7]

Running parallel with the narrative of British history is an alternative 'mystical' version. The alternative history tells of the Drake, the naval hero, waiting to be called by the sound of his drum to return to protect the shores of England from invasion.

There are stories told of the Stone of Scone, the seat of the coronation throne, which had originally been the stone on which Jacob had rested his head when he had the dream of the ladder connecting heaven and earth.

One of the most persistent legends, and one which resurfaces at times of national crisis, is that of King Arthur, the once-and-future king who lies sleeping beneath English soil waiting for his call to return.

Reading the mystical runes of Diana is not a science. Prophecies and secrets abound, as do strange and fanciful interpretations. But the death of Diana has an undoubted resonance. There is nothing logical about the connections made. Nothing rational in the way in which she is made out to be a faerie queen, a cosmic omen, a new chapter in the mystical history of Britain.

It becomes relevant however when seen in the context of the pre-millennium years. It was a time of strange irrational fear. These fears became widespread and in the most famous instance a whole industry grew up exploiting the fear of what was known as the millennium bug. All computers would crash as the third millennium dawned, or so it was said, and even the government endorsed the warnings. In the event nothing happened. It was a massive example of irrational self-delusion, of superstition in the technological age.

More understandable perhaps were the fears among followers of the Christian faith. The return of Christ was associated with a millennium, his thousand-year reign on earth. It was neat numerology to link the change of calendar year with the prophesied millennium of the book of Revelation. In the death of Diana there was additional reinforcement of the idea and she became in some Christians' eyes identified with the woman described in 12:1–6.

And there appeared a great wonder in heaven; a woman clothed with the sun, and the moon under her feet, and upon her head a crown of twelve stars: And she being with child cried, travailing in birth, and pained to be delivered. And there appeared another wonder in heaven; and behold a great red dragon, having seven heads and ten horns, and seven crowns upon his heads. And his tail drew the third part of the stars of heaven, and did cast them to the earth: and the dragon stood before the woman which was ready to be delivered, for to devour her child as soon as it was born. And she brought forth a man child, who was to rule all nations with a rod of iron: and her child was caught up unto God, and to his throne. And the woman fled into the wilderness, where she hath a place prepared of God, that they should feed her there a thousand two hundred and threescore days.[8]

Saying that Diana is the Woman Clothed with the Sun is saying more than that she is a saint or an angel, or even the goddess Diana – it is setting her at the level of the Feminine Principle in all its archetypal glory, a level for which the 'Blessed Mary Ever-Virgin' of Catholicism has until recently been the only human contender.

'A woman clothed with the sun' combines several meanings – the glitter and sparkle of modern evening dresses, which Diana was famous for, the accompanying flash of hundreds of cameras going off whenever she appeared at night, her intensely blonde hair. Perhaps the clincher is that Prince William's birthday is 21 June, the summer solstice, a potent prophetic symbol for Britain. The sun is a royal sign, so this ties 'the woman' in with royalty, kingship and, in particular, the fact that William is heir to the British throne.[9]

The death of Diana, Princess of Wales triggered trains of fantasy in the minds of those prone to fantasise. There are websites and bookshops full of unorthodox ideas masquerading as scholarship. Many tend to fall back on the same well-trodden paths – Arthur, Nostradamus and the book of Revelation. Diana provided a wealth of new material. There were coincidences to be found and conspiracies to be mined. Symbolism, allegory, myth and legend, whenever they could be related to the Princess, became cycled and recycled into new symbols, allegories and legends. There is nothing more appealing to a person looking for profound signs than to be able to light upon a news story of significance to their own mystical journey. Storms and earthquakes provide such material on a regular basis, but the mysterious death of a one-time fairytale princess is unmatched in its potential for new myth making.

Yet myth making is not the domain of the obsessed few. Stories have always been the means by which all human cultures at all stages of history have sought to understand and convey the deeper meaning of life.

Diana myths spread rapidly. During the pre-millennium hiatus, at a time of spiritual uncertainty, fear and expectation, Diana's death occurred as a seismic event. It was not simply a media-generated outbreak of emotion, hyped up but unsustainable. It tapped into what Charles Cameron called

> . . . deeper recesses of psyche and imagination . . . the clearest evidence for Carl Jung's theories of projection, archetypes, and the Anima. I believe we are witnessing a revival of what he would call the Feminine Principle. I believe that all this adds up to a pervasive popular disgust with and reaction against the 'bottom line' mentality which rules so much of our lives, and speaks to an interest in human values, communication, and respect. I believe it also corresponds to an increased concern for the planet we live on.

> As with all millennial hopes and expectations, I am reminded of the Sufi saying that hope and fear are two sides of the same coin. I believe that this cult of Diana is not without its darker aspects, that the archetypes themselves are literally 'awesome' – opening onto terror as well as love, spitefulness as well as generosity.[10]

And so events unfolded. Diana evolved in popular imagination into a faerie, a star of the night, a queen of heaven, or whatever form a devotee might wish.

One Australian writer went so far as to talk of events that may propel the 'Memory of Diana well beyond stardom, to Authentic Sainthood and APOTHEOSIS IN GLORY'. The fairytale, the legend and the myth have just begun, maintains

George Viktor. 'We are living in an epoch of spiritual, cultural and environmental crisis of unprecedented scope and dimension. That we are approaching the Period of End-time. Right now, we are looking for The Beacon.'[11]

Prince Charles meanwhile attempted to separate himself from the extraordinary mêlée of emotion and mystical speculation. He had day-to-day concerns: the upbringing of his sons; his duties as Prince of Wales; and his relationship with Camilla Parker Bowles.

As the years passed after Diana's death it became more a matter of when, rather than if, a marriage would be appropriate. Increasingly Camilla appeared at his side as hostess at Highgrove and as partner in public. She was divorced. She had met William and Harry. Even the Queen was no longer maintaining her distance.

With his sister Princess Anne having been remarried by the Church of Scotland, at first Prince Charles thought this might be the route he would need to take. In 2000 he was appointed by the Queen to carry out the ceremonial duties of Lord High Commissioner to the General Assembly of the Church of Scotland. It is a curious role in that the holder of the office has the status of the monarch in Scotland for the week in May when the Assembly sits. Normally the person appointed to the office is from the great and good of Scotland. For Charles, the heir to the throne, to be appointed was unusual.

As Lord High Commissioner, the Duke of Rothesay (Prince Charles is known by his Scottish title north of the border), took up residence at Edinburgh's royal palace, Holyrood House. It was not a happy time. First of all he antagonised the staff normally employed to look after the Lord High Commissioner and arrange the formal dinners, by insisting his own staff were used to run the palace for the week. Then, without consulting the church leaders, he invited Camilla Parker Bowles to join him. Many kirk elders disapproved of what they considered his blatant adulterous behaviour. Any chance the Prince might have had to sound out discreetly Scottish opinion on a church wedding north of the border quickly evaporated.

Prince Charles found an ally in Dr George Carey. Soon after the death of Diana, the Archbishop of Canterbury, in the role he perceived for himself as the royal family's parish priest, became concerned for Camilla Parker Bowles. He was sure she was not the ogress portrayed by the popular press and that she and Charles were genuinely in love. He wrote to her suggesting a meeting. Camilla agreed as long as the meeting could be a totally private occasion. It was arranged for Mrs Parker Bowles and Dr Carey to meet in a terraced house in Peckham. It was the home of the Archbishop's son Andrew and seemed a suitably secure location. Dr Carey later described Camilla as 'a most attractive and charming person, warm-hearted and intelligent, with a down-to-earth attitude . . . We were to meet several times . . . We came to appreciate the deep and affectionate relationship that existed between her and Prince Charles; she was a more dependable person, and probably more aware of the importance of Charles's role in the nation than Diana ever was.'[12]

In order to marry, Prince Charles, by law, needed his sovereign's – his mother's – permission. Well aware of Camilla's involvement in the break-up of her son's first marriage, she was not minded to give her permission hastily.

It was not until seven years after Diana's death that the moment seemed right to allow the wedding to take place. In that time Camilla had met and come to know the young Princes. She had met the Queen in a formal and public setting. The Queen Mother, who might have harboured the strongest objections, had died. Over the seven years Camilla had become established as the Prince's partner and had not put a foot wrong. Occasions had been manufactured for her to be seen in public with the Prince of Wales, and the public reaction from the ensuing media coverage did not indicate a significant groundswell of objection to the partnership. The loyal Dianaphiles were not convinced, but the royal advisers could detect no substantial body of objection to the Prince of Wales marrying again.

The wedding announcement, when it eventually came, triggered a series of embarrassing problems that revealed a remarkable degree of incompetence by the royal advisers.

The legalities of an heir to the throne taking part in a civil marriage had been inadequately researched. The venue for the wedding had to be changed in a very public about-face. Legal challenges to the match were raised and in a stroke of sheer bad luck, the Pope died shortly before the wedding day and the date had to be changed so that the wedding would not clash with his funeral.

The Prince of Wales and his new bride were eventually married by registrar Clair Williams at Windsor's Guildhall, in the building where a few months later Sir Elton John was to contract his civil partnership with his same-sex partner.

Most senior members of the royal family were present to witness Charles and Camilla exchange vows, including Prince William and Prince Harry. Camilla's children by Andrew Parker Bowles were also there.

The Queen and Duke of Edinburgh were notably absent, but did attend the service of marriage blessing which was conducted shortly afterwards by the new Archbishop of Canterbury, Dr Rowan Williams and televised from St George's Chapel, Windsor.

The blessing was attended by around eight hundred guests, including political figures, show-business celebrities, members of the royal family, even a collection of Prince Charles's former girlfriends. There were however no representatives of the Spencer family in the congregation.

The actor Timothy West went so far as to describe the occasion as a 'fairytale'!

It is now a common procedure for Church of England clergy to bless the marriages of couples where one or other of the parties has been divorced and a former partner is still living. Guidelines issued to the clergy give the option for a blessing to be refused if a new spouse was involved in the break-up of the previous marriage. Dr Williams did not exercise this option.

However, the service included a general confession of sin, which several commentators highlighted in the context of the couple's previous adulterous relationship. The couple also made solemn vows.

'Charles and Camilla, you have committed yourselves to each other in marriage, and your marriage is recognised by law. The Church of Christ understands marriage to be, in the will of God, the union of a man and a woman, for better, for worse, for richer, for poorer, in sickness and in health, to love and to cherish, till parted by death. Is this your understanding of the covenant and promise that you have made?'

Prince Charles and the new Duchess of Cornwall replied: 'It is.'

Turning to Charles, the Archbishop continued: 'Charles, have you resolved to be faithful to your wife, forsaking all others, so long as you both shall live?'

Prince Charles replied confidently: 'That is my resolve, with the help of God.'

The Archbishop then asked Camilla: 'Camilla, have you resolved to be faithful to your husband, forsaking all others, so long as you both shall live?'

In a quiet voice, she replied: 'That is my resolve, with the help of God.'

Police estimated that around 20,000 people lined the streets of Windsor to catch a glimpse of the couple. The mood was one more of curiosity than supportive of the couple. Fears that large numbers of Dianaphiles might have targeted the occasion to organise a protest were not realised.

Since the wedding Camilla's presence at her husband's side has become a familiar sight in Britain. As things stand, when Charles becomes King, Camilla will be known as the Princess Consort. Although if her absorption into the British royal scene goes well she may, one day, become Queen.

In 2005 her first major test of acceptance outside Britain was a visit scheduled for the United States. America was and remains Diana territory where thousands of the most 'Di-hard' Dianaphiles are to be found.

The Princess, said Kitty Kelley, 'ruled the country's celebrity-obsessed culture. Americans were transfixed by the royal soap opera of her marriage to the prince.'[13] Few will forget the image of Diana dancing with Hollywood star John Travolta.

Would a new bride, a woman in her late fifties with the reputation as the marriage-breaker, the woman who hounded Diana as the third person in the marriage, be accepted? 'Some will never forgive the woman the Princess of Wales once called the Rottweiler', Kitty Kelley wrote. 'But Diana's death and the passage of time have softened resistance to the extra-marital love affair of Charles and Camilla. Once the young princes, William and Harry, gave their blessing, others followed suit.'[14]

In the event, Camilla was judged to have done well. She met the Bushes, said the right things and made no attempt to outshine her husband's first wife. Nothing of course would have satisfied the most devout Dianaphiles, but to the majority of Americans, those who took notice of the visit at least, Camilla passed the test.

By Christmas 2005 Camilla's public engagements were beginning to become routine. She was invited to switch on one of London's sets of Christmas lights and the occasion proved unremarkable. Even her stepsons were speaking of her in public in affectionate and supportive terms. 'She's made our father very happy,' said Prince Harry in an interview given on the occasion of his twenty-first birthday. 'We're happy to have her around. She's not the wicked stepmother. I'll say that right now. Everyone has to understand that it's very hard for her. Look at the position she's coming into. Don't always feel sorry for me and William – feel sorry for her.'[15]

10

WHO GUARDS THE LEGEND?

Following the funeral of the People's Princess, who was to be the official keeper of the Diana memory? It was in the interests of the royal court to keep the exploitation of that memory within tight bounds. It would be undignified for there to be a commercial free-for-all and the sensitivities of Diana's sons had to be borne in mind. The Spencer family had its own ambitions and agenda. There was no willingness to cede the initiative back to the House of Windsor following the events of the funeral when Earl Spencer's oration had been applauded by the public. An important player in this tussle for power was Diana's former butler and confidante, Paul Burrell. He was utterly loyal to Diana's memory, to the boys and to the Royal House. He was also well aware of the fact that Diana and her mother, Frances, had not been on speaking terms at the time of her death and regarded Earl Spencer's address as being an exercise in hypocrisy.

He later described his thoughts as he listened to the Earl's address. What came to Paul Burrell's mind as the Earl's grand words echoed around the abbey were the very different words of Charles Spencer angrily addressed to his sister eighteen months earlier. 'Your mental problems . . . your fickle friendship, I was a peripheral part of your life and that no longer saddens me . . . Our relationship is the weakest I have with any of my sisters.'[1]

Round One went to the Spencers when Diana's Will was read. The main beneficiaries were the two Princes, but Frances and Diana's sister Lady Sarah McCorquodale were the executors. Paul Burrell became agitated when he saw the two of them take control of Diana's memory and shred numerous documents – many of them items of Diana's personal correspondence. 'I witnessed history being destroyed by a family that was already intent on seizing control of her world from the Windsors. I felt it was wrong.'[2] Burrell was also unhappy that the celebrated wedding dress was not given to The Victoria and Albert Museum, but ended up in the Spencer private Diana Museum at Althorp.

As recognition of his close relationship with the Princess, Paul Burrell was invited to join the Diana, Princess of Wales Memorial Committee to help advise the government on appropriate ways in which the life of the Princess might best be commemorated. It was to work alongside another body, the Diana, Princess of Wales Memorial Fund which had been set up to manage the large sums of money being spontaneously given by members of the public. In 1998 Burrell was appointed a paid member of the fund. However, despite throwing himself wholeheartedly into the work and the charity fund raising, as months past he did not feel that he was being encouraged by fellow members to contribute as fully as he wished.

There came a point when he felt that he was losing control over a world the Princess, he believed, had trusted him to control. Had he not in life been 'the rock' on which she depended for so much? In his anxiety he asked for an audience with the Queen. A private audience was granted.

He spoke to the Queen at length and shared his anxieties. They discussed a whole manner of issues relating to Diana and her life. He told his sovereign how there were items once owned by Diana he had decided to keep in his own safe-keeping. Little did Paul Burrell realise as he was confiding in the Queen how important that meeting and exchange of information would be in later months, when he found himself in the dock at the Old Bailey charged with theft. Perhaps only then did he realise what the Queen had meant when she said to him, 'Be careful Paul. No one has been as close to a member of my family as you have. There are powers at work in this country about which we have no knowledge. Do you understand?'[3]

Paul Burrell's most immediate danger however came from members of the Memorial Fund. Did they feel the former butler was getting above his station? Did they think his attempts to control Diana's memory were inappropriate or obsessive? Whatever the reason, it was decided he should resign. As he left, an angry Burrell's parting words were an accusation-cum-observation. 'This fund bears no resemblance to the person I knew. It does not fulfil her wishes or her requests.'[4]

On 18 January 2001, the police made an early morning call at the Burrell's home. The house was searched and later Burrell was arrested. Hundreds of items were taken, tagged and bagged and later used to frame charges against the former butler to, and confidante of, the Princess.

What the officers appeared to be most interested in was finding a box that had previously been at Kensington Palace. The house was a treasure trove of royal memorabilia. Many items were personally inscribed to the Princess. The police also scanned numerous documents, personal letters that Paul Burrell had pledged himself to guard.

'The police were ripping through the Boss's most personal items, it was obscene. In my eyes I had let her down by allowing them through my door. I have never felt so useless. So numb. So physically sick.'[5]

On 14 October 2002 Paul Burrell stood accused at Central Criminal Court of the theft of 310 items from the Prince of

Wales, Prince William and the estate of Diana, Princess of Wales. 'Butler in the dock', 'Diana's Secrets' and 'What's in the box?' were among the newspaper headlines the case generated.

The trial was 'as sensational as I expected',[6] tabloid editor Piers Morgan wrote in his diary. He spoke of the evidence heard as 'juicy stuff' and noted 'They must be mad allowing Burrell to potentially take the stand. Cornered and desperate, he might say anything, and he knows a lot because he was there.'

The testimony from Frances, Diana's mother and Diana's sisters for the prosecution hurt Burrell most. Frances, in Burrell's view, demonstrated her woeful knowledge of life in royal service and the way in which it was commonplace for superfluous royal gifts to be given to staff. He found her evidence both wounding and misleading.

For a long time there had been no love lost between Frances and her daughter's butler. She found him controlling and suspected that before Diana's death he had prevented her from talking to her daughter. This may indeed have been true, but whether he was acting as the 'obsessed' protector of his employer or on her instructions is not clear.

The case collapsed in unprecedented and bizarre circumstances before Paul Burrell himself was due to give his evidence. The prosecution, after a lengthy and nail-biting delay, withdrew all accusations. It appeared that the case was being pursued under a false premise. The prosecution told the court that it had recently been informed that during a private meeting with the Queen, Paul Burrell had informed her that he was taking certain items into safe-keeping. 'The proper course would be to invite no further evidence against Mr Burrell and invite the jury to find him not guilty.'

Paul Burrell was mightily relieved.

What lay behind the legal fiasco? Who tipped off the police to search the Burrell family home? Was there a hidden agenda? Did the royal family insist on a prosecution and if so, was it because they were wrongly told that Burrell had been selling some of Diana's personal items for personal gain?

Was it all an act of jealousy and backbiting which got out of control? Was it really the Spencers who wanted to put Burrell, the uppity butler, in his place, to discredit him and his claim that he was the true guardian of Diana's memory?

Whatever explanation there might be as to why the case was brought, the consequences of its collapse were immediately apparent. Relief all round. The royal family would have been as relieved as Paul Burrell, spared what might have been said in open court by the former Palace servant to save his reputation and preserve his liberty.

What confidential information might have been put in the public domain? And would it have been more damaging than the letter Paul Burrell was later to release?

In his memoirs he published the text of a letter received by him ten months before the fatal crash from the Princess. It included the lines: 'This particular phase in my life is the most dangerous. [The Princess then identified where she felt the threat and danger would come from] is planning "an accident" in my car, brake failure and serious head injury in order to make the path clear for Charles to marry.'[7]

The blanked out words were later published by a national newspaper, 'My husband'.

The Burrell trial and his subsequent account of it and of his life with Princess Diana did much to fuel the conspiracy theories surrounding the circumstances of the car crash. Polls have shown that around 25 per cent of the British people believe that Diana was murdered.

The whole episode had confirmed in suspicious minds that the British establishment was capable of ruthless and malicious activity against those it wished to discredit. If it was prepared to sacrifice Paul Burrell, then could it not have been responsible for some even more sinister crimes?

The most suspicious mind was that of Mohamed Al Fayed himself. Fired by grief and motivated by an abiding distrust of the British establishment, which had, so he believed, denied him British citizenship, he was convinced that the deaths of Diana, his son, and his employee were murder.

When, six-and-a-half years after the event, a British coroner, Michael Burgess, called the police in to help him unravel events, Al Fayed was triumphant. 'I suspect not only Prince Charles but Prince Philip, who is a racist,' he told the media. 'It is absolutely black-and-white, horrendous murder.'

At a stroke the coroner had given a plausibility to the conspiracy theories which up until then had been largely entertained only by Al Fayed, Diana devotees, conspiracy websites, Colonel Gaddafi and a range of Middle Eastern media outlets.

'Coroners are sober folks,' wrote Stephen Bates in *Time Europe*,

> . . . representatives of one of the oldest and most independent arms of the arcane English judicial system. They usually work in dusty rooms at the back of courthouses, establishing the cause of unexpected deaths. Few ever find themselves in the glare of the world's TV cameras. But Burgess might as well get used to it. A grey-haired, bespectacled lawyer, he is a pivotal figure in the latest chapter of the Diana saga. Not only is he Britain's royal coroner, in which capacity he is looking into Diana's death, but he is also coroner for the county of Surrey, where Dodi is buried, and is thus responsible for finding out his cause of death as well.[8]

A year later, all concerned were still waiting for a verdict. When it comes it is hard to see how the coroner will be able to satisfy every interest. If he throws any doubt on the conclusion reached by the French authorities after their exhaustive two-year investigation, he will trigger a phenomenal response. Not only will he be implying that the French were either corrupt or incompetent, but also that the death of Diana was not the straightforward accident previously claimed: that it was not caused by the car being driven too fast by a driver who was under the influence of drink and medication.

Mr Burgess will need to address the issue of the mysterious white Fiat Uno. It was never tracked down by the police, although it is strongly claimed that it was seen at the time, could have been involved in the crash and that paint from a white Fiat was found on the wrecked car. He will need to examine the theory that the driver Henri Paul was fit to drive and had had a flashgun fired at him to disorientate him. He will also have to ask why Diana was not taken to hospital more rapidly. He will not be required to determine what happened after the death, or consider the suggestion that formaldehyde was injected by the French into Diana's body to preserve it and disguise any chemical evidence of her pregnancy will not be for him to examine.

If, on the other hand, Mr Burgess concurs with the French findings, the conspiracy theorists will immediately disbelieve him and conclude that he too as royal coroner, is part of the cover-up.

The first website peddling the conspiracy theory was online within thirteen minutes of news of her death. Over the following months the royal family, MI5, MI6, the CIA and French secret service, the Freemasons, the Vatican, and even the global arms industry have been accused of involvement in murder.

Another parallel but incompatible set of theories have suggested that Dodi and Diana were not killed at all, that the accident was a hoax and diversion to allow them to escape the attention of the world and live in peace together.

Mohamed al Fayed himself is convinced that the deaths were murder – he is '99 per cent certain it was no accident'. He has offered a massive reward to anyone who can provide proof to substantiate his view and also hired a team of top lawyers. He is in no doubt about the motive: it was all part of the vendetta against him by the British establishment. They were horrified not only that Diana might marry a Muslim, but that she might also have been carrying his child.

As the police enquiries continue the royal family must just wait. In the meantime Prince Charles has realised his ambition of marrying Camilla. Even that has not gone unnoticed by the conspiracy theorists. Did Charles and Camilla get married before the coroner reported just in case anything was thrown up by the inquiry which did not look good and which would have turned the public against Charles, preventing him from ever marrying his mistress?

As the *Time Europe* Stephen Bates' article concluded: 'Michael Burgess's decision to hand the conspiracy theories over to the police means that the straightforward explanation for the accident can never win. Even if the theories are fully discounted and dispatched, that will only be seen as incontrovertible proof of a cover.'

One reason that it will be hard to convince everyone that the deaths of Diana and Dodi were simply a tragic accident, if indeed that was the case, is that Diana's murder fits far more convincingly into the mythology of Diana.

As with Diana in life, the real person is now no longer important; the Diana of myth and legend has superseded her.

It is far more appropriate for a mythological Diana to meet a sinister and unnatural end than for her life to have been snuffed out by the tragic, but mundane actions of a drunk driving too fast.

Diana's death has been described as a sacrifice. It was a parable for the final years of the twentieth century. The writer Jeremy Seabrook described the story of her death as 'one of human sacrifice in the primitive society that is late capitalism. The photographers who were following on motorbikes were competing for the best shot. And competition, according to the economic dogmas of the age, is the supreme motor of all creativity and achievement.'[9]

Diana was a global icon whose likeness was as familiar in the villages of India as on the streets of London. She embodied an iconography of wealth and success allied to a deep humanitarian commitment. She was the perfect emblem of the age in which she lived and yet her sudden death rendered worthless everything she stood for. If the mega-famous, the famously beautiful and the beautifully compassionate can be snuffed out in an instant, what lasting value do those qualities possess?

In the original religious meaning of the word a sacrifice was a bloody business. It was the taking of life for a spiritual purpose. In the Old Testament the slaughter of animals was performed in a specific way for blessings to accrue and obligations to be met. In the New Testament Jesus was seen as the sacrificial lamb and through his death humankind was redeemed. Animal sacrifice is common in many religions. It can come in several forms. A sacrifice might be a ritual to expel an impurity. The scapegoat was seen as a symbol of evil and sent out into the desert to die. A sacrifice can be of the best animal in honour of a god, or the gods; or a sacrifice can be a communal activity designed to bond a tribe together. Another way of classifying sacrifice is not by purpose, but by victim. Is it a domestic animal being killed, or a human being? Over the centuries humans have been killed for many ritualistic purposes. Sometimes slaves are killed to accompany their masters to the next world. Young men were sacrificed to propitiate the sun. Virgins were killed to ensure the soil remains fertile. The ultimate form of human sacrifice was the slaying of the king both to honour and to appease the deities.

Is it possible to see the death of Diana as a form of modern blood sacrifice? A royal figure who died amid the rituals of media stardom, whose death took on a redemptive purpose? Her death caused many in the media to pause for thought. Psychologist Carol Sellars suggested that everyone who read the papers and watched television was culpable. 'If the public's insatiable interest in Diana had not been there, she would not have been pursued by the paparazzi . . . Much of the public's grief may have its roots in guilt . . . Her tragic fate has highlighted the fact that the media only reports what we seek to know.'[10]

Diana did not of course willingly offer herself as a sacrifice as Christ had done, which rules out one crucial comparison. She did not die from a landmine explosion or from contracting a disease from one of the patients she had comforted. She died, as the tabloids did not hesitate to point out, in the pursuit of her own pleasure in the back of a rich boyfriend's chauffeur-driven car on her way to spending a night of adulterous passion with him.

There was no resurrection either, although after Diana's death there was a remarkable resurrection of her reputation.

No examination of Diana's death in its mythical setting would be complete without looking at the dark side, the Faustian element to the story. Faust was given earthly power, wealth and glory in exchange for his soul. Diana had a pact with the public, through the media. The press was both enemy and ally. As well as knowing how to manipulate her image, what photo opportunities to offer and to what end, she also used carefully selected reporters as a conduit for her views and spin on events. She used the press against Charles and the Palace establishment, and when she was sidelined by the House of Windsor she turned to the media to get her views across. She chose an interview on *Panorama* to bare her soul and confess to adultery, which she did so skilfully that at the end little blame attached to her. Public sympathy was with her when she spoke of Camilla being the third person in the marriage. She professed to hate the photographers who chased her. She told the tabloid editor Piers Morgan how she knew most of them and would support 'an anti-stalking bill tomorrow. Then she took me to the window and started showing me the various media cars, vans and motorbikes lurking outside.'

'But when I asked her why she doesn't go out of one of the ten other more discreet exits, she exposed her contrary side: "I want to go out the front like anyone else. Why should I change my life for them?" '[11]

Ultimately, like Faust she had to repay the debt, and it might be said that she was snatched at the height of her wealth and beauty and dragged down to hell. Although of course in folk imagination, as expressed in the messages left with the flowers, she was assumed straight into heaven. In Diana cosmology, in her Marian role, she is now the Queen of Heaven.

To suggest that her life and death followed a Faustian pattern directly contradicts the suggestion that in her life and death she was the lamb led to the slaughter.

As in every analysis of her contradictory life there are elements of truth and enlightenment to be found in a whole range of myths and allegories. No single interpretation of the legend can be taken as the ultimate explanation of her complex appeal and influence. Yet both images, of Diana the blood sacrifice and Diana the modern-day Faust, contain echoes of truth.

11

PROTECTING
THE IMAGE

In medieval times it was well known that to give an otherwise nondescript object a special cachet it needed a connection with a well-known saint or holy person. Trading in relics was big business. The most expensive items were those that were not only rare but made the greatest claims. For instance, pieces of the cross on which Christ was crucified commanded the greatest respect and price.

In modern times the trade in relics and religious keepsakes is no less intense. Visitors to San Giovanni Rotondo in Italy, for instance, where the twentieth-century saint and stigmatic Padre Pio lived, will find numerous shops selling Padre Pio statues, calendars, tapes, videos, portraits and a whole host of pious merchandise. On display in the cell in the monastery where he lived, tourists can see the most prized and valuable items, those things used by the saint himself. These include the whip with which he scourged himself. On special occasions the saint's bloodstained mittens are put on display and the devout queue to touch them.

The Diana collectables and relics started coming on the

second-hand market almost as soon as the funeral was over, and the interest continues. Original copies of newspapers and magazines carrying Diana photos and stories are at the affordable end of the Diana scale. Copies of the official invitation to the funeral or the wedding are auctioned for hundreds of pounds.

Thousands of people around the world are collectors. Some buy pottery, plates, mugs, figurines and thimbles with Diana connections. Others prefer the Diana dolls. Then there are Diana teddy bears, candles, jigsaw puzzles, T-shirts, tea-towels and replica clothes. Even tape cassettes of television programmes involving Diana have their buyers.

The internet auction site eBay provides a constant supply of items. Occasionally a true rarity is offered – a handwritten letter from Diana perhaps, or a genuine snippet of material from Diana's 'Elizabeth Emanuel' wedding dress framed with a collage of other souvenirs – but mostly it is run-of-the-mill souvenirs put up for sale.

The Princess's private address book was auctioned and was bought by a Japanese millionaire for £40,000. He now has access to dozens of numbers and addresses for Diana's closest friends plus contact details for some very well-known names such as Colin Powell, Margaret Thatcher, Lord Attenborough and the singer Bryan Adams. Astrologers, faith healers, dress designers and photographers are among the other numbers. How it came to be in the public domain remains a mystery, although there are at least two stories of address books belonging to the Princess going missing, including the one which Paul Burrell is said to have read from during his all-night vigil alongside the Princess's coffin shortly before the funeral.

At any one time, even eight or nine years after her death, the eBay auction site will have hundreds of individual items. On a typical day the auction list might include: a Charles and Diana gilt wedding mug; a commemorative Lady Diana bookmark; an HRH Prince Charles and Lady Diana Spencer whiskey; a mint condition crown; a Royal Doulton Lady

Diana figurine; a Diana look-alike Sindy doll; a Franklin Mint plate. Few are expected to raise more than a few pounds, but nevertheless there is an active market.

Some of the items produced during and after her lifetime are on the borderline of artistic good taste. There is the 'Chuck and Di have a Baby' paper-doll book with drawings of the Prince and Princess of Wales in their underwear on the cover. Other items are remarkably elaborate, as in the case of the Princess Diana Royal Wardrobe Collection – twenty-four replica outfits as worn by the Princess, plus an eleven-and-a-half-inch tall Diana doll to wear them.

'Patronising rubbish' is how Stephen Bayley, who once ran The Design Museum, describes much of the 'collectible' market.[1]

Some businesses have made a great deal of money from producing Diana memorabilia and in the process have maintained an uneasy relationship with those wishing to be the arbiters of good taste and preservers of Diana's memory.

Some defenders of Diana's good image and reputation have questioned the right of commercial enterprises to produce merchandise exploiting the Diana image. Following her death, the Diana, Princess of Wales Memorial Fund was involved in a controversial and expensive legal battle with the American based company, the Franklin Mint. The Fund wished to make the point that the Diana image was not open to anyone to use and abuse. The Mint was the manufacturer of several souvenir lines including plates, jewellery and a Diana doll, dressed in a sparkling white dress and jacket, which sold for £145.

In 1998 the Fund accused the Franklin Mint of unauthorised exploitation of the Princess's property rights. When the action started, the Fund insisted that it was important to send a message to others in the market that the Fund would strongly assert its rights to the Princess's name.

The case did not go well for the Fund and a Californian court ruled that the Franklin Mint had not violated the law by using the Princess's image. Legal costs have been estimated at over £4 million and after its legal victory the Franklin Mint accused the Fund of wasting money in pursuing the battle.

Dr Andrew Purkis, the Fund's chief executive, defended the Fund's determination to protect the Princess's image from commercial exploitation, and 'to assert our legal rights for the sake of vulnerable people who depend on the fund's efforts to continue the Princess's humanitarian work around the world. 'Those who profit from the Princess's memory commercially should respect the wishes of her estate and make a portion of the profits available for charity, as of right, through her Memorial Fund.'

A spokesman for the Franklin Mint told the BBC that the company had already donated £2.5 million to some of Diana's favourite charities.

'We would never do anything to harm Princess Diana's image nor the respect that we know the British people have for her memory,' he said.

But the case did not end when the Franklin Mint had its case upheld. The American company then turned the legal guns on the Fund's trustees accusing them of waging a 'most nasty PR campaign against us and we think they should be held accountable'.

The owners of the Franklin Mint, Stewart and Lynda Resnick, had taken the case personally and been incensed by criticism in the British media suggesting they were like vultures feeding on the dead and that they were stealing the Princess's name and likeness.

A counter suit for malicious prosecution followed with the Fund being sued for £15 million. The Pennsylvania-based firm included Diana's sister Lady Sarah McCorquodale in its action, accusing her of acting 'maliciously, wantonly . . . and with the intent to oppress' the Mint.

The Fund became seriously worried about the open-ended financial implications of the battle and in July 2004 froze its charitable funding. The freezing of cash awards was described by the Charity Commission as a 'massive blow' to voluntary organisations. The Mint responded by saying that it had no intention of hurting the charities helped by the Fund, and pledged to give any money it should win to charity.

The Mint's UK spokesman, Steven Locke, said the lawsuit was necessary, despite the legal costs involved. 'I think they (the trustees) have pushed the Diana Fund into financial paralysis, basically to try and find a Cinderella who will rescue them, (or) alternatively to scare us into dropping our action.'[2]

The accusation was dismissed by the Fund, which said: 'We're not in a financial crisis, we have £46 million of uncommitted money. 'But because we don't know the maximum liability or timeframe (of the action) we can't continue to spend at the same rate that we have been spending.'

Many of the affected charities – which worked with landmine victims, refugees, young offenders and people with learning disabilities, among others – expressed dismay. In its first five years, the Fund had awarded £40 million to good causes, with much of the money having been donated by Diana supporters in the wake of her sudden death.

The matter was eventually settled in November 2004 when the case was dropped just as a jury was being prepared to hear the evidence. The details of the out-of-court settlement were not made public. The immediate consequence was that the Fund could resume its programme of donations to the causes Diana had supported. It announced the release of £525,000 for a number of UK and international projects, which had already been earmarked but put on hold, and said that it would begin offering new grants in 2005.

The Fund and the Franklin Mint issued a joint statement saying that the 'energy and resources' needed for a court battle would be better spent on a 'mutually agreed international programme of humanitarian work' in honour of the Princess.

The Mint withdrew its claim that the Fund and its trustees, including Lady Sarah, acted with malice saying that the Fund's trustees had acted in 'good faith' and 'on advice received from their former American attorneys'.

The high-profile case has not deterred other companies from producing some quite outrageous items; in fact it might have had the opposite effect. The lawsuit had left the Fund in no mood or state to take legal action against any other party it might consider to be exploiting Diana's image. However, the Fund may have been cheered by the fact that following the court case the Franklin Mint had to face some difficult financial times. The worldwide market in collectibles had fallen by 40 per cent, and the Franklin Mint had been hit very hard.

Two thirds of the workforce was laid off and the company refocused its business. It now concentrates on marketing model classic cars and aeroplanes. Much of the decline in the market was due to the increasing popularity of eBay. Customers have discovered they need not pay exorbitant shop prices for souvenirs and knick-knacks. The impulse to collect appears to be as strong as ever. It is the willingness to pay high prices that has evaporated.

As any look at the eBay site will confirm, the image of Diana is now firmly in the public domain. Artists feel free to exploit it in any way they choose.

At one end of the artistic spectrum there are the jokey tributes, tongue-in-cheek works like 'Diana: Warrior Princess'. It is a comic-strip and role-play game-book illustrated by Aaron Williams, a gentle satire with Prince Charles, the Queen and Margaret Thatcher as the cardboard villains.

At the other end there are grand designs intended to be long-lasting memorials. These almost inevitably draw strong opinions from the public. The Harrods statue of Diana and Dodi is one example. It was unveiled on the eighth anniversary of the couple's death, to mixed reactions. 'Naff,' said some; 'ghastly,' said others; 'a magnificent tribute,' said those to whom it appealed.

However the most famous and controversial memorial has undoubtedly been the Diana Fountain. From its inception to its latest closure and reopening it has been a multi-million-pound headache for the royal parks and the government

In July 2003 the Culture Secretary Tessa Jowell agreed to select the winning design, following the failure of Diana's friend Rosa Monkton and her independent committee to decide between two possible winning designs chosen from sixty ideas.

'As the Minister responsible for the project,' she said, 'I will be . . . recommending a winner. It is now time to deliver a fitting memorial to the life of Diana.'

Would she have been so keen to take responsibility had she known what the future had in store, culminating in political terms with a stinging report from her parliamentary colleagues? The fountain, built in Hyde Park, went £2.2 million over its £3 million budget and will cost £250,000 a year to run.

Edward Leigh, chairman of the House of Commons Public Accounts Committee, branded the memorial 'an open drain' and asked why it ended up 'like a muddy bog' after the first couple of weeks.

Tessa Jowell's department admitted that the bill for the opening ceremony alone cost £318,000, and that work to rectify the fountain's 'teething problems' had cost another £700,000.

'Was the monument a fiasco?' asked Sadiq Khan, a Labour member of the Committee, Tessa Jowell's top civil servant. Dame Sue Street asked. She admitted, 'There were difficult lessons to learn . . . but I don't think it can be described as a fiasco . . . It has been a troubled project with a good and lasting outcome.'

Initially the fountain had been a popular new attraction in the park. In her address on the occasion of the fountain's opening the Queen congratulated the design team in its imagination and said 'I believe that you have given the park, at the very heart of our capital city that Diana knew so well, a highly original memorial which captures something of the essence of a remarkable human being. I think Diana would have enjoyed it and I believe she would want all of us to do so too.'

Thousands of visitors came to see the huge water feature when it was first opened one hot summer's day in July 2004. It did not go unnoticed that it was the first occasion both the Windsor family and the Spencers had appeared together in public since Diana's funeral.

The fountain was designed by American landscape architect Kathryn Gustafson. It takes the form of a large sloping granite ring with water welling up into the structure at the top and running in two directions. The shallow channel, around 200 metres (660 feet) in circumference, was designed to allow visitors, particularly children, to splash around in its circular water flow before the two streams join again in a reflecting pool.

'Chic' and 'dignified' were the descriptions given by some of Diana's friends. A 'storm drain', said its detractors.

In practical terms the fountain failed to pass its first real test. When children played pooh-sticks in the flowing water with twigs from the park, the drains became clogged. The stone sides of the water channels also became slippery and there were some minor accidents.

Within days of opening it was closed for adaptations following meetings between park officials and health and safety advisers.

The fountain's future is now assured, but not quite as envisaged when the design was accepted. Access to its flowing waters for children is now restricted. It is not so much fun as it was. It is for looking at, not playing in as Diana might have preferred.

The readers of one national newspaper have actually called for the whole project to be dismantled and the money written off.

Eighty-four per cent of readers polled called for it to be bulldozed as the fountain's numerous faults were marring the memory of Diana.

Comment solicited included:

It's an ugly blot on the landscape. Scrap it and sack a few people at the same time for allowing such a vast sum of money to have been wasted on creating so little. It's a national disgrace.

Princess Diana would not have wanted such a waste of money spent on her, she'd have wanted a donation made in her name or a hospital ward built and named after her, to portray her care for the sick and her passion in helping others, not a fountain that nobody can use or enjoy.

Another public project to commemorate Diana received such an unenthusiastic welcome that it was scrapped before work on it was ever started.

Plans for a Diana, Princess of Wales Memorial Garden, to be built on a 2.7 acre site near Kensington Palace, were scrapped after people living nearby complained about the numbers of visitors it would attract.

The £10 million proposal was replaced by a suggestion from The Diana Memorial Committee that a playground and a memorial walk should be built through London's parks near the palace linking Kensington Gardens, Hyde Park, Green Park and St James's Park.

Paris however proposed honouring the Princess with a garden – a vegetable garden – the purpose being to teach children how to cultivate the land. As in London, the suggestion had its doubters. A city councillor was quoted as saying dismissively that Diana was being awarded a thousand square metres of leeks.

Words of encouragement for the French idea came from the publishing director of *Burke's Peerage*, Harold Brooks-Baker.

'The French saw her as an individual very close to nature . . . she represented Mother Nature to them. From the point of view of a Princess it seems strange but to the French she was not a princess but a goddess and a goddess is supposed to create life from the earth.'

Of all memorial suggestions the one that would appear from polls and surveys to have the widest support is for a major, dignified, realistic statue to be erected prominently in London.

As one of the *Daily Mail* readers polled put it, 'I think it's now time to have a statue of our dear Diana, after all London is full of them. Diana deserves a very special memorial, she was unique.'

Yet *Daily Mail* readers are unlikely to have welcomed one statue that went on public show in Liverpool. In a pastiche of a Roman Catholic statue of the Virgin Mary, the sculptor, Luigi Baggi, showed Diana as the Madonna. It was part of a provocative exhibition that also included a fifteen-foot fibreglass statue of Jesus Christ.

Liverpool peer, Lord Alton said the exhibition was 'deeply offensive'. The Bishop of Liverpool, the Right Reverend James Jones, was more reflective. 'This controversial exhibition is a sign of our times. It reflects our culture and shows the huge gap that exists between traditional beliefs and the spirit of a new age.'

The Roman Catholic Archbishop of Liverpool, the Most Reverend Patrick Kelly found he was too busy to visit the exhibition himself, but in a statement made three points.

> Firstly, Roman Catholic devotion to Mary is rooted in the Gospels which set before us Mary of Nazareth, her poverty, and her surrender to the word of God.

> Secondly, over the course of 2,000 years appreciation of Mary has been expressed in many forms of art not one of which would ever claim to tell the whole story.

> Thirdly, comparisons might be made between the story of Mary, guaranteed to aspire the Gospels, and the story of anyone else, for example Princess Diana, and that would determine the authenticity of linking these stories through an art form.

Diana art takes many forms. At one end of the spectrum there is the Andy Warhol portrait of the young Diana that has become a popular poster. At the other end is what can best be described as folk art, paintings in a primitive or naïve style often found incorporated into Diana tributes. There is a genre of Diana art that has evolved for public display on the gates of Kensington Palace and at Althorp.

These tribute pictures use heart and rose motifs to symbolise Diana as the Queen of Hearts and the English Rose. The accompanying text is frequently in verse and places Diana in heaven as a guardian angel or caring mother figure.

Many of the poems written are overly sentimental – not great poetry, but written with great feeling. Where photographs of Diana are used they show her in the classic Madonna-and-child pose, hugging a sick child. Alternatively the photograph is cut out and her head is placed in a decorative halo – the traditional and instantly recognisable Christian device that suggests holiness.

The art is spontaneous and often untutored, amateur in the best sense of the word, executed out of love. It resembles the art associated with Elvis Presley and left at the graveside in the memorial gardens at Graceland. The same iconography and images are utilised. Other examples of the style can be seen in drawings of the saints in some Latin American countries. Similar bold colours are employed plus gold and silver glitter of all kinds and plastic or paper flowers.

Art and collectibility come together in one very active Diana market, the buying and selling of coins and stamps. Diana was seen by many countries around the world as an obvious revenue earner. Special issue stamps are widely sought and some unexpected countries have cashed in. For $23.50 philatelists can buy a complete Princess Diana Mint set of six stamps plus two souvenir sheets from Kyrgistan and a similar set from Turkmenistan.

One dealer advertises over six hundred different stamp issues, from wedding sets to those marking her death. A set of stamps from Tuvalu shows Diana in a black low-cut evening gown; from Grenada comes a set showing Diana dressed as a pilot; Dominica has her standing in an array of international flags; Gibraltar opts for a stamp showing William as a baby; St Kitts and Nevis opts for Diana showing off gowns and jewellery; and Gambia has marketed a stamp showing Diana with Princes William and Harry holding white roses.

The British government has not been averse to raising some extra revenue from Diana, although in the case of the £5 coin, a cut from sales went to the memorial charities. The Royal Mint issued the coin in her memory; on one side is a portrait of Diana by David Cornell and on the other the standard portrait of her mother-in-law.

The coin came in three versions, base metal, silver and gold, ranging in price from £9.95 to £595. A fourth minting of the coin was put into general circulation at face value.

As well as collecting the more highly-priced Diana souvenirs, many of the Dianaphiles' most treasured items are their own scrapbooks, which they have compiled from published newspaper and magazine photographs. Some scrapbooks run to many volumes and have been compiled over more than twenty years. Diana was well aware of the power of the single image and, as described earlier, used it to great effect on several occasions: at the Taj Mahal to illustrate her unhappy marriage; to promote a better understanding of AIDS; and in her anti-landmine campaign.

Many of the best-known portraits of the Princess parallel the images of classical and religious art. Not only did she sit with a child as if posing as the Madonna with the Christ child, her body language could convey, sorrow, suffering, empathy – whatever emotion she chose. And because a photograph is taken in an instant and only intended to represent an instant, she was under no obligation to hold a pose for long. She could laugh one minute and cry the next. She could change her mind and mood. She could be consistently contradictory, forever inconsistent and make a virtue of it. And publishers would, and continue to, select whatever image of her suits their immediate purpose.

The Dianaphiles who undoubtedly made the best investment were those who bid successfully for one or more of her dresses at the auction held in New York shortly before her death. These dresses have now become almost priceless relics. While some have been loaned to museums and public exhibitions, many remain in their owners' possession. One dress is considered to be so valuable that a security guard accompanies it whenever it leaves the owner's house. Another is kept in a bank vault. Each dress has a story linked to an event and is testimony to Diana's constantly changing moods and self-image.

12

SHRINES AND
HOLY PLACES

It helps with all religious observance to have a place where prayer can be offered and towards which there can be a spiritual focus. In Islam the holy places are in Mecca and at Medina. For Christians, Bethlehem, Jerusalem and Nazareth contain the important sacred sites. In recent times, with the growing religious devotion to Elvis Presley, large numbers of people go to Graceland, Memphis and Tupelo.

Followers of Diana visit three special sites and, when in London, often add two other 'shrines', or memorials erected in her honour. The three sacred sites of Diana are the ornate gates outside Kensington Palace, her London home; Althorp, the Spencer family home where Diana's body is buried; and the Place D'Alma in Paris where she died. The two additional shrines are the Diana Fountain in London's Hyde Park and the memorial to Diana and Dodi in Harrods in Knightsbridge.

Kensington Palace is situated on the western edge of central London's royal parks. The ornate gates face Hyde Park itself and have become the main focus of devotion on the anniversaries of Diana's death. It is where flowers and messages are left all the year round, but especially on the last day of August. Three centuries ago the palace was at the heart of court and government affairs. It was the monarchs' retreat from Whitehall and used regularly by the king, or queen, from the late seventeenth century through to the accession of George III in 1760. Later, it was where Queen Victoria was born and where she was living on the morning she was awoken to be told she was queen.

The palace is divided into apartments for various members of the royal family and was Diana's home up until her death. Parts of the palace consist of state apartments and they, along with a collection of royal dress are open to the public.

A short walk across the park is the Diana Fountain. As suggested earlier, it is a controversial addition to the park, described by many Diana followers as 'the ditch'. Mohamed Al Fayed has called the Princess Diana Memorial Fountain a 'sewer'.

He commissioned what he believes to be a more appropriate memorial and in September 2005 a bronze statue depicting the late Princess and her lover Dodi Fayed was unveiled at his London store Harrods..

The sculpture, by Bill Mitchell, is life-sized and has been described as showing Diana and Dodi gazing lovingly into each other's eyes as they release an albatross into the sky. It is called 'Innocent Victims', a direct reference to Mohamed Al Fayed's conviction that his son and the woman he claims would have been his future daughter-in-law were murdered. 'This is a statue to stay here forever. Until now nothing has been done to preserve her memory and legacy. She was an amazing woman who brought joy to the whole world.'

The Harrods memorial can be seen in the course of shopping at the store; to visit Althorp involves a whole day. While the Harrods shrine might be seen to be brash and gaudy, everything at Althorp is presented in impeccable English good taste – although traditionalists might rue the legacy of Raine who, as Countess Spencer, sold several

Spencer family artistic heirlooms and redecorated the mansion house.

Set in rolling parkland seven miles from Northampton the historic country estate of the Spencer's exudes affluence, privilege and tradition.

In the stables there is an exhibition dedicated to Diana's life. Photographs, old toys, school reports, shoes and dresses and in a section dedicated to the wedding, pride of place is given to the famous wedding dress itself. There is also a room devoted to the tributes paid to Diana at the end of her life, and at the end of their tour visitors are invited to buy some of the tasteful souvenirs on sale.

Writing six years after Diana's death, Frances Shand Kydd's biographers described how people often left the exhibition in tears,

> . . . perhaps moved by the carpet of dried aromatic petals strewn across the floor (widely but wrongly assumed to be from flowers left in tribute at Kensington Palace and Althorp after the Princess died), or by the sight of her extraordinary wedding dress, or messages from people of all ages and stations in life in several books of condolence from all over the world laid out for people to read. Most simply absorb the atmosphere in silence.[1]

'I am very proud of what has been achieved at Althorp,' Diana's brother Earl Spencer wrote in his letter of introduction to visitors.

> It was always my hope that my family and I would be able to meet the hopes and expectations of those coming to pay their respects to, or simply learn more about, Diana. At the same time I was determined not to approve anything that would besmirch Althorp's name, as an unspoilt place of beauty, in its classically English setting . . . Enormous thought and effort is focussed on

these matters . . . so we can meet the fundamental objectives that honour a great lady and maintain the integrity of the deeply atmospheric setting for her final resting place.[2]

Out of season the Althorp exhibits also travel. In 2005 an exhibition, selected from the Althorp collection and entitled, 'Diana – A Celebration', was flown to the USA. It went to Florida and Texas and proved highly popular.

The highlight was the Diana wedding gown, complete with twenty-five-foot train, diamond tiara, shoes and parasol. Outfits that had escaped auction were also included: twenty-eight dresses, suits and gowns designed by Versace, Valentino, Chanel and Azagury. In addition there were personal items of jewellery, Spencer home movies of her childhood, letters and photographs.

Other artefacts associated with Diana included the musical score and handwritten lyrics of the Elton John and Bernie Taupin composition dedicated to Diana, which was adapted from the song 'Candle in the Wind'.

The truly dedicated and wealthy Diana fans are now able to negotiate with Earl Spencer to be allowed to stay the night at Althorp and even sleep in the bedroom once used by Diana herself.

Diana's grave is sited on an island in the middle of a lake. At one end of the lake is a replica classical temple where visitors leave flowers and messages. It is a place of quiet dignity, but also at night or out of season must seem extraordinarily empty and lonely.

The island site gives the grave the sense of a forbidden place, set apart from the world where no-one may walk or venture. There is no bridge across and the island is only reached by rowing boat. The island has been left as a natural habitat. There is deep symbolism in the choice of a moat to protect the grave. In classical mythology the dead must go across water to the place from which no living person can return. In Arthurian legend King Arthur's last journey is by boat. He floats across the water and into the mists, to be lost from view until the day comes when he is summoned. He will then return to defend his kingdom.

The Place D'Alma in France is where Diana, Dodi and Henri Paul died. Or, more precisely, the accident occurred in the underpass beneath Place D'Alma. In the centre of the Place there is a large golden sculpture of a flame. It was there before the crash but has now been adopted as an unofficial memorial and visitors might think it was erected in Diana's memory. Around the anniversary of the accident the sculpture is covered with messages and flowers. Most of the year-round there are tourists leaving notes and paying their respects.

In the weeks following Diana's death, the Place D'Alma became a special focus of devotion. It was there that people claimed they could still sense the presence of Diana. One retired police officer spent time by the golden sculpture every day as he said that it was there he could feel Diana was with him.

Fans of Elvis Presley say much the same thing about the gardens at Graceland where they are close by the place where Elvis died. Some fans have taken one step on from having a profound sense of the presence of the dead Elvis; they say that they have seen him too. He has appeared in a window of the mansion house. In the case of Elvis there have been many other claimed sightings away from Graceland. In the case of Diana there is an equal profusion of claims.

One of the earliest claims emerged when it was said that Diana's image had been seen in a portrait hanging at St James's Palace in London. Shortly afterwards claims of sightings were posted on the internet and claims continue to be posted from around the world.

This report from Kosovo in 2001 is typical: 'I was at morning mass. A lady sat next to me and gave to me a nice smile. I could not believe it. "You are her," I said. "Yes, but we must not tell anyone." She was like an angel. She was the Princess.' Also in Kosovo it is rumoured that a mysterious nurse has been offering help to homeless families. She is said to be British and to resemble Diana. In Albania a man described how he was led safely home in the dark through a minefield by a Princess Diana figure.

A Diana figure offering help is a familiar theme; take this example:

> I was on my way to the orphanage to donate some toys for Christmas. Out of nowhere some drunk driver bumped me off the road and into a ditch. I went unconscious until I was awoken by what seemed to be Princess Di. She told me to get out of the car slowly, and painfully I unbuckled and crawled out of the wreck. When I got out the cops were there and my car had caught on fire. I searched and looked for her, but I never saw her again. I feel she has saved me and I owe my life to her. God bless you princess Di.

In some instances the sighting can be explained as wishful thinking mixed with mistaken identity. This is a report of a sighting in New York in 2001:

> I was taking a stroll down Central Park when I saw a woman from behind. I got an eerie feeling immediately and said to myself that is Princess Diana. When I walked in front of her I looked at her face. She had large black sunglasses on and she said with a British accent to me 'Good Day'. I don't know if it was really her but the resemblance was uncanny.

The stories are similar to those that have been told over the years about angelic intervention in earthly affairs. As Diana is frequently referred to as an angel in letters and cards, this is an unsurprising parallel. In other folk-tales little people or animals have taken the role of the angels, as beings from another realm who offer guidance to humans in extreme need. Often angels are described as messengers and sometimes Diana has an important speaking role. 'There was Princess Di in a radiant flowing gown and sparkly shoes, she smiled and said "Don't worry, peace will come and all mankind will rid the earth of war."'

Some of the claims of Diana sightings have the same extraordinary, yet mundane, ring to them as in the famous 'I saw Elvis at the gas station' stories. She has been spotted in a car at traffic lights in Orlando, USA; test driving a Volvo in Wagga Wagga, Australia; on a thriller ride at Thorpe Park, Surrey; on a yacht in Malta; in a charity shop in Edinburgh; and in Marks and Spencer in Derby. This last case was described thus, and includes a very plausible human response to the event. 'She looked at me and smiled. I jumped, shouted "GHOST" and ran like hell. I wish now that I had not.'

In other accounts, the Diana is quite definitely an ethereal as opposed to material being. 'I found myself staring straight up into the eyes of Princess Di! She was glowing and she seemed to smile right through me.' 'My friends were the first to see Princess Di. She was covered with a kind of light all around her.' 'I looked up and there was Princess Di. She was real bright, like she had a halo.'

Other Diana sightings are quite clearly the product of dream or hallucination. Perhaps the heat of the outback had something to do with this one.

Me and me dingo were rounding up a few stray sheep in the outback when I see me some kangaroos not far off. They were lying in the shade of a coolibah tree, escaping the midday sun. Me dingo fetched me rifle and I took careful aim. Looked like 'roo for dinner! Then stone the crows!! The tall blonde 'roo stands up on her back legs and I realise it's Princess Di! 'Ocker, put down the rifle!' she calls out.

And this account is of a similar nature:

> She done moved in here wit' me an' my dogs where we
> don't do nothin' all day but sit in the shade drinkin' beer
> and smokin' a little dope and maybe fool around a bit
> and watch the TV and wait on our welfare checks and
> food stamps. Oh, yeah. And now she goes by Sally Ann.

The Diana of vision or hallucination is not always a
comforting figure:

> I first saw her hair was really a mass of snakes. Then I
> saw her eyes. I was mesmerised. She spit in my face and
> yelled something about bloody bastards and then ran
> into the woods. I followed her and came across a little
> throne surrounded by fairy nymphs and sparkling roses.
> Elton was standing on a stump with a pipe wrench in his
> hand telling me not to come any closer. I was scared and
> ran away.

It can help to be thinking of Diana for a vision to occur.

> I was just thinking about whether to take the Princess Di
> bus tour with my friends Kelly and Lily who travel with
> me all the time. Last year, we went to Hong Kong, but
> this year we wanted to walk the Last Mile with Princess
> Di. Well, to make a long story short, we saw what we
> think may have been Princess Di, alive and walking
> around, right on the grounds of the Spencer family
> estate. Could it have been a relative?

Without necessarily endorsing the idea that Diana has truly
been seen in spiritual form, the following story seems entirely
plausible.

> Since my late husband passed away I've fallen into the
> habit of eating lunch alone at the restaurant where we

first met. Silly but I find it comforting to be in the familiar surroundings . . . Usually I sit in the back near the kitchen where the singles are relegated. This last Tuesday the . . . place was almost empty. This meant I could sit in the window booth where my husband and I first ate. Halfway through the meal I felt a strange tingling. At first I thought it was my Harry. I was so excited. But when I looked in the window I could very clearly see the reflection of Diana sitting across from me in the booth. I couldn't see her if I looked directly, but she was very clearly there in the reflection. Don't think me silly for reporting this. She seemed so sad sitting there all alone. I hope everything is alright.

Although other reports are clearly not to be taken seriously:

While taking a shower – a monthly thing for me – the soap I was using started to change shape. First it looked like Elvis, then, Richard Nixon, then suddenly it turned into a tortilla with the image of Princess Di.

An internet rumour has been spreading for four years that a vision of Diana will be seen at Althorp and witnessed by hundreds. It would be an event comparable to the mass sighting of the Virgin Mary at Fatima, Portugal, when in 1917 thousands of pilgrims reported seeing the sun dance and the face of the Virgin. So far nothing remotely similar has happened.

While to date sightings of Diana have been relatively common, they have also been low key. How the claims will evolve in years to come is difficult to predict. In terms of Marian visions it is normally the case that sightings proliferate when other external social and economic problems impinge. A mass sighting can divert attention from those problems and be a shared cathartic experience. The Fatima vision took place in the third year of the First World War. The most famous angelic vision also took place during the war years in 1914 when the Angel of Mons intervened between the allied and German trenches.

Under what circumstances might a significant Diana vision come about? Possibly during a period of economic recession and at a time when the House of Windsor is facing unpopularity. The sighting might start as a spontaneous, populist occurrence and then take on wider political and religious significance. The initial witnesses may well sincerely believe they have seen something of significance. It could be a case of mistaken identity or a natural phenomenon with a simple explanation, the rational explanation will not matter. There need not be many witnesses – the Medjugorje legend of sightings of the Virgin Mary started with only six children claiming to see a vision. What will be crucial is how the witnesses' accounts are interpreted and authenticated. If a report emerges and solidifies which can be taken to be either literally true, or heavily symbolic of a wider truth, and that account captures the imagination and mood of the public, a story of a Diana vision could be exceptionally powerful.

13

DIANA OF THE
NEW AGE

During her life Diana consulted numerous astrologers and New Age therapists. She poured out her heart to many of them, and some repaid her trust by publishing tapes of her consultations. Others behaved more honourably and have kept her secrets to themselves.

Her interest in the New Age philosophies was not a secret; she talked openly about it and used New Age idioms in her speech. She talked of 'energies' and of the personalities of her friends being determined by their star signs. In some ways she had much in common with Prince Charles. He too was interested in ideas outside the mainstream consensus, and was much mocked in the press when he mentioned, for instance, that he had talked to his plants. Where the Prince and Princess diverged was in how they fitted their interests into their wider philosophical landscapes. Prince Charles professed an interest in all matters ecological. He studied Jung and searched for an intellectual framework in which to fit his ideas. Diana, by contrast, was not inclined to look for the over-arching theories. She lived by instinct and intuition.

Her attempts to read and study around the subject were short-lived, as, reputedly, was her attention span.

Yet Charles and Diana shared one aspect of their mutual fascination with alternative ideas. They exhibited the same inconsistency. Charles in particular was prone to philosophising about deep ecology one minute, and the next driving an expensive car or commandeering a helicopter to travel to an engagement when a train would have done. Diana similarly would empathise with the suffering of the marginalised and downtrodden of the third world one day and jet off the next to enjoy a no-expenses-spared hedonistic holiday.

Charles is an ecumenist. His comment about wishing, as King, to be defender of faiths, was no throw-away remark. He sees many of the world's religions as having valid insights and appears not to accept that the Protestant Christian tradition, which at his coronation he will have to swear to uphold, has the exclusive claim to truth.

But what of Diana, what did she really believe? Did she have a faith, an understanding of a god? Like everyone of her class and background she had been given a conventional religious upbringing. She was baptised as a child into the Church of England and attended church services as and when required. For many people this grounding is sufficient for life. The Queen is a faithful and traditional Christian. She attends divine worship on a regular basis, in Scotland as a Presbyterian and in England as an Anglican, says her prayers and is a regular communicant. However, from a young age, Diana had entertained ideas that were not encouraged by church teaching. She felt, in some undefined way, that she had a destiny to fulfil and in later life she talked on several occasions of being spiritually guided. Such ideas would be described by Christians as occult and thus to be discouraged.

Her guide, Diana said, was her grandmother, Cynthia, Countess Spencer. She had a clear memory of her in life and recalled enjoying her company on her early visits to Althorp. She was 'sweet, wonderful and very special'. Cynthia, Lady Spencer, was well-known for her good works. She visited the sick and offered encouragement to the less fortunate. As Andrew Morton observed, Diana inherited her grand-mother's qualities of compassion. And it was in the taped memoirs she prepared for Morton that she confirmed the identity of her spirit guide as her paternal grandmother.

'She looks after me in the spirit world. I know that for a fact.'[1]

At one consultation with a medium she believed that her grandmother had contacted her, as had one of her uncles and the protection officer, Barry Mannakee, to whom she was particularly close and who died in a motorcycle accident.

There is another reference to her belief in spiritual guidance to be found in a little noted section of the notorious 'Squidgy' tapes. She told James Gilbey about a conversation she had had with the Bishop of Norwich in which she had told him, 'I'm aware that people I have loved, and [who] have died, and [who] are in the spirit world, look after me.' His reaction, according to Diana, was one of horror!

In the same conversation with James Gilbey she spoke of her belief in reincarnation, again a subject that had arisen during the conversation with the Bishop. The Bishop had wanted to know how she coped with talking to people who were dying.

'I said: "I know this sounds crazy, but I've lived before." He said: "How do you know?" I said: "Because I'm a wise old thing." '

It was Gilbey, in the course of the same taped conversation, who introduced the subject of astrology. He had seen a horoscope referring to Diana that had included the obser-vation that Cancerians turn to 'less materialistic, and more spiritual things'.

Diana consulted several astrologers, but took from the consultations only what she needed to hear. She enjoyed the trappings and rituals of astrology, but did not study the underlying theory or attempt to understand the process in any great depth. She once said of her sessions with astrologer Debbie Frank, 'She doesn't advise, she just tells me from her angle and with astrology. I listen to it but I don't believe it totally.'[2]

Diana did however firmly believe that she had premonitions. Most famously that, even at the moment she accepted Prince Charles's proposal of marriage, she knew she would never be queen. 'A voice said to me inside: "You won't be queen but you'll have a tough role."'[3]

Omens were also important to her and one strange story is told of events that occurred during Prince William's christening. The weather abruptly changed from sunshine to threatening storm. A candle being passed to the godparents as part of the service flickered as a cold gust of wind blew in through a window. The candle almost went out, but not quite.

'The candle symbolised not only life, hope and light, but William himself. And, as William is heir to the throne, the candle also represented the monarchy. The candle flickering indicated a grave crisis, but the fact that it wasn't blown out indicated that William would survive coronation.'[4]

This omen was not one that went unnoticed by Prince Charles, according to his mentor the late Sir Laurens van der Post, who compared the event to a Jungian dream.

Astrologer Nick Campion, the President of the Astrological Association, wondered if the candle flickering was a warning of Diana's death.

The awful loss of his mother will forever remain the defining trauma of William's life and as he adjusts to it over the coming years and decades, so will the monarchy.

As we are quite clearly dealing with imagery and cosmology of an arcane nature, there is one other curious event which needs to be described. In late August 1982 a portrait of the new Princess was hung in the National Portrait Gallery, an occurrence which attracted considerable publicity at the time. At 10.20 am on the morning of the 29th of August a man walked into the gallery, knife in hand, and slashed the Princess's image.

This struck me as a bizarre event at the time, an omen equivalent to, for example, the breaking of Czar Nicholas II's gold chain at his coronation.[5]

In terms of astrological timing, it is said, the attack on the painting and the moment of her death coincided.

A lively description of Diana's interest in New Age pursuits and the trappings of astrology has been provided by her butler. During one period when Diana was attempting to 'find herself', 'I seemed to open the door to an ever-growing band of lifestyle gurus, health experts, healers, astrologers and psychics.'[6]

Paul Burrell wrote of what he called the melting pot of ideas, zodiac information, power of crystals, messages from the spirit world and energies around her.

The scent of incense from burning joss-sticks in the Princess's bedroom wafted through the first floor . . . I became used to the astrologer Debbie Frank arriving . . . and the floor of the drawing room . . . being scattered with Zodiac charts. She felt that Cancerians, like their symbol the crab, had a hard outer shell and a soft centre. She told Debbie, 'This house is full of Geminis. William is Gemini, Paul is Gemini, and it's not easy.'[7]

One acupuncturist phoned in a state of alarm following one session fearing she had left a needle in the Princess's head – which fortunately she had not.

While always sensitive to religious atmosphere, to spiritual people and sacred places, Diana's religion was not that of a deep thinker. Hers was an intuitive acceptance of spirituality rather than a cerebral conviction. She did however go through an experience that could be likened to a spiritual awakening. It came ten years after her marriage and happened when she tended a dying friend Adrian Ward-Jackson. This was no superficial encounter with the problem of AIDS. She made a commitment to stay alongside Adrian through his final days and hours and it made a profound impact on her. When news reached her that his condition was finally deteriorating Diana was in Scotland. She drove through the night from Balmoral, breaking protocol by not telling the Queen of her departure, arriving at 4 a.m. at the hospital where Adrian was being treated. She began a bedside vigil lasting many hours. She acknowledged after his death that she had 'reached a depth inside which I never imagined was possible. My outlook on life has changed its course and become more positive and balanced.'[8]

Few people who witness the death of a friend or relation remain unmoved by the experience. If the death is a slow process of decline, the dying person and the witnesses can form an extraordinarily close bond. Dying remains a mysterious business. What is happening to the mind and the spirit as the body slowly shuts down? Watching someone dying peacefully can be a form of prayer. It is a shared spiritual experience. For Diana, who up until then had been largely sheltered from the realities of death, attending Adrian Ward-Jackson through his final illness was her first experience of this kind. It enabled her to rethink her life and to ask those basic questions about mortality which people normally shy away from.

A few years earlier when her father had suffered a stroke and was seriously ill in hospital, Diana was not able to bond with him in the same way. The fiercely protective Raine was always at hand. Diana and her sisters had to battle for every moment with their father. In the event Earl Spencer recovered. He was well enough to walk his daughter down the aisle at her wedding. When he died in 1992 Diana was away in Austria on a family skiing holiday. He suffered a heart attack. It was a time when Diana and Charles's marriage was going through a particularly difficult time and Diana's grief was invaded by arguments with her husband about what role he should play. Should he return with her to London and then accompany her to her father's funeral? Diana thought that in life he had taken no interest in her father's health, why should he feign interest after his death? All he was interested in was his public image and not wanting to give the press the opportunity to criticise him for appearing indifferent to his wife when she had just lost her father. They travelled to London together, but Charles went immediately to Highgrove while Diana stayed in Kensington Palace. They travelled to the funeral separately, Diana by car and Charles by helicopter.

Around this time Diana's mother too was undergoing a period of spiritual reappraisal. Her second marriage had failed. Her reflections on her life and her time alone led her in the direction of Roman Catholicism. She found the local Roman Catholic congregation in Oban to be welcoming and was attracted by the church's teaching on repentance and forgiveness.

'She was looking for something that required her complete commitment, something all-consuming, a belief that would never desert her, ideals that she could trust and live by, for ever.'[9] Being received into the church was to her a home-coming.

Frances became an active member of her local congregation. She was a reader at Mass and also helped with other parish duties, making tea, coffee or offering hospitality to visiting clergy. After her death the Scottish Cardinal Keith O'Brien recalled her 'dedication to the sick and handicapped on her regular visits to Lourdes and the inspiration, which she gave to many suffering people, having suffered herself in various ways throughout her life'.[10]

Diana was also attracted to the outward trappings of Roman Catholicism, if not the commitment and discipline. Pictures of the veiled Diana meeting Pope John Paul II and reports of her conversations with several leading Catholic clerics led to speculation that she, like her mother and the Duchess of Kent, might seek to be received into the church.

She often walked the short distance from Kensington Palace to her local Roman Catholic church, attached to a Carmelite priory, to light a candle at an altar dedicated to St

Thérèse of Lisieux. Her visits started in 1985, the year of the sixtieth anniversary of the saint's canonisation. Perhaps she felt a connection with St Thérèse.

At first glance the pious young French nun, born in 1873, and the glamorous, promiscuous modern Princess, might appear to have little in common. They both claimed to have had no special talents, both were remarkably determined and scheming individuals, both produced accounts of their own lives, both died young and both, in death have become mythologised. There is an active Thérèse cult, not dissimilar in many ways from the embryonic one currently focused on Diana. It is a popular movement, often dismissed as over sentimentalised, in which Thérèse's supposed simple holiness is paraded and she is called the Little Flower.

Feeling an empathy with St Thérèse of Lisieux and lighting candles in a Roman Catholic church does not however amount to serious evidence that Diana was seeking to convert. After her death much was made of the fact that a Catechism was found among her belongings at Kensington Palace. The red-bound book is the manual of teachings of the Roman Catholic Church and would be read by a serious enquirer. It was thought to have been given to her by Father Anthony Sutch, whose guidance on Catholicism Diana had sought. Yet this discovery too does not of itself strengthen the case that Diana was looking to become a Catholic. The fact is, it was not the only book found. Diana admitted once to having over one hundred spiritual manuals waiting to be read covering the widest range of Christian and New Age ideas.

When she did make a form of commitment to the church it was not through membership, but by action and involvement in the church's practical work. It began, as her former equerry Patrick Jephson recalls, following a visit she paid to Westminster Cathedral. Jephson was a particularly close and informed observer of the Princess's moods, infatuations and superficial obsessions. From his account her visit that day to the cathedral had an unusually profound and long-lasting impact.

He described the atmosphere of the occasion – the dark cavernous cathedral with the organ playing softly and the scent of incense in the air.

> While the Princess played her part flawlessly as a conventional royal performer at the engagement . . . the experience also opened up the possibility of a more spiritual answer to the public and private pressures that were gathering around her. Mainstream, traditional royal duty has always involved religion. There was surely potential for combining public duty with personal enlightenment.[11]

After her tour of the cathedral Diana took coffee with the Cardinal Archbishop, Basil Hume. The result of that conversation was that Diana decided to involve herself with the Cardinal's charitable work for London's homeless. She gave money and made many unofficial visits to night shelters and hostels, even taking Prince William on one occasion. The young Prince's ability to cope with meeting some of the least loved and most unlovable of his grandmother's subjects was remarked upon by the Cardinal as 'extraordinary'.

'The Cardinal's quiet but practical holiness made a deep impression on her and she would have given a great deal to be able to emulate it, and to know the peace of mind that was its reward.'[12]

What Diana achieved in her charitable work, undoubtedly bringing cheer and comfort, was, Jephson noted, through instinct rather than any formalised response to any structured religious influence on her life.

> Sadly, she did not feel the happiness she deserved from the good work she did. The compassion she showed others was too often just compensation for the attention she seemed to feel she had always been denied herself. In addition, because she was the catalyst rather than a direct cause of good, she did not develop the disciplined

215

thinking necessary for spiritual growth, or feel the satisfaction that might have been of solid benefit to her in return.

I think it was an instinctive need to redress this imbalance that led her to seek spiritual answers from her various therapists and astrologers – but they demanded little in the way of disciplined thinking either, or if they did, their services were quickly dispensed with.[13]

Diana dabbled in spirituality in a manner typical of what is generally described as New Age. She grabbed at whatever spiritual ideas and proffered guidance appeared exciting, novel and superficially comforting. New Age spirituality can be described as the spirituality of the consumer age. Competing religious ideas jostle for attention in an open marketplace to be bought and consumed as any other product. Diana was a spiritual shopper in a New Age mall.

Diana attempted to read some of the books that had inspired the New Age, but did not have the required powers of concentration to make sense of them or the academic training to question them. She had no resources of intellectual rigour. At this stage in her life she might have found a conversation with Prince Charles on spirituality useful, but the backlog of ill-feeling prevented either taking the initiative. Both, in their separate ways, had come to realise that despite the fact that they were immensely rich in the material sense, that wealth did not bring contentment. Charles believed he had a more disciplined mind than Diana, but throughout his life has never managed to reconcile his intellectual interest in spiritual matters with his enjoyment of material pleasures. He is attracted by the idea of the simple life, he is genuinely alarmed by the dangers of rampant consumerism in the world, and yet, as suggested earlier, his actions frequently contradict his principles. As a young man he fell under the spell of Laurens van der Post, a man seen by many during his life as an inspired thinker on spiritual and environmental issues, and was disappointed to find that he could not interest Diana in these ideas. Perhaps Diana instinctively sensed something bogus about the man, who despite being regarded as a deep philosopher in his lifetime was exposed after his death as the pedlar of fraudulent claims.

Or perhaps, whatever hope there might have been that Charles and Diana would have shared a common spiritual path, that hope was extinguished at source by his insensitive decision to take seven van der Post books with him to read on his honeymoon and Diana's intuitive resistance to her husband's guru.

It was not until after her death that van der Post was most brutally exposed in a biography, entitled *Faking it – Storyteller: the many lives of Laurens van der Post* written by J. D. F. Jones.

Frank McLynn's New Statesman review pulled no punches.

When Laurens van der Post died in 1996, aged 90, the received view was that he was a distinguished explorer and traveller, also a mystic and sage, a guru to both Prince Charles and Margaret Thatcher. But, as this bio-graphy makes clear, he was in fact a fraud, charlatan, impostor and Grade-A phoney. The depressing tale begins with his many lies. He falsely claimed to be descended from Dutch aristocracy; to be an expert on Japan and the Japanese; to have explored virgin territory and gone where no white man had gone before; to be an expert on the Bushmen; to have been Mountbatten's political and military officer; to have been C G Jung's close friend and confidant; to have served on a whaling ship; to have met D H Lawrence; to have been an architect of the 1980 Lancaster House agreement. The list goes on and on. He even lied about his age and wartime rank . . . As J D F Jones remarks, there have been other notorious recent liars . . . but they did not put themselves forward as teachers of high spiritual and moral values.[14]

If Camilla Parker Bowles was the third person in the marriage as Diana later complained, van der Post was, for a time, the fourth.

> Charles used to want to go for long walks around Balmoral the whole time when we were on our honeymoon. His idea of enjoyment would be to sit on top of the highest hill at Balmoral. It is beautiful up there. I completely understand; he would read Laurens van der Post or Jung to me, and bear in mind I hadn't a clue about psychic powers or anything, but I knew there was something in me that hadn't been awoken yet and I didn't think this was going to help! So anyway we read those and I did my tapestry and he was blissfully happy.[15]

Over the years, despite her instinctive interest in matters spiritual, and longing to make sense of her confused life, she made little progress in her search for religious knowledge.

At one stage towards the end of her life she even made enquiries about Islam. This was during her affair with Hasnat Khan when she visited his family. There was much speculation that had she married Dodi Fayed she would, like her friend Jemima Goldsmith, have embraced the religion. Indeed one of the first murder theories to emerge after her death originated in Egypt and claimed that she was killed by the British establishment precisely because she wished to become a Muslim.

What makes it unlikely that she would have converted to Islam is that like Roman Catholicism it is a religion that requires commitment to regular prayer and devotion. There is nothing in Diana's life story that suggests she would have been inclined to or capable of following a strict religious discipline.

The two religious systems are also authoritarian, in the sense that they rely in religious discourse on their two respective and immutable authorities, the Koran in the case of Islam and the historical teachings of Pope and Church in the case of Roman Catholicism. There is nothing in her life to suggest that Diana would have wanted to submit herself to any religious authority. Conversion to either appears out of character. Diana felt little attraction towards religious institutions and, while nominally Anglican, she felt little affinity with the Church of England, which requires far less submission to either teaching or leadership.

Her aversion to formalised religion was something Robert Runcie, as Archbishop of Canterbury, understood. His own wife was not one for religious institutions. Talking to Diana, the Archbishop tried, as he said, to get on her side. The royal family he knew were people of formal piety so he reassured Diana that it was not necessary to worry about religious language and liturgy.

> You may have more spiritual insight than your cerebrally inclined husband. The trouble is that you believe that to be religious you have to be capable of handling ideas, religious ideas. But that's not necessarily true at all . . . I have a wife who is very, very bright . . . but she's not an ideas woman – she hates an idea when she sees one![16]

Diana, Runcie considered, needed encouragement and not instruction. 'When you began on abstract ideas, you could see her eyes clouding over.'[17]

Diana's personal faith was utterly ungrounded in theory or training. It was intuitive and fickle. She moved from one counsellor to another, one astrologer to the next, a new theory or therapy according to whim and fashion.

She encountered transcendent moments on her journey through life, taking inspiration as and when it came from the outstanding people she had the opportunity and good fortune to meet. On meeting Cardinal Hume she declared, 'That man, he's so holy,' adding, in case she was seen to be too intense, 'just like a great big teddy bear!'

Today, Diana's name is often associated with that of Mother Teresa of Calcutta. Diana's first contact with the work and reputation of Mother Teresa had come through a remarkable Irishwoman Oonagh Shanley-Toffolo, an acupuncturist who had trained in Chinese medicine, a former nun and midwife, who had known the Duke of Windsor. Oonagh used her consultations with Diana to develop the Princess's spiritual confidence. She believed Diana had a mission in the world to help humanity and Mother Teresa was presented to her as a role model.

In 1992 Diana had visited Calcutta and had described the visit to Mother Teresa's home as a life-changing experience that had placed her on a humanitarian and spiritual path. It was where, she told Paul Burrell, she had found her direction in life. She regarded the sisters of Mother Teresa's community as saints and knelt with them to pray in the chapel. She learned from them the importance of simple gestures when comforting the young, sick and poor.

On returning from Calcutta she said she was driven by a deep need to help the sick and dying on a global scale. It had been her awakening. From 1992 onwards she began, Paul Burrell observed, to talk more and more about spiritual beliefs.

But the saintly nun and the Princess came to be linked most closely by the sheer coincidence of their deaths, occurring as they did within days of each other in 1997.

They did meet in life and in her quiet knowing way Mother Teresa was well aware of the shallowness of Diana's faith, and suspicious too that Diana was capable of using associations with her work to bolster her own public image.

There was also a certain undignified competition between Diana and Charles to win the nun's attention. When she was taken ill in 1992 the Prince sent her a bouquet of flowers and pointedly instructed his staff not to associate Diana with the gesture. At Christmas in 1995 Diana decided on a whim to fly to Calcutta to offer to help her with her work. Mother Teresa shrewdly, but diplomatically declined the offer by suggesting Diana visit the order's projects in London to save herself the inconvenience of flying to India. When the news of Mother

Teresa's response was conveyed to Diana, Patrick Jephson recalls 'a long, hurt and unloved silence' at the other end of the telephone line.

Patrick Jephson never saw Diana discover a faith to sustain her in times of real doubt and loneliness.

> It was probably the only way in which she could have gained genuine satisfaction and happiness from the good that was so often laid at her door. Here, perhaps, was the greatest lost potential of all. The Princess's quest for personal fulfilment grew increasingly desperate. In the absence of solid faith that could comfort her, she took refuge in impulsive bouts of mysticism and psychology. Without a reliable framework of knowledge and support, or wise guidance she was prepared to trust, these too were bound to fail her.[18]

In the final year and a half of her life Diana saw far fewer therapists, although there is no evidence that her belief in New Age ideas ever diminished. When Piers Morgan in May 1996 asked her outright if she had stopped seeing therapists, she said 'Yes, I stopped when I realised they needed more therapy than I did.'[19]

The roll-call of astrologers, clairvoyants and New Age healers and therapists consulted by Diana during her life is a long one. It includes Penny Thornton, Betty Palko, Felix Lyle, Debbie Frank, Simone Simmons, Rita Rogers, Roderick Lane, Sue Beechey, Chrissie Fitzgerald, Oonagh Toffolo and many more covering specialities from astrology to colonic irrigation, aromatherapy to acupuncture.

As a consequence of her endorsement of so many spiritual disciplines and fads, Diana has in death attracted an astonishing interest from the world's clairvoyants, astrologers and New Age practitioners, ranging from the most respectable through to the seriously cranky. Some have claimed to have made direct contact with Diana and channelled messages from her.

In the most widely-publicised case in 2003, the British psychics Craig and Jane Hamilton-Parker featured in a televised séance. Parts of the show, called *The Spirit of Diana*, were filmed at the Livery Hall of the Stationers Guild, near London's St Paul's Cathedral. The programme was described by critics as ghoulish and the very worst sort of exploitation.

14

FROM BEYOND
THE GRAVE

Lurid scenes showing the psychics supposedly making contact with the dead Princess were cut from the final version of *The Spirit of Diana* for the British Living TV audience. They contravened the regulatory guidelines to which British television channels have to adhere. However, a sequence filmed in the tunnel in Paris where the Princess died showing the clairvoyants attempting to make psychic contact with the event, remained in the programme.

In the show it was claimed that Diana was, in the afterlife, working with children while watching over her own sons from the 'other side' and that she was 'having fun' and spending time with Mother Teresa.

Specific questions were supposedly put to her. The Princess denied she was pregnant at the time of her death, but said that she had been intending to marry Dodi. According to the psychics she defended the Queen, who had been criticised at the time of her daughter-in-law's death for showing too little emotion and said that she still cared for her former husband, Prince Charles.

This was not the first claim by clairvoyants to have made contact with Diana. Messages purporting to come from the Princess appeared very shortly after her death from various sources. Some clairvoyants no doubt believe they bring comfort. People disposed to believing in spiritualism might experience feelings of reassurance from hearing messages from beyond the grave. It is a personal thing.

In the case of Diana, messages supposedly coming from her were for public consumption. Some of the mediums claiming contact spoke of seeing the Princess in heaven and watching over her sons. Others claimed to reveal secrets. In 1998 a medium called Rose Campbell believed she had had revealed to her the true meaning behind Diana's life and work.

As so often happens with channelled messages, spirit sayings are unconvincing blends of banality and religious pastiche and Rose Campbell's reportage is no exception.

'I wasn't given the choice before,' Diana is claimed to have told the medium, 'but now I can continue with my true work and make the world feel their own guilt at having poverty and war within their kingdoms and making the princes and princesses more important to the story than the paupers. There is no one more important than the paupers for they are the kingdom.'[1]

And in another message Diana talks in a similarly unconvincing way.

> I am hoping to see the gift that my children possess to make their choices to live in the fairy tale, but not in the land of make believe. To be a prince or princess is to live in the fairy tale, but that does not mean that one has to live in the land of make believe where there are no mistakes, no desires, no urges, and therefore no humanity. I was living proof that to make believe is to make mockery of the fairy tale. There is no castle that has no dragon, and if you pretend that it doesn't, then you live in the land of make believe.[2]

While such messages probably reveal little, if anything, about Diana, they reveal a lot about the post-Diana age. Judging from the interest shown in the psychic websites devoted to Diana, it would seem thousands of people believe that eight years after her death Diana is still capable of communicating with the world.

She does so in two ways: through alleged channelled messages and by new tapes and transcripts of her real conversations being leaked. Former clairvoyants and New Age therapists consulted by Diana in her lifetime continue to release information about the Princess into the public domain.

Simone Simmons was widely accused of betrayal when she published information about Diana which she claims to have been told during private conversations with the Princess. Simone is an 'energy' healer and clairvoyant who was frequently consulted by the Princess between 1993 and 1997. She claimed that Diana had confessed to using cocaine and had had an affair with John Kennedy Junior, the son of the assassinated American President.

The admission concerning John Kennedy came, Simone says, during an intimate conversation with the Princess about her need to give and receive love.

Diana and I were in her sitting room at Kensington Palace. She was wearing a pair of stylish yet comfortable beige suede ankle boots, a pair of jeans and a V-necked cashmere sweater that cost a great deal of money. We were sitting for a change on the sofa rather than on the floor when she brought up the subject . . . She had met him in New York in 1995 when he was trying to persuade her to give an interview to his magazine . . . When Kennedy arrived she was bowled over by his easy American charm and the physique he worked so hard to keep in shape. She told me, 'We started talking, one thing led to another – and we ended up in bed together. It was pure chemistry' . . . Not every woman is aware of her sexuality, and Diana really was not aware that she had any real sex appeal. With Kennedy it was different. He made her feel desirable, wanton and very womanly. It was, she admitted, a moment of pure lust – the only time in her life that she succumbed in that way. My mouth dropped open. I was so flabbergasted that for a few seconds I couldn't say anything.

Being Diana, she naturally wanted to take the relationship further. She started fantasising about what a powerful team they would make, and how, if everything went right, she could have become part of America's 'royal family' . . . When she got back to England she had John's astrological chart prepared and discovered that because he was a Sagittarius and she had Sagittarius rising, they were compatible in a number of respects, but not enough to sustain the relationship.[3]

One of the few people to back her claim was Ivan Fraser, a one-time collaborator with David Icke who runs a website dedicated to publishing the news he claims the mainstream news suppliers prefer to suppress. Fraser has himself claimed a psychic encounter with Diana. His defence of Simone gave him the opportunity to link Diana with President Kennedy and Marilyn Monroe, three people around whose deaths potent conspiracy theories have been developed. He thought Simone's claim was being discredited because she was a psychic and concluded:

Contrary to the vile media assaults on Simone, she is not an evil witch or lonely publicity-seeker, or out to make a buck by betraying the memory of Diana. She is using the book to clarify what she knows to be the truth, to dispel certain false popular rumours (such as Harry not being Charles's son), and to bring back into the public consciousness the issues that Diana was so passionate about, to resurrect the issue of landmines.

She is also donating 10% of what she makes in profit from the book to charities to help both animals and humans.[4]

There are many New Age practitioners who still proudly claim, like holders of the royal warrant, to have been 'by appointment' to Diana. Little deters them from squeezing from their past connections every current drop of publicity. Not even a proven record for having been wrong suggests caution. Diana was introduced to Penny Thornton by Sarah Ferguson. She reassured Diana that one day she would be 'allowed out' of her position 'as opposed to divorcing'. Despite having been proved wrong by events – Diana and Charles did indeed divorce – she continues to study Prince William's astrological chart.

In 2001 she described how at the time of William's birth the sun had just entered the sign of Cancer demonstrating the overriding importance of his mother in his life. William's relationship with his father, she said, suffered because of the state of his parents' marriage. And only in these last four years since Diana's death has he been able to forge the close relationship he needed with Charles.

'Only the brave astrologer sticks her neck out,' she concluded, 'and faces ridicule when none of it pans out or cynicism when it does!'

But undeterred she predicted:

William may well fall in love – and with someone who is not wholly acceptable to the Royal family; He may drop out of university. He may find himself at odds with authority; He may suffer an accident.; He may take on a much more serious role within the Royal family . . . I have long believed that he will take on the mantle of the monarchy when the Queen dies and events during the next twelve months may take us ever nearer that eventuality.[5]

Four years later it can be seen that her predications have not been impressive.

Of course astrology is not primarily about predicting the future. It is, say many practitioners, a catalyst to self-awareness and self-understanding. The one-to-one relationship with the astrologer is the means by which the client can come to a point of self-realisation.

Astrologers use the metaphor of the cosmos, and the position of the stars and heavenly bodies as a tool to understanding self and the wider cosmos.

It is interesting that no astrologer, either before the event, or with hindsight, has ever claimed that the study of the heavens was able to predict Diana's death. Some have said that with hindsight they can now see Diana as a person of cosmological significance, but there was no indication of her death and the impact it would have on the world. Like Elvis Presley, now regarded by many followers as a messiah, Diana too is described as having a favoured position within the divine scheme. In it she has been granted the status of one of the Earth's great teachers.

The American medium, Marcia McMahon claims to receive messages from Diana and in 2003 to have gone one further, to have received a communication from Christ in which he talked about Diana.

Know too, woman, that I felt as you did, burdened with a very great message! In search of how to reach the masses, while not offending those in power. Be aware then that it is always those in power who will be most offended. Their smallness next to you is even smaller. They quiver at the thought that my Beloved Princess Diana speaks to humble servants like you, and they strive to be greater than your great message! And their attempts are feeble; their words as nothing but sand in a desert battlefield. Can the grain of sand shriek at the wind as it is tossed about? No. These grains of sand, then see your power, and envy you. They have no wisdom to match Diana's and yours! Your book is full of wisdom, like you both!

And the wise are confounded, and the meek inherit the Kingdom of God! It has always been this way. My prophets they kill and cast out! Then the people hear the prophets and they rise up, and they worship them, and proclaim my prophets, God! And so goes the cycle; the teacher, the gurus, the worshipers. Earth has had many great teachers; you are now among them! Be watchful then in the days ahead for sandstorms in the desert! There are many grains moving in the wind, as these are hard times! But then the desert will bloom and your flower Diana, England's Rose will bloom again upon the Earth.

Many will hear you, then my child. Peace be with you, my peace I leave you.[6]

Marcia McMahon, despite being something of a psychic names-dropper – she is on channelling terms with Mother Teresa, Dodi Fayed and John Lennon as well as Diana and Jesus – confessed herself totally flabbergasted at being chosen to convey the message to the world.

The whole process of being able to hear from Princess Diana is absolutely astounding even to me. I am very blessed with a friend like this and so are you, the reader, blessed by her intervention into human affairs. She was a very lovely person on earth and she continues her causes from the heavens. Her message is so typically Diana; her causes are those who are suffering . . . and the future of our children, especially those underprivileged children in third world countries, world peace and world war, politics as it affects real human lives, and yet there is something about this channelled material from Diana that we don't know about. The unique spiritual wealth of information she is privileged to share with us now, insights into the afterlife, the order of universe, other universes, higher beings, saints, and God. Diana addresses Colin Powell, Tony Blair, Mr. Bush and Kofi Annan about the current world situation. Her messages have gone around the world and are being read by just those diplomats who need her solutions! This work is awesome![7]

Political leaders are quite capable of taking advice from the most unlikely sources. President Reagan listened to his wife Nancy's astrologer and Tony Blair has in Carole Caplin his own New Age adviser. However, no public admission has ever been made by any of the named world leaders that Diana speaks to them.

It is easy to dismiss Marcia McMahon as being on the crankier end of the Diana spectrum. She is of significance because she has readers and because she is not the only person making these curious and outlandish claims. There is as yet no network of Diana religious cults, there is, however, evidence of a sizeable number of individual followers of Diana behaving in a religious way towards her. Like Diana's own quest for spiritual awakening, those who search for religious meaning through Diana do so on an individual and ad hoc basis. They mix and match ideas in much the same way she did.

Is there ever likely to be a Diana religion? Religions tend not to start with well-formed doctrines and cosmologies, but grow out of followers banding together to remember a spiritual inspiration and to perform rituals. In the early days of Christianity groups of disciples met together to recall the ministry of Jesus and to break bread as he had commanded. It was three hundred years before the creeds were finalised.

Today, followers of Diana simply do things in remembrance of their Queen of Hearts. They visit places, offer flowers, write messages, meet together, share books, cherish relics, go on pilgrimage and erect shrines. These are all standard forms of expression and any attempt to define what is meant by 'religion' would contain references to all these elements.

Within months of Diana's death a Church of Diana was set up and at one time claimed 7000 followers. It was an internet church based in America and its founder Richard Yao, who retitled himself Chairman Yao, claimed that the church would teach its members to 'stay young and live longer'. The Church's Bible was called 'DianaSpeaks' in which followers were told, 'Your Princess will speak to you. She will be your angel.'

The church now appears to have been removed from the internet and it is very possible that Yao, who made it very difficult to be contacted in person at the time the church was launched, was playing an elaborate hoax.

Any church of Diana, should one ever emerge, would undoubtedly be dismissed by leaders of the mainstream churches. If not condemned as a serious heresy it would be laughed out of court as a joke. Yet it was Christian leaders who at the time of her death gave Diana her spiritual credibility. In some ways they started the whole process.

Most ministers felt they had no option but to preach about Diana on the Sunday following her death. In the mood of the moment many of them spoke of Diana in profoundly religious language. Given some of the things they said in all seriousness, it is not surprising that followers of Diana have felt permitted to seek a spirituality for themselves in Diana and to make some amazing claims.

Dr Tom Wright, now one of the Church of England's senior bishops, said that Diana's actions pointed [ironically] to an older and deeper message.

He drew a comparison between Diana and Mozart, suggesting Diana, as Mozart before her, had lived an unorthodox life, met a tragically early death and left an extraordinary legacy.

But such figures catch at our hearts not least because they remind us, if only subconsciously, of another young man, one with the tag of royalty, yet who didn't behave as royalty should; one celebrated by the masses, but deeply threatening to the establishment; one who brought healing and hope, but who was cut down, in his prime, by the forces he had challenged. To evoke this parallel is certainly not to canonise Diana. It is to explain the deepest reason for the public reaction to her life and death.[8]

He spoke of the parable of the Good Samaritan and how at a deep level of interpretation it could be said that Jesus took two roles in the story. He was the good neighbour, the man who offered help and healing, but he was also the victim, the man set upon, stripped and left for dead.

He brought the parable up to date. There was a young boy who went for a walk in a field and stepped on a landmine. It exploded and severely injured him. A politician saw him and walked by keeping his upper lip stiff. A photographer came on the scene and took pictures from every angle.

'But a young and beautiful girl came and took him in her arms and bound up his wounds. And she went to the inn-keepers and said, "Look after him; and don't put those things in your fields again." Jesus' conclusion might be Diana's last words to us, "Go and do likewise." '[9]

The rituals performed at the time of Diana's death were religious in outward appearance, involving prayer, the lighting of candles, the offering of flowers and so on; but collectively the rituals could not be said to have conformed to any recognisable religious practice. They were spontaneous and fitted the occasion. They were not rituals that could be recognised as having been drawn from any one specific doctrine of faith. The religion was there by implication and not by declaration.

The collective reaction to Diana's death was a sign of the vast reserves of 'implicit religion' lurking just below the surface of contemporary life, according to Church of England bishops.[10] But what is that religion? Can it be said to be Christian?

'The religion which Diana articulated through her words and deeds and the religion which seems to have resonated with so many of those who mourned her, was perfectly explicit,' claims Linda Woodhead. 'And although it owed a debt to Christianity, it was not Christianity in any traditional sense.'[11]

The Diana religion, suggested Woodhead, was discernable and widespread and superbly adapted to the modern age. 'It could be called a "Religion of Tender Loving Care" or a "Religion of Tender-hearted Humanitarianism" but Diana's own words suggest instead the simpler "Religion of the Heart".'

The two saints of the religion might be said to be Diana and Mother Teresa. Their lives intertwined in many ways, especially at the end through the coincidence of their deaths, and in the public's mind both women were identified with offering love to the unloved.

Diana's vision however focused on the sacredness of the human, Mother Teresa's vision was centred on a transcendent God incarnate in Jesus. As Linda Woodhead puts it, 'Where Diana looked within to find God, Mother Teresa looked up; where Diana saw human loveliness, Mother Teresa saw sinful humanity; and where Diana saw uniquely valuable human beings, Mother Teresa saw Christ.'[12]

Mother Teresa's model of charity was one of paternalism. God the Father providing for the needs of his children. Diana's model was of one suffering human offering love to another. When in Africa photographers asked to show Diana handing out food to children. She objected saying it patronised the children and endorsed the 'begging bowl' image of Africa.

That Christ was at the centre of Mother Teresa's life and work is unmistakeable. She was also willing to remain obedient to the institution she had joined. Independent and opinionated, a radical pioneer, but never would she have wanted to step outside the protection or authority of the church.

By contrast, Diana was eventually to defy the institution she had joined. She became independent and opinionated and a radical pioneer. In the end she was impelled to step outside the protection of the royal family and forfeit her status as a member.

It could be unkindly said that Diana was not Christ-centred, but self-centred. Her heavy employment of New Age therapists to discover and pamper her inner-self suggests this most strongly. Woodhead however suggests that for Diana, her self-absorption was an integral part of her capacity to give love to others.

> It was necessary to love self in order to love others; it was necessary to love others, and to be loved by others, in order to fulfil self. Diana's Religion of the Heart was not simply a religion of self: it was a religion of loving kindness directed to all needy human beings, self and others.[13]

It contained echoes of Christianity's second command-ment of Christ to love one's neighbour as oneself, but it omitted the first of those commandments, to love God. Instead it took love as a human emotion, focusing on warm, tender, emotional and reciprocal love. Heart love has 'little to do with the head and even less to do with rules or with duty'.[14]

Heart love is to do with self-empowerment and intuition. It does not require learning or education; indeed the lack of either is viewed as its virtue. It is a proud declaration of the principle of 'dumbing down'. As a set of ideas it would never attract endorsement from academic or social elites. It lays no claim to structure or logic. It is proud of its irrationality. There are no hierarchies and anyone, whatever their back-ground, class, gender, training or ethnic group, it is claimed, is able to demonstrate heart love. It is a natural human instinct. In these terms, the Religion of the Heart has an immediate appeal to those in society who have previously felt marginalised. Furthermore, in another rebuff to the leaders of institutionalised religion, those who practise the Religion of the Heart are open, indeed encouraged, to admit to and share their own uncertainties and fallibilities.

Again the admission of failure is turned on its head and deemed a virtue. 'It seems to have been precisely her willingness to admit failures, embarrassments, vulnerability and humiliations which made many people love, admire and even revere Diana.'[15]

The Diana Religion of the Heart has been described as a religion of empty sentiment, devoid of intellectual content. Insofar as it does have a metaphysical stance it is fluid and imprecise. 'It can take either a theistic form, in which the ultimate value of the human is inscribed by its creator, or a non-Theistic, New Age, form in which the human is seen as participating in the divine.'[16]

It raises an age-old question: is God outside and separate from, or is God the divine light within each human being? Diana would never have formulated that question in her own mind, but in her words and deeds appeared to provide an answer. He could be said to be both. And within the context of the Religion of the Heart, what is wrong with holding contradictory views?

While the Religion of the Heart has no teachings or dogma it has certain tendencies. Followers tend to believe, for instance, in the afterlife. Several tributes to Diana talk about her watching over the earth from heaven and some assume she has an ability to hear the petitions of the faithful. The tribute imagery is drawn from Christianity, with Diana frequently cast in the role of an angel.

The modern Western world is characterised by the operation of the market economy and the practice of democracy. The Diana Religion of the Heart meshes well with both social forces.

It fits with the market economy by being fully compatible with . . . 'spiritual shopping' rather than asceticism or self-sacrifice. And it fits with democracy through its hostility towards authorities . . . And its empowerment of each individual in his or her ordinariness and 'humanity' . . . Through its sacralisation of the sphere of intimate and domestic relationship the Religion of the Heart fits well with the process . . . Whereby religion's sphere of activity shrinks from the public . . . to the private.

Diana acted as a sort of magnifying glass of popular tastes and trends, of commonly held beliefs and widely cherished ideals.[17]

A further underlying text can be read into this argument. The sphere of intimate and domestic relations is also the territory of the feminine. A challenge to institutionalised religion is also a challenge to notions that God is masculine.

'The realm of the mythic or sacred arguably provides the power source for Diana Spencer's remarkable interaction with a global public and with history', wrote Jane Caputi. She pointed out that

. . . an extensive resonance exists between the ancient myth of the Goddess Diana and the myth unfolding around the Princess. Popular response to Diana is often dismissed as media manipulation, but it represents an oral tradition . . . Many ancient Goddess traditions, like that of Diana, are antecedents of contemporary ideas of the . . . sovereign female subject, both human and divine. The turning of Princess Diana into a modern myth reflects a yearning for a return of female divinity.[18]

With a commitment to the feminine aspects of the spiritual, as implied in the Religion of the Heart, comes a potential sea change in society. Replacing masculine values of competition, achievement, speed, physical power with compassion, tolerance, nurturance, community, and being one's true self.

When Princess Diana died more women responded than men. There were more female names than male names signing the cards at Kensington Palace. Internet chatrooms were visited significantly more often by women than men. Women rather than men were giving free rein to their emotions.

Hostility to what some described as media over-kill tended to be expressed by men. There was one American discussion forum called, 'I Don't Give A Rat's Ass About The Death Of Diana!' and three quarters of the comments recorded came from men.

Was this because women sensed the blow Diana had been striking for feminism in her life, or was it because Diana had talked so often and publicly about her personal life that many women felt as if they had been her confidante – the female friends with whom she shared her worries over coffee and who had also experienced problems with husbands, lovers, in-laws, children and dieting?

It is interesting to note that in the last quarter of the twentieth-century Britain produced two remarkable women who went on to command a world stage. Diana, Princess of Wales and Margaret Thatcher, British Conservative Prime Minister. Both were powerful women, but they selected radically different routes. Diana appealed to the feminine, caring side of the human condition. Lady Thatcher became an honorary man, more forceful and masculine than any modern man might dare to be. Diana was the Queen of Hearts. Margaret Thatcher was the Iron Lady. What is remarkable is that while both lived in the same country, indeed the same city at the same time for sixteen years, the two women's paths seldom crossed. They were both fantasy figures and the subject of dreams and nightmares. They were the zeitgeist of the nation. Yet in Andrew Morton's authorised account of Diana's life there is just one passing reference to Mrs Thatcher and in the lengthy volume Lady Thatcher wrote about her premiership, Diana receives not a single mention. Nothing of the influence Diana was having on the British nation during her time at Downing Street appears to have been noticed by Lady Thatcher or considered by her to have been of any importance. They undoubtedly attended many of the same state events and throughout the 1980s the two women dominated public life, and yet they appear to have had absolutely nothing in common. One can imagine Lady Thatcher giving the Religion of the Heart short shrift.

In the early days of New Labour, many of the characteristics of the Religion of the Heart became respectable. New men were encouraged to play a full role in child rearing. Admitting to weaknesses and apologising for mistakes became acceptable. Indeed it evolved into a political tactic that Tony Blair mastered to perfection. He successfully rode the anti-Thatcher tide. She had been in power long enough. The electorate wanted a change. A change not just in personalities, but political style as well, although policies stayed much the same.

It could be said that Diana only truly emerged in her confident guise once Mrs Thatcher had departed the political arena. It was John Major as Prime Minister who announced the separation of the Prince and Princess, and Tony Blair who captured the mood on the day Diana died by talking of 'the People's Princess'.

'The departure of both Thatcher and Diana does leave a huge vacuum,' said Anthony Sampson, author of *The Anatomy of Britain* series of classic portraits of the British political scene.

'Blair now stands as the one person able to fill that vacuum,' wrote American commentator Dan Balz. 'But even people close to Blair argue that this is not a role any politician can easily play. Diana "was the new Britain", one Blair adviser said. "There is not a politician who can fill that role. From that point of view, it's a great loss." '[19]

Yet is the Religion of the Heart solely a phenomenon of the present age? Arguably there have been forerunners, one of special relevance due to the coincidence of name. Two thousand years ago there existed a religion devoted to Diana of the Ephesians.

Diana, or Artemis, in the Ephesian context, is best known today through the involvement of Paul and Timothy in the New Testament accounts.

'Ephesus might seem to be the showcase church of the New Testament', wrote Professor Eugene Peterson. 'It was a missionary church established by the eloquent and learned Jewish preacher Apollos.[20] Paul stopped to visit this fledgling Christian community on his second missionary journey.'[21]

'We don't know exactly what went wrong with the Ephesian church; nothing is spelled out. What is clear is that the religion of the culture had overturned the gospel. The gospel.'

What resulted, it is suggested, is that the Christian congregation turned to a form of gnosticism; the cultural values of the society around seeped back into the church.

'In 1997 we had a remarkable encounter with this old Ephesian stuff,' Professor Peterson maintains.

Diana was the perfect goddess for a religion that didn't want anything to do with the God and Father of our Lord Jesus Christ, but was desperate to worship someone or something . . . In Edinburgh I watched long lines of men and women carrying bouquets of flowers to place on appointed shrines throughout the city. They were silent and weeping, unutterably moved by the death of their goddess. I read the meditations on Diana in the daily newspapers.

I'm not suggesting that the Diana cult of Ephesus and the Diana cult of 1997 have the same content, but the effect is the same. The Ephesian Diana cult, a pastiche of stories, superstitions and systems of thought endemic to the ancient East, served the city's religious needs. The recent Diana cult is also a pastiche of stories and longings and public relations efforts that serves the religious needs of an astounding number of people. Her death brought into the open just how wide her influence extended. Diana evoked the best of people – but only the best of what they want for themselves, not of what God wants.[22]

Only one event since 1997 has matched the death of Diana as a pan-national 'where were you when you heard?' event: the destruction of New York's twin towers.

Like the death of Diana the world went into shock. The news media became saturated with the one story. Conspiracy theories of all kinds were born. Heroes and villains emerged. There was however one difference. Diana's death elicited the Religion of the Heart response. The fall of the towers triggered a call for vengeance. The war on terror was declared and troops mobilised to invade Iraq. The conservative right in the USA interpreted events in apocalyptic terms: Biblical prophecies were being fulfilled; the day of judgement was at hand.

The Religion of the Heart has no such eschatological doctrine. It is a here-and-now practice with no concept of God's wrath. Any examination of the future of the Religion of the Heart, any thought of a Diana spirituality surviving, needs to consider the post 9/11 world climate. It was the event that turned the Blair government on its head. From its early position appearing as a new sensitive party, in tune with people's feelings and needs, it became the loyal ally of a conservative American president intent on waging war. Masculine values were reasserted and the 'touchy-feely' world of Diana seemed out of tune with the age.

Again, encouraged by Diana's own interest and example astrologers have made similar observations on the feminine influence of the Princess on world affairs, but coming of course from a very different direction.

Reviewing her birth chart the Goddess-astrology website described how Princess Diana manifested the energies of the feminine planets and asteroids.

Artemis, the Greek goddess of the Moon, was named Diana in the Roman mythology. Goddess of the hunt and of the hunted . . . Lady Diana exhibited the qualities of her namesake. As the hunter, she persisted in her quest to better the world for those less fortunate. As the quarry, she led photographers and reporters on a chase around the world . . . Her life was closely tied to the moon's phases. Some major events of her life occurred during eclipses: her marriage, the birth of her William, and her death.

Ceres represents motherhood and nutrition, both of which were focal points for the Princess. One of Diana's most important duties, according to her in-laws and royal tradition, was to produce heirs for the throne. Her fertility was an important factor in her being chosen by the royal family as a mate for the prince, although she was also required to be a virgin bride. A Cancer, Diana was drawn to children and worked in a day-care centre before her marriage and the birth of her two sons. Diana struggled with nutrition for a long time. Her bulimia was very public, but she eventually recovered and learned to nourish herself.[23]

To quote from an astrological source is not to endorse the practice, be it art or science. It is to illustrate two points. The first, that a huge interest in Diana survives among that New Age subculture which exists just below the horizon of mainstream debate, but that can claim substantial popular support. And second, that the growth in this subculture, and the fact that it is no longer a marginalised and taboo area of interest, can be attributed in part to Diana. She endorsed the ideas and spoke the language of the New Age.

A poll conducted in 2000 examined religious beliefs in Britain and how they had changed since 1980. The period coincided almost exactly with the two Diana decades. The results highlighted a gradual reduction in a belief in the personal God of Christianity, but this did not simultaneously show a growth in total disbelief. Only 8 per cent, a small minority of people declared themselves to be 'convinced atheists'. Many expressed faith that science would help mankind, but they did not think science was capable of explaining the mysteries of life. On the contrary, the movement was in the opposite direction. The survey demonstrated very clearly that there had been a significant rise in the number of people who classified themselves as being 'spiritual', as opposed to being 'religious'.

Many people, the survey indicated, had a wide spectrum of beliefs, the majority of which encompassed historic Christian teachings, but which included such ideas as reincarnation taken from Eastern religions.

The survey showed that claims to have had spiritual experiences were not on the wane as many might have predicted. They were, if anything, on the increase.

> Yet whilst people hold these beliefs, they do not necessarily want to be labelled 'religious' and even less do they associate themselves with a particular denomination. Only 9 per cent of the population believe that they have the only path to God. Two thirds believe either that all religions offer a path to God, or that there is a way to God outside organised religions.[24]

While there had been a decline in church attendance, confirmed by the survey, 'people are discovering a spiritual side to their lives, so much that they declare prayer to be the most important of all their spiritual experiences'.[25]

It is an undoubted trend that increasingly people believe in the spiritual realm without wishing to commit themselves to a religious institution. Professor Grace Davie uses the phrase 'believing without belonging' to describe the phenomenon. Not that this is a pattern of behaviour unique to religion. Believing without belonging characterises the involvement of people in a range of other non-religious activities. There is for instance no major reduction in interest in politics, but there is a marked reduction in membership of political parties across Britain.

In church terms this trend need not spell terminal decline for faith in Britain, it simply presents new challenges.

'Those that minister to a half-believing rather than unbelieving society will find that there are advantages and disadvantages to this situation,' Professor Davie told a Bishops' Conference in 2002. 'Working out appropriate ministerial strategies for this continually shifting and ill-defined context is the central and very demanding task of the religious professional. A firm and necessary grasp of the sociological realities is but the starting point.'[26]

Examining the details of the changes underway in society throws up some unexpected findings. Traditional church-going normally attracts the old rather than the young. However European surveys quoted by Professor Davie suggest that where institutionalised religion is in greatest decline,

. . . the relative confidence among the young that there is something (not very specific) after death and that the tendency to believe in an afterlife is increasing rather than decreasing. They also reveal the predilection of the young for an immanent rather than transcendent understanding of God (God is inside each person, rather than external).

With this in mind, the future becomes extremely difficult to predict. What seems unlikely, however, is the emergence of a society in which secular rationalism becomes the overriding norm.[27]

Measurements of church attendance measure only the tip of

the religious iceberg. The hidden iceberg beneath the waves represents a great mass of unseen belief.

It only becomes visible, it could be argued, at specific and significant moments, such as the death of Princess Diana. These were times when, not only did latent spirituality emerge into view, but the church institutions rediscovered a role. Cathedrals and parish churches around the country became places were flowers were laid and books of condolence opened. And at the heart of her funeral rite was the ancient abbey at Westminster. Its Dean and Chapter were the impresarios for that unique blend of high liturgy and popular culture devised to mourn the loss of a beautiful young woman and celebrate her extraordinary life.

> The churches became an important, though not the only, gathering point for a wide variety of individual gestures of mourning in which Christian and less Christian symbols became inextricably mixed, both materially (candles, playing cards and Madonnas) and theologically (life after death was strongly affirmed, but with no notion of judgment). More significant, however, was an awareness in the population as a whole that multiple and well-intentioned gestures of individual mourning were inadequate in themselves to mark the end of this particular life (as indeed of any other). Hence the need for public ritual or public liturgy (in other words a funeral) and where else but in the established church.[28]

Under normal circumstances the established, historic, churches might feel they are losing their influence and certainly their capacity to lead and shape the religious thinking of large sections of the population. People today, especially the young, prefer to shop at a religious supermarket of ideas, reverting to the traditional brands only on rare occasions.

There is a shift, Professor Davie notes, from an understanding of religion as a form of obligation to an increasing emphasis on consumption.

> I go to church (or to another religious organization) because I want to, maybe for a short period or maybe for longer, to fulfil a particular rather than a general need in my life and where I will continue my attachment so long as it provides what I want, but I have no obligation either to attend in the first place or to continue if I don't want to.[29]

Diana was indeed the epitome of the spiritual shopper. But, to what extent did Diana's promulgation of New Age spirituality shape the trends of the age? Or was she simply reflecting them? It is not possible to say.

However, as a result of her support for unconventional spirituality, she became and continues to be the target of fierce attack from those who believe they are defending orthodox Christianity.

While leading Anglicans identified Christ-like qualities in the Princess, those on the more intolerant outer-edge of evangelicalism went so far as to suggest her death was a form of divine retribution, for her lax lifestyle, her New Age beliefs and, in the end, for forming a romantic relationship with a Muslim. The three suggested causes of God's wrath were brought together by one Australian internet ministry.

> Diana was an approachable God, who didn't demand repentance or exhibit holiness . . .

> Diana was an icon of the humanists' goddess, exquisite, glamorous, New Age in every way, kind and gentle . . .

> Diana was able to live life to the full with all its naughty little pleasures, and her wealth was mind-boggling.

> God surely removed this woman, as she would have

married a Muslim and become a Muslim . . . She who is
the mother of the Prince who is the heir to the throne of
Great Britain . . . Would there have been pressure to
teach William and Harry the Islamic religion? Diana
stood for every New Age concept of these latter days.
She was a champion for interfaith, New Age mediums
and astrologers, New Age alternative medical treatments,
she wanted unity and 'peace' in a New Age world.

Diana's death showed that she was mortal, a mere
human being after all. The devastation of the sudden
discovery of this fact – over-night the goddess has
fallen, dead – had left an awful black hole in the lives
of the godless! Yet, she lives on! Satan will make her live
on, as an object of worship and awe she is larger than
life![30]

Again to quote is not to endorse, but the above Christian
quote makes the same point as the quote on page 241 from
the astrologer. Diana lives, whether as goddess or demon, in
the minds of thousands whose ideas inhabit a realm of
thinking, scholarship, interest and polemic outside the
normal boundaries of mainstream theological discourse.

Yet increasingly it is mainstream theological discourse that
is becoming marginalised, claims one Anglican cleric. The
Reverend Chris Chivers is Canon-chancellor of Blackburn
Cathedral and recently described a chasm existing between
the doctrinal centre in the main world faiths and the fringes
of faith.

The so-called religion of the fringes – often disparagingly
dismissed as spirituality of folk religion: the flowers and
teddy-bears left at roadside shrines, the self-help
volumes that fill the 'mind, body and spirit' sections of
our bookshops – this is actually now the predominant
form that religion of any kind is taking.[31]

Is it therefore possible, or even likely, that over the coming decades the religion of the fringes will become the new orthodoxy. And if it does, what will unite the disparate elements? What, or who will provide its focus?

15

LONG LIVE DIANA

Is the story of Diana now over? The Prince of Wales and the Duchess of Cornwall are married. The two Princes have completed their education. In both cases they agreed to follow royal precedent and undergo military training as officer cadets at Sandhurst.

In August 2007 the tenth anniversary of Diana's death will be recalled. What will the mood of the nation be? Will the shadow she has cast over the House of Windsor for twenty-five years have faded?

It is tempting to suppose that every attempt will be made by royal officials to use the occasion of the anniversary to draw the final line under the Diana saga. There will be a desire to view the occasion as the end of an era.

An attempt to 'achieve closure', to quote Patrick Jephson, has been made before, notably when the Queen and the royal family stood alongside the Spencer family at the ceremony to mark the opening of the memorial fountain. But on that occasion a combination of public unwillingness and engineering mishaps thwarted the plan.

'The sadness in the hearts of the people will take longer to fade', Jephson wrote at the time. 'This may, I fear, exasperate

248

any anti-Di diehards who hope the ceremony will nail the lid on her coffin once and for all.'[1]

For twenty-five years, Diana as bride, wife, mother, charity worker, fashion symbol, icon, will have dominated the affairs of the 'family business'. Of course, the two Princes and many thousands of their grandmother's subjects will, on 31 August, remember the Princess with sorrow, but the royal establishment will be looking for signs that the notorious 'loose cannon' in their midst will have been finally stilled. They will hope sincerely that the fickleness of the general public, combined with short-term memory, will have consigned Diana to history.

They will hope that in due course Diana will be of little more consequence than Queen Alexandra is today. In her lifetime she did much good charitable work and she attracted considerable sympathy as the wife of another Prince of Wales who was a notoriously unfaithful husband. But in less than a hundred years she has become a footnote in history.

It will be accepted that there will remain a hardcore of devotees who will never forget Diana. The anniversary ceremonies may continue, albeit on a small scale, for generations. It should not be forgotten that devotion to King Charles the Martyr, beheaded in 1649, has not faded after three and a half centuries. Every January he is recalled in ritual and prayer. His possessions are venerated as relics and there are even churches dedicated to him as a saint.

There is every reason to suppose that in the year 2350 people will still be gathering at the gates of Kensington Palace to lay posies of flowers.

But how big will that faithful band of devotees be? As the third millennium unfolds, will Diana retain her wider following? Will churches of Diana be created as some have fancifully speculated? Will all future members of the royal family be judged against standards set by an idealised Diana? The answers to those questions depend on at least five, unknown factors.

First, how long will it be before Charles is crowned King?

The signs are that the Queen will have the health and longevity of her mother and Charles may ascend the throne as an octogenarian, if at all. By then there will be few people left to care whether he is accompanied to his coronation by 'Queen Camilla'. It will be assumed the reign will be short and all eyes will be on the new heir, Prince William. In this scenario, King William V will, at his coronation, be older than his mother was when she died. He will be crowned in the abbey where his mother's funeral was held. Diana will be much spoken about and questions will be asked, especially this one: Has William developed the mannerisms and concerns of his mother? Does he, in appearance and style, resemble his mother?

He is today a tall and good-looking young man who has inherited characteristics from his mother and the Windsor family. When, in the interview he gave to mark his twenty-first birthday, he talked of his future destiny as King, he used words and phrases learned, so to speak, at his paternal grandmother's knee.

> All these questions about do you want to be king? It's not a question of wanting to be, it's something I was born into and it's my duty. Wanting is not the right word. But those stories about me not wanting to be king are all wrong. It's a very important role and it's one that I don't take lightly.

> The monarchy is something that needs to be there. I just feel it's very, very important, it's a form of stability and I hope to be able to continue that.

His mother's influence too was there. She had been careful in her lifetime to offer her sons a broader and warmer upbringing than the one she and their father had experienced. 'I want to bring them up with security . . . I hug my children to death . . . I always feed them love and affection, it's so important.'[2]

'My guiding principles are to be honest, genuine, thoughtful and caring,' William said on coming of age. He described how he had been greatly influenced by his visits to homeless hostels as a teenager with his mother.

'I learned a lot from it, more so now than I did at the time. My mother used her position very well to help other people, as does my father, and I hope to do the same.'[3]

It must be hard on the young Prince to know that his parents are not only his to love in life or memory, but public property as well. As well as the mother he and his brother recall and mourn, there is another Diana, the mythical one. 'Of all the unfair cards . . . they have been dealt,' observed Patrick Jephson, 'the knowledge that their mother, the People's Princess, is now in the people's possession must be one of the hardest to contemplate.'[4]

Prince William will know too that he is bound up in the fantasies and expectations of those who have taken possession of his mother's memory.

Prince William, whose name is William Arthur, was born on the summer solstice; if he were to follow the ancient custom of kings using their second name, he would become King Arthur. Thus through Diana, the ancient British royal bloodline would be restored to power, with a new King Arthur.[5]

The position might be rather different if by some unexpected turn of fate his brother Harry becomes King. Both Kings George V and V1 in the last century were second sons and it is not rare for the 'spare' to succeed and not the 'heir'. Prince Harry does not look as much like his mother as his elder brother William does. As a young man he has not had a good start on the public relations front having been caught up in the unfortunate incident of the Nazi uniform. He had to make a public apology after he chose to go to a fancy dress party wearing a German Second World War outfit complete with swastika armband. To make matters worse, the incident happened on the sixtieth anniversary of the liberation of Auschwitz. 'I am sorry if I offended anybody. I'd like to put it in the past now,' he said in his twenty-first birthday interview. He appeared to want to make amends and talked in the interview of carrying on his mother's work by helping orphans in Lesotho.

The second unknown factor is much broader. The world will change over the coming years in ways that cannot at present be anticipated. In all probability the catalyst for change will be global warming. This will trigger social and economic problems of great magnitude. A high-cost British royal family, still steeped in the values of privilege and empire, might be among the first disposable 'luxuries' on the agenda. In such a climate of reform and frugality the simple human-scale model of royalty as practised by Diana might be the attractive replacement. Again much will depend on Prince William and his inclinations.

The early signs are mixed. Unlike his father at the same age, when William went to university he declined to be served by a valet or chauffeur. He shared a flat in St Andrews with three other students, shopped at the supermarket and cycled around town. By and large the media respected his private life, although he could never be entirely off-guard.

He has opted not to use the title His Royal Highness, explaining, 'I don't want all the formalities because they're not needed for the time being.' Perhaps he is also mindful of the way his mother was deprived of the title. In the interviews he gave at the time of his twenty-first birthday he wore jeans and a casual shirt.

However he cannot ever hope to live an ordinary life. He needs police protection and is destined for a life of public scrutiny. 'There's been a lot of speculation about every single girl I'm with and it actually does quite irritate me after a while, more so because it's a complete pain for the girls . . . I don't want to put them in an awkward situation because a lot of people don't quite understand what comes with knowing me.'[6]

Because of the gossip and intrusion he will have to fall back on the protection of the royal palaces and court if he is to enjoy any form of privacy. This will distance him from real life and the signs are there already that he takes his pleasures from such activities as polo and throwing extravagant parties for rich friends. His brother found himself in deep trouble over the Nazi costume incident, demonstrating that he was not sufficiently in touch with the feelings of most ordinary people to realise that his choice was in serious bad taste. Prince William's continuing education for his future role will include a range of short work attachments specially designed for him. He has already completed work experience in London's financial centre and with a mountain rescue team.

Not many young men have their coming of age celebrated with the issue of a special coin, a £1,000 face-value gold piece, of which twenty-one were minted to be sold for £14,500 each; or with a poem by the Poet Laureate. Andrew Motion marked Prince William's twenty-first birthday with a rap and a sonnet.

The sonnet ended with the wish:

. . . that you'll be free to claim your life
While destiny connects with who you are
A prince and yet familiar common clay;
Your father's heir but true to your own faith;
A mother's son and silvered by her star.

Third, there could be a revival of religion in Britain. Around the world there is ample evidence of a younger generation turning to spiritual answers to the fundamental questions about the meaning and purpose of life. Whether it is the Christianity of the Bible belt in America or Islam in the Middle East, religious practice is on the increase. Should that interest in religion take a new form, and be one focused on the feminine attributes of God, an iconised Diana might have a prominent role to play. This is not to say that a sizeable

Church of Diana will become established, or that she will become canonised by the Christian Church, only that her example might be taken as an inspiration by those seeking to explore their softer spiritual natures. Concurrently there might also be an anti-Diana backlash triggered by the orthodox faiths. She has already been demonised by several conservative Christian organisations aghast at her support for New Age practices and at the way new spiritual movements draw support from her example.

This is typical of several Christian websites commenting on Diana.

> The flowers thrown at the cars after Diana's Westminster Abbey memorial were in honour of a goddess figure, not the Lord Jesus Christ. This was in response to that deceptive service at the abbey. The goddess worship alone was enough to bring the wrath of the Almighty on London! People indeed are standing at the crossroads of something immense. Choose Christ and His Sacrifice, or choose the beautiful face of evil . . . and the Goddess worship of the New Age.

> Now, there is an island shrine to the Goddess Diana . . . The very atmosphere of this world is so evil, so seductive that it cannot be long before the Church of the Lord Jesus Christ is Raptured.[7]

Fourth, new and titillating information, or speculation, about Diana might emerge. The American security forces hold a large file on her. Under the Freedom of Information Act some of the material it contains might be prized into the public domain. More former employees might write memoirs. Other 'secrets' might emerge which would reflect badly on Prince Charles or other members of the royal family.

There are also undoubtedly new revelations to be made about Diana. Her former butler, Paul Burrell, hinted strongly that he had a further secret he was not yet ready to reveal. If he is withholding a royal equivalent of the third Fatima revelation, might it be because it does not reflect well on his former employer? If at any time the rumour, which spread at the time of her death, should be confirmed that Diana was pregnant with Dodi's child, this would rebound both on Diana's reputation and the House of Windsor, for it would fuel the conspiracy theories that she was murdered by the royal family to avoid the possibility of the future King having a Muslim brother.

The fifth factor however, linked as it might be to the fourth, presents the most immediate threat and could herald a rapid upsurge of sympathy for the dead Princess of Wales. It is the publication of the official enquiry into the circumstances of the accident in Paris. Those who have prejudged the issue and have signed up to one or more of the conspiracy theories will not be convinced by anything other than a confirmation of their own entrenched position. But, when the official findings are published, should anything be said which could be construed by a reasonable, fair-minded citizen to in any way give credence to the suggestion that Diana's death, and the deaths of Dodi al-Fayed and Henri Paul were the consequence of anything other than a tragic accident, the consequences for the Windsor family will be huge. At best there might be a call for Prince Charles to be bypassed as heir and for Diana's son William to succeed to the throne on the death or abdication of the Queen. At worst it could be the end of the monarchy in Britain and signal a public demand for a republic or some style of British equivalent.

Some sections of the mainstream British press mirror the internet obsession with the conspiracy theory. The *Daily Express* in particular has been stirring the pot of rumour.

'Police cannot rule out murder' was the front page headline on 23 May 2005. The story beneath was pretty thin, quoting senior police officers saying they could not disprove the welter of conspiracy theories. On page five the paper claims that one of the key areas of concern among the police officers investigating the crash was the suggestion that the driver, Henri Paul, regularly worked for MI5 and MI6.

In September 2005 the paper was focusing on the rumours that Diana was pregnant at the time of the crash. 'British authorities ordered Princess Diana's body to be embalmed illegally to prevent tests revealing whether she was pregnant, the *Daily Express* has learned.'

By October, the newspaper was telling readers that Diana and Dodi were secretly planning to marry. This, it was hinted, was the surprise announcement the Princess had been promising the press corps shortly before she died.

There is much conjecture, but there are few facts. And if the past is an enigma, what of the future? It is unknown, but all things are possible.

The least likely sequence of events is that none of the above will occur. Diana will stubbornly refuse to fade from memory. The Diana story is far from over, but in keeping with the character and style of Diana, Princess of Wales herself, what will happen next defies prediction.

NOTES

1: The improbable myth

1. Camilla opted on marriage not to be known as the Princess of Wales.
2. Pierre Delooz, 'Towards a sociological Study of Canonised Sainthood in the Catholic Church' in Stephen Wilson ed., *Saints and their Cults: Studies in Religious Sociology, Folklore and History* (Cambridge University Press, 1983), p. 195.
3. www.princess-diana.com
4. November 2005.
5. Rayelan Allan, *Diana, Queen of Heaven*, Chapter One (self published).
6. Mary Ratcliffe, extract from poem 'Diana, carve her name with pride' written for eighth anniversary of Diana's death.

2: The disappointing daughter

1. Max Riddington and Gavan Naden, *Frances* (Michael O'Mara Books, 2003), p. 42.
2. ibid., p. 43.

3. ibid., p. 23.
4. ibid., p. 25.
5. Lady Colin Campbell, *Diana in Private* (GK Hall, 1993), p. 57.
6. ibid., pp. 58–59.
7. Andrew Morton, *Diana: Her True Story in Her Own Words* (Michael O'Mara Books, 1998), p. 24.
8. Robert Lacey, *Princess* (Times Books, 1982), p. 11.
9. Lady Colin Campbell, *Diana in Private* (GK Hall, 1993), p. 63.
10. Andrew Morton, *Diana: Her True Story in Her Own Words* (Michael O'Mara Books, 1998), p. 34.
11. BBC Television, 20 November 1995.
12. Lady Colin Campbell, *Diana in Private* (GK Hall, 1993), p. 125.
13. Lord Blake.
14. Archbishop's chaplain, later Bishop of London who attended the Princess in death and sat with her body through the night before her funeral.
15. Humphrey Carpenter, *Robert Runcie* (Hodder and Stoughton, 1996), p. 223.
16. Andrew Morton, *Diana: Her True Story in Her Own Words* (Michael O'Mara Books, 1998), pp. 40–41.
17. BBC Television, 20 November 1995.
18. W. F. Deedes, *Brief Lives* (Pan, 2004), p. 68.
19. Jonathan Dimbleby, *The Prince of Wales* (Warner Books, 1994), p. 220.
20. Tim Miles, newstip@globefl.com
21. Hugo Vickers, *Elizabeth the Queen Mother* (Hutchinson, 2005), p. 423.
22. Gyles Brandreth, *Philip and Elizabeth: Portrait of a Marriage* (Century, 2004), p. 406.
23. Andrew Morton, *Diana: Her True Story in Her Own Words* (Michael O'Mara Books, 1998), pp. 35–36.
24. Jonathan Dimbleby, *The Prince of Wales* (Warner Books, 1994), p. 348.
25. ibid.

26. Hugo Vickers, *Elizabeth the Queen Mother* (Hutchinson, 2005), p. 424.
27. Andrew Morton, *Diana: Her True Story in Her Own Words* (Michael O'Mara Books, 1998), p. 42.
28. ibid.

3: Magic and mystery

1. BBC Television, *Panorama*, 20 November 1995.
2. Jeffrey Richard, *Diana: The Making of a Media Saint* (I. B. Tauris, 1999), p. 63.
3. A. N. Wilson, *The Rise and Fall of the House of Windsor* (Sinclair-Stephenson, 1993), p. 41.
4. Piers Morgan, *The Insider* (Ebury Press, 2005), p. 153.
5. BBC Television, *Panorama*, 20 November 1995.
6. Andrew Morton, *Diana: Her True Story in Her Own Words* (Michael O'Mara, 1998), p. 57.
7. Jonathan Dimbleby, *The Prince of Wales* (Warner Books, 1994), p. 359.
8. W. F. Deedes, *Brief Lives* (Pan, 2004), p. 69.
9. BBC Television, *Panorama*, 20 November 1995.
10. A. N. Wilson, *The Rise and Fall of the House of Windsor* (Sinclair-Stephenson, 1993), p. 42.
11. Ian Bradley, *God Save the Queen* (Darton Longman and Todd, 2002), p. 68.
12. *National Examiner*, January 1996.
13. Andrew Morton, *Diana: Her True Story in Her Own Words* (Michael O'Mara, 1998), p. 65.
14. Nicholas Davies, *The Princess who Changed the World* (Blake, 1997), p. 13.
15. Ted Harrison, *Defender of the Faith* (Harper Collins, 1996), p. 105.
16. Private letter, now in public domain.
17. Ian Bradley, *God Save the Queen* (Darton Longman and Todd, 2002), p. 48.
18. G. Bennett and A. Rowbottom, *Born a Lady, Died a Saint* (Fabula, 1998), p. 208.
19. Robert Lacey, *Princess* (Times Books, 1982), p. 21.

20. Liturgy of the Coronation – the words of the Archbishop of Canterbury.
21. Robert Lacey, *Princess* (Times Books, 1982), p. 1.
22. ibid., p. 1.
23. ibid., p. 24.
24. Lady Colin Campbell, *Diana in Private* (GK Hall, 1992), p. 194.
25. Sir James Frazer, *The Golden Bough* (Macmillan, 1922), p. 347.
26. Jonathan Dimbleby, *The Prince of Wales* (Warner Books, 1994), pp. 590–91.

4: The wounded healer

1. BBC Television, *Panorama*, 20 November 1995.
2. Andrew Morton, *Diana: Her True Story in Her Own Words* (Michael O'Mara Books, 1998), p. 46.
3. BBC Television, *Panorama*, 20 November 1995.
4. Andrew Morton, *Diana: Her True Story in Her Own Words* (Michael O'Mara Books, 1998), p. 51.
5. Nigel Dempster and Peter Evans, *Behind Palace Doors* (Orion, 1993), p. 148.
6. www.royalarchive.com
7. *James Hewitt: Under Hypnosis*, Channel Five, 22 September 2005.
8. Letter, Prince Charles to Lord Lewin, 1982.
9. Jonathan Dimbleby, *The Prince of Wales* (Warner Books, 1995), pp. 463–64.
10. Andrew Morton, *Diana: Her True Story in Her Own Words* (Michael O'Mara Books, 1998), pp. 143–44.
11. Jeffrey Richard, 'The Hollywoodisation of Diana', in *Diana: The Making of a Media Saint* (I. B. Tauris, 1999), p. 59.
12. Arthur Edwards, Q and A, BBC Online.
13. ibid.
14. W. F. Deedes, *Brief Lives* (Pan, 2005), p. 67.
15. Gyles Brandreth, *Philip and Elizabeth: Portrait of a Marriage* (Century, 2004), p. 411.

16. ibid., pp. 410–11.
17. Hugo Vickers, *Elizabeth the Queen Mother* (Hutchinson, 2005), pp. 471–72.
18. Andrew Morton, *Diana: Her True Story in Her Own Words* (Michael O'Mara Books, 1998), p. 150.
19. ibid., p. 179.
20. Piers Morgan, *The Insider* (Ebury Press, 2005), p. 162.
21. Andrew Morton, *Diana Her True Story in Her Own Words* (Michael O'Mara Books, 1998), p. 60.
22. ibid., p. 160.
23. Jonathan Dimbleby, *The Prince of Wales* (Warner Books, 1994) pp. 504–05.
24. Andrew Morton, *Diana: Her True Story in Her Own Words* (Michael O'Mara Books, 1998), p. 161.
25. ibid., p. 63.
26. ibid., p. 11.

5: The beginning of the end

1. George Carey, *The Times*, 3 June 2004.
2. BBC Television, *Panorama*, 20 November 1995.
3. ibid.
4. Patrick Jephson, *Shadows of a Princess* (Harper Collins, 2000), p. 273.
5. Paul Burrell, *A Royal Duty* (Michael Joseph, 2003), p. 175.
6. Patrick Jephson, *Shadows of a Princess* (Harper Collins, 2000) p. 257.
7. ibid., p. 258.
8. Address as patron of Turning Point, June 1993.
9. www.feminist.com/askamy
10. Patrick Jephson, *Shadows of a Princess* (Harper Collins, 2000) p. 282.
11. Max Riddington and Gavan Naden, *Frances* (Michael O'Mara Books, 2003), p. 144.
12. Earl Spencer's funeral oration, September 1997.
13. *Daily Telegraph*, 14 July 1993.
14. Paul Burrell, *A Royal Duty* (Michael Joseph, 2003), pp. 217–18.

15. Piers Morgan, *The Insider* (Ebury, 2005), p. 160.
16. ibid.
17. ibid., p. 161.
18. George Carey, *The Times*, 3 June 2004.
19. Patrick Jephson, *Shadows of a Princess* (Harper Collins, 2000), p. 96.
20. ibid., p. 97.
21. Patrick Jephson, *Shadows of a Princess* (Harper Collins, 2000), p. 304.
22. ibid., p. 97.
23. 'Don't Cry for me Argentina', Andrew Lloyd Webber and Tim Rice.
24. Speech to Headway lunch, 3 December 1993.
25. Patrick Jephson, *Shadows of a Princess* (Harper Collins, 2000), p. 318.
26. *Evita*, Andrew Lloyd Webber and Tim Rice.
27. Beatrix Campbell, *The Guardian*, 8 December 2002.
28. BBC Television, *Panorama*, 20 November 1995.
29. ibid.
30. Patrick Jephson, *Shadows of a Princess* (HarperCollins, 2000), p. 340.
31. Private letter, Prince Charles to Jonathan Dimbleby, 17 July 1994.
32. BBC Television, *Panorama*, 20 November 1995.
33. ibid.
34. Piers Morgan, *The Insider* (Ebury, 2005), p. 120.
35. Anna Pasternak, *Princess in Love* (Signet, 1995), p. 88.
36. Tony Benn, *Free at Last!* (Arrow Books, 2002), p. 341.
37. Patrick Jephson, *Shadows of a Princess* (Harper Collins, 2000) p. 367.

6: A timely death
1. Paul Burrell, *A Royal Duty* (Michael Joseph, 2003), p. 221.
2. ibid., p. 229.
3. Earl Spencer's funeral oration, September 1997.
4. Paul Burrell, *A Royal Duty* (Michael Joseph, 2003), p. 236.
5. Private letter to Paul Burrell, 28 August 1996.

6. BBC Television, *Panorama*, 20 November 1995.
7. Patrick Jephson, *Shadows of a Princess* (Harper Collins, 2000), p. 352.
8. BBC Television, *Panorama*, 20 November 1995.
9. Tony Benn, *Free at Last!* (Arrow Books, 2003), p. 370.
10. Max Riddington and Gavan Naden, *Frances* (Michael O'Mara Books, 2003), p. 151.
11. Hugo Vickers, *Elizabeth The Queen Mother* (Hutchinson, 2005), p. 482–83.
12. Patrick Jephson, *Shadows of a Princess* (Harper Collins, 2000), p. 352.
13. ibid., p. 326.
14. ibid.
15. Piers Morgan, *The Insider* (Ebury, 2005), p. 163.
16. Earl Spencer's funeral oration, September 1997.
17. *The Guardian*, 2 September 1997.
18. Dan Balz, *Washington Post Foreign Service*, Friday 5 September 1997, p. A29.
19. Tony Benn, *Free at Last!* (Arrow Books, 2003), p. 341.
20. Nigel Fountain, *Observer*, 27 July 1997.
21. Rosalind Brunt, in Jeffery Richard, ed., *Diana: The Making of a Media Saint* (I. B. Tauris, 1999), p. 21.
22. Nigel Fountain, *Observer*, 27 July 1997.
23. Professor Richard Fenn, in *Diana: The Making of a Media Saint* (I. B. Tauris, 1999), p. 140.

7: 'Mines kill children, don't they Mummy?'

1. Paul Burrell, *A Royal Duty* (Michael Joseph, 2003), p. 261.
2. W. F. Deedes, *Brief Lives* (Pan, 2004), p. 74.
3. 'Responding to Landmines: A Modern Tragedy and its Solutions', keynote address at seminar co-hosted by the Mines Advisory Group and the Landmine Survivors Network, 12 June 1997.
4. www.bbc.co.uk
5. W. F. Deedes, *Brief Lives* (Pan, 2004), p. 75.
6. ibid.
7. 'Responding to Landmines: A Modern Tragedy and its

Solutions', keynote address at seminar co-hosted by the Mines Advisory Group and the Landmine Survivors Network, 12 June 1997.

8. ibid.
9. Piers Morgan, *The Insider* (Ebury, 2005), p. 164.
10. W. F. Deedes, *Brief Lives* (Pan, 2004), p. 76.
11. Paul Donovan, *Observer Worldview*, 25 August 2002.
12. ibid.
13. 'Responding to Landmines: A Modern Tragedy and its Solutions', keynote address at seminar co-hosted by the Mines Advisory Group and the Landmine Survivors Network, 12 June 1997.

8: With the angels
1. Gyles Brandreth, *Philip and Elizabeth: Portrait of a marriage* (Century, 2004), p. 421.
2. Piers Morgan, *The Insider* (Ebury, 2005), p. 169.
3. ibid., p. 170.
4. Rosi Braidotti, 'In the Sign of the Feminine: reading Diana', *Theory and Event* 1997, vol. 1 issue 4.
5. ibid.
6. Gyles Brandreth, *Philip and Elizabeth: Portrait of a Marriage* (Century, 2004), p. 422.
7. Tony Benn, *Free at Last!* (Arrow Books, 2003), p. 437.
8. A reference to the decision to decommission *Britannia*, which cost £9 million a year to run.
9. George Carey, *The Times*, 3 June 2004.
10. ibid.
11. Very Reverend Dr Wesley Carr, Dean of Westminster, Opening address at funeral, September 1997.
12. Earl Spencer's funeral oration, September 1997.
13. The University of Oxford Centre for Suicide Research, 'Effect of death of Diana, Princess of Wales on suicide and deliberate self harm.' *British Journal of Psychiatry* 2000, vol. 177, issue 469.
14. 'Suicides rise after Diana's death', *BMJ* (News) 2000, vol. 321, issue 1246.

15. Jeremy Seabrook, *Resurgence*, January 1998.
16. Engraved glass panels inside the north porch entrance of Salisbury Cathedral.

9: The myth spreads

1. Gyles Brandreth, *Philip and Elizabeth: Portrait of a Marriage* (Century, 2004), p. 432.
2. Nostradamus, Century IX, quatrain 12.
3. ibid., Century II, quatrain 28.
4. In 1987 the track was released by The Smiths as a single.
5. Dr Alain Pavie, head of the Cardiology department at Hospital de la Pitie Salpetriere in Paris.
6. Mixhalis through Lauren Brockway, 'Diana, Queen of Hearts: Farewell, Faerie Princess', *Sedona: Journal of Emergence* 1997, vol. 7, issue 11, pp. 48–49.
7. Charles Cameron, *She Became an Icon: the Life and Death of Princess Diana in Millennial Discourse*, Center for Millennial Studies, 1997.
8. Revelation 12:1–6, King James/Authorised Version.
9. Charles Cameron, *She Became an Icon: the Life and Death of Princess Diana in Millennial Discourse*, Center for Millennial Studies, 1997.
10. ibid.
11. George Viktor, *The Defining Moment* (Megatrends Enterprises, Sydney NSW 1997).
12. George Carey, *The Times*, 3 June 2004.
13. Kitty Kelley, author of *The Royals*, quoted in *The Guardian*, 27 October 2005.
14. ibid.
15. *The Times*, 15 September 2005.

10: Who guards the legend?

1. Paul Burrell, *A Royal Duty* (Michael Joseph, 2003), p. 298.
2. ibid., p. 314.
3. ibid., p. 318.
4. ibid., p. 333.

5. ibid., p. 339.
6. Piers Morgan, *The Insider* (Ebury, 2005), p. 358.
7. ibid., p. 322.
8. Stephen Bates, *Time Europe*, 11 January 2004.
9. Jeremy Seabrook, *Resurgence*, January 1998.
10. Carol Sellars, *The Psychologist*, November 1997.
11. Piers Morgan, *The Insider* (Ebury, 2005) p. 120.

11: Protecting the image
1. *Daily Telegraph*, 9 November 2004.
2. BBC Radio 4, *Today*, July 12 2003.

12: Shrines and holy places
1. Max Riddington and Gavan Naden, *Frances* (Michael O'Mara Books, 2003), p. 190.
2. Althorp visitor guide.

13: Diana of the New Age
1. Andrew Morton, *Diana: Her True Story in Her Own Words* (Michael O'Mara Books, 1997), p. 65.
2. ibid., p. 66.
3. ibid., p. 34.
4. *Astrology* 1983, vol. 57, issue 1, p. 37.
5. www.astrologer.com
6. Paul Burrell, *A Royal Duty* (Michael Joseph, 2003) pp. 188.
7. ibid.
8. ibid., p. 176.
9. Max Riddington and Gavan Naden, *Frances* (Michael O'Mara Books, 2003), p. 133.
10. Cardinal Keith O'Brien, statement, 3 June 2004.
11. Patrick Jephson, *Shadows of a Princess* (Harper Collins, 2000), p. 164.
12. ibid., p. 166.
13. ibid., p. 167.
14. Frank McLynn, *New Statesman*, 8 October 2001.

15. Andrew Morton, *Diana: Her True Story in Her Own Words* (Michael O'Mara Books, 1997), p. 43.
16. Humphrey Carpenter, *Robert Runcie* (Hodder and Stoughton, 1996), p. 225.
17. ibid., p. 222.
18. Patrick Jephson, *Shadows of a Princess* (HarperCollins, 2000), p. 168.
19. Piers Morgan, *The Insider* (Ebury, 2005), p. 122.

14: From beyond the grave

1. www.angelfire.com
2. ibid.
3. Simone Simmons with Ingrid Seward, CBS News extract (website, 29 September 2005) from *Diana – The Last Word* (St Martin's Press, 2004).
4. Ivan Fraser, *Why I believe Simone Simmons and her Revelations about Diana*, www.truthcampaign.ukf.net (accessed, July 2005).
5. www.geocities.com/astrologyprincewilliam
6. www.angelfire.com
7. www.angelfire.com
8. Bishop Tom Wright, sermon preached in Lichfield, *Church Times*, 12 September 1997.
9. ibid.
10. *Church Times*, 24 October 1997.
11. Jeffrey Richard, *Diana: The making of a media saint* (I. B. Tauris, 1999), p. 120.
12. ibid., p. 122.
13. ibid., p. 128.
14. ibid.
15. ibid., p. 130.
16. ibid., p. 134.
17. ibid., p. 137.
18. Jane Caputi, 'The Second Coming of Diana', *NWSA Journal* 1999, vol. 11, issue 2, p. 103.
19. Dan Balz, *Washington Post Foreign Service*, 5 September 1997, p. A29.

20. Acts 1:24.
21. Marva Dawn and Eugene Peterson, *The Unnecessary Pastor* (Christian Century, 11999).
22. ibid.
23. goddess.astrology.com
24. Spiritual profile of Britain commissioned by the BBC and supported by *The Tablet* and the University of Nottingham, 2000.
25. ibid.
26. Grace Davie, *Only Connect – Communicating the Christian Faith in the 21st Century, From Obligation to Consumption: Patterns of Religion in Northern Europe at the Start of the 21st Century*, Bishops' Day Conference, September 2002.
27. ibid.
28. ibid.
29. ibid.
30. Website of Endtime Ministries, Queensland, Australia.
31. Reverend Chris Chivers, *Church Times*, 2 December 2005, p. 10.

15: Long live Diana

1. *Sunday Telegraph*, 4 July 2004.
2. Andrew Morton, *Diana: Her True Story in Her Own Words* (Michael O'Mara Books, 1997), p. 68.
3. Press Association.
4. *Sunday Telegraph*, 4 July 2004.
5. G. Bennett and A. Rowbottom, quoting a member of British Order of Druids in *Born a lady, died a saint* (Fabula, 1998), p. 207.
6. Press Association.
7. Website of Endtime Ministries, Queensland, Australia.

INDEX